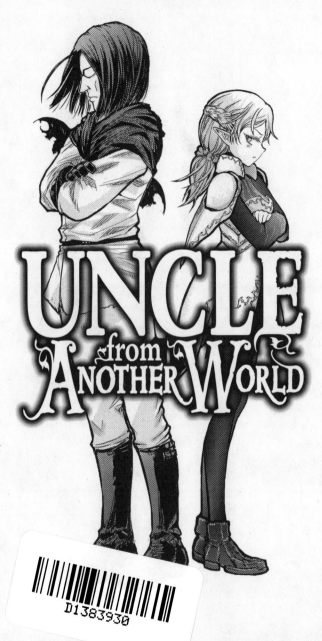

UNCLE from ANOTHER WORLD

Hotondoshindeiru

A Man Who Survived

CONTENTS

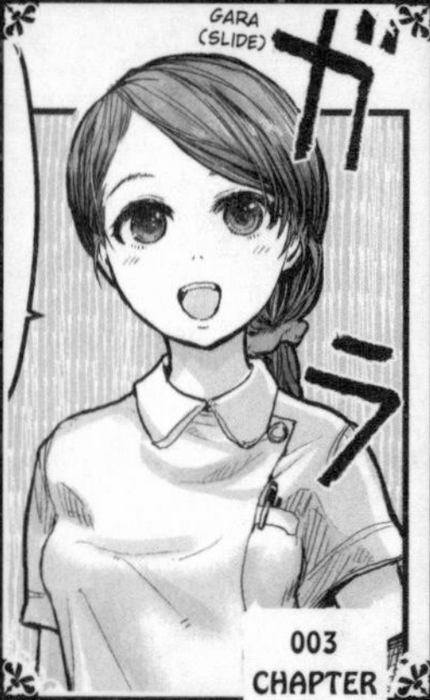
GARA
(SLIDE)

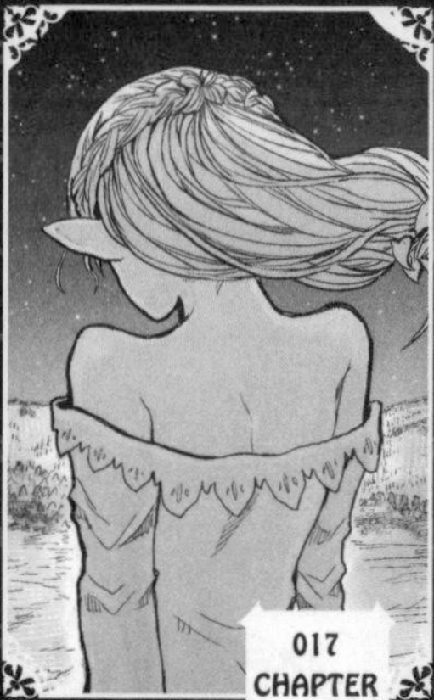

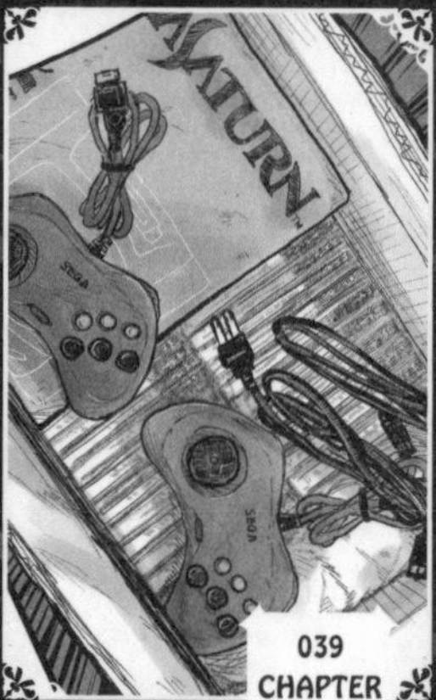

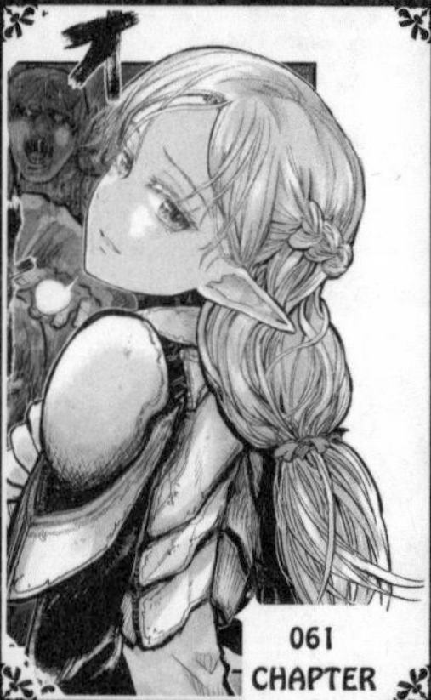

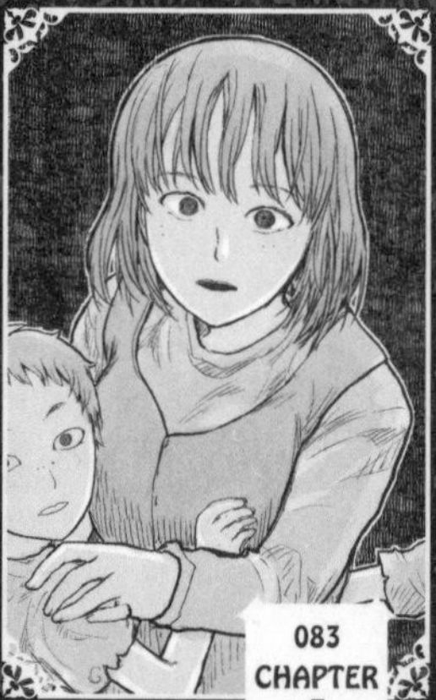

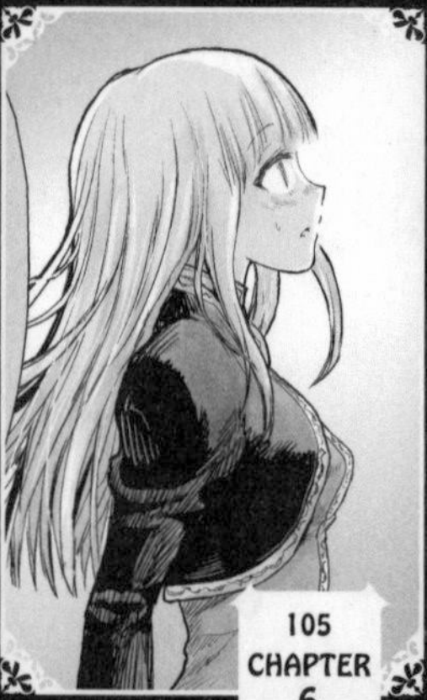

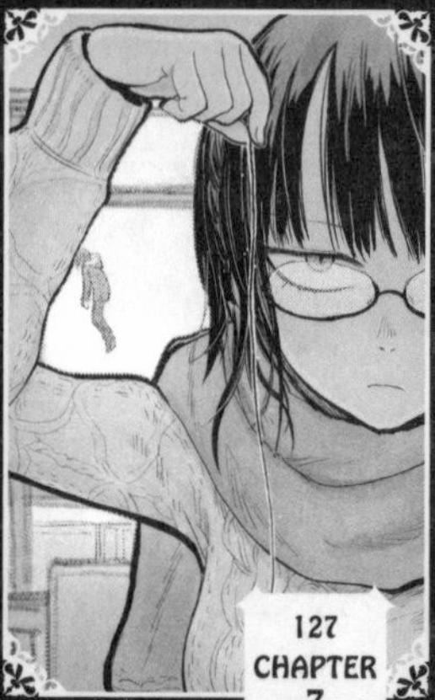

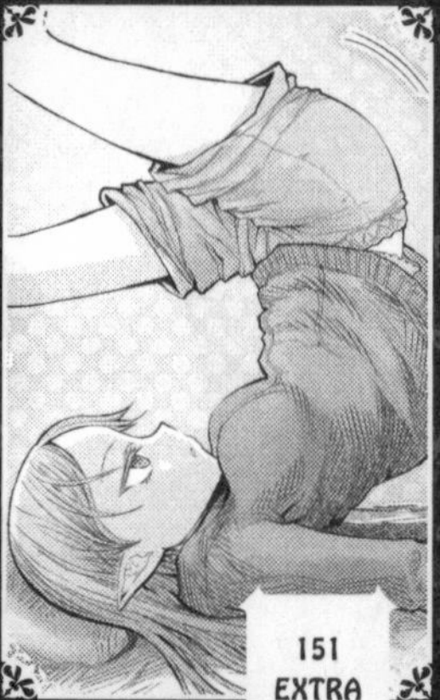

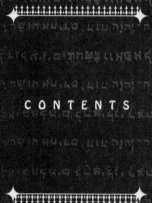

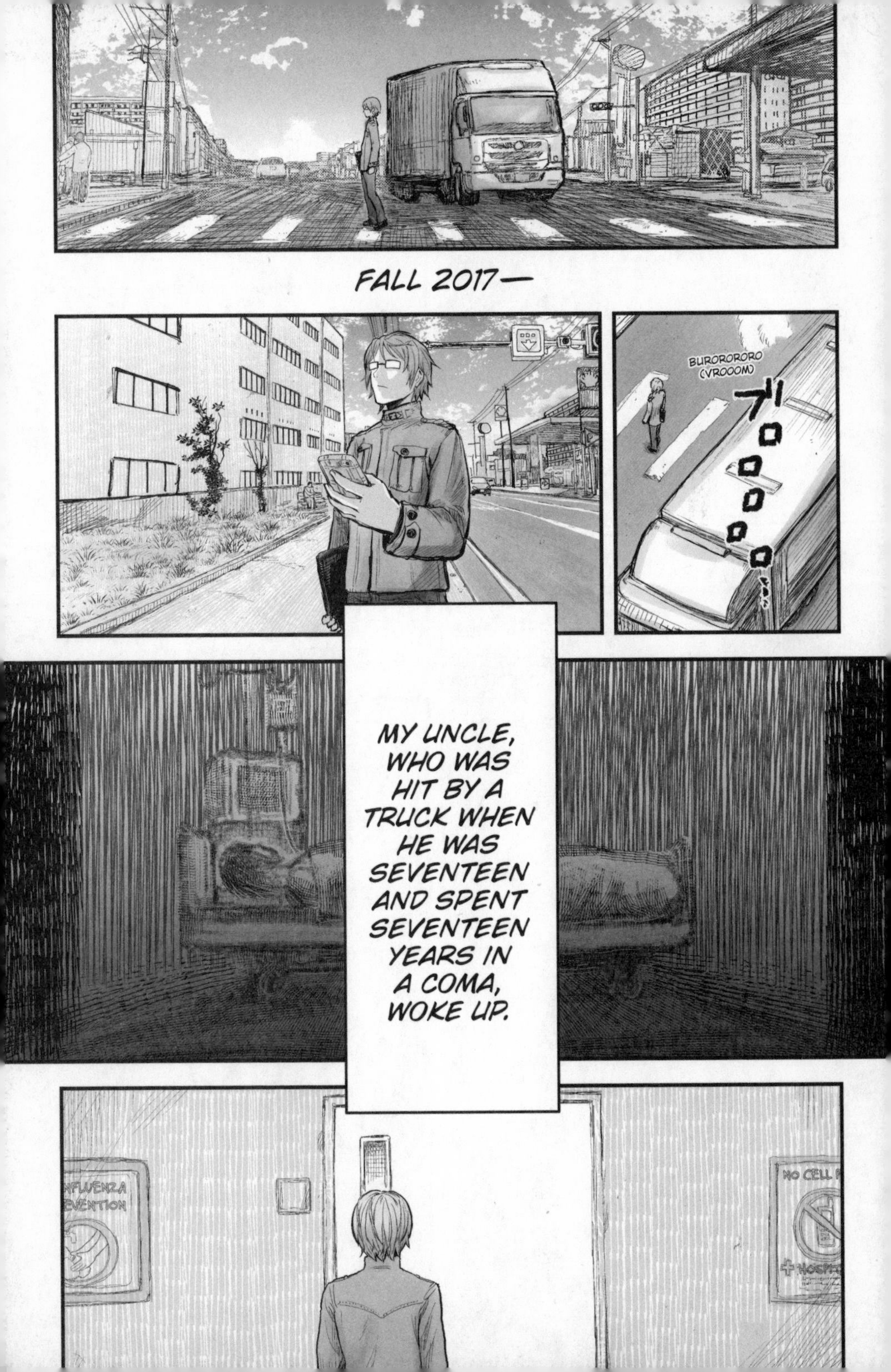
FALL 2017—
BUROROROR
(VROOOM)
ブロロロロ
MY UNCLE, WHO WAS HIT BY A TRUCK WHEN HE WAS SEVENTEEN AND SPENT SEVENTEEN YEARS IN A COMA, WOKE UP.

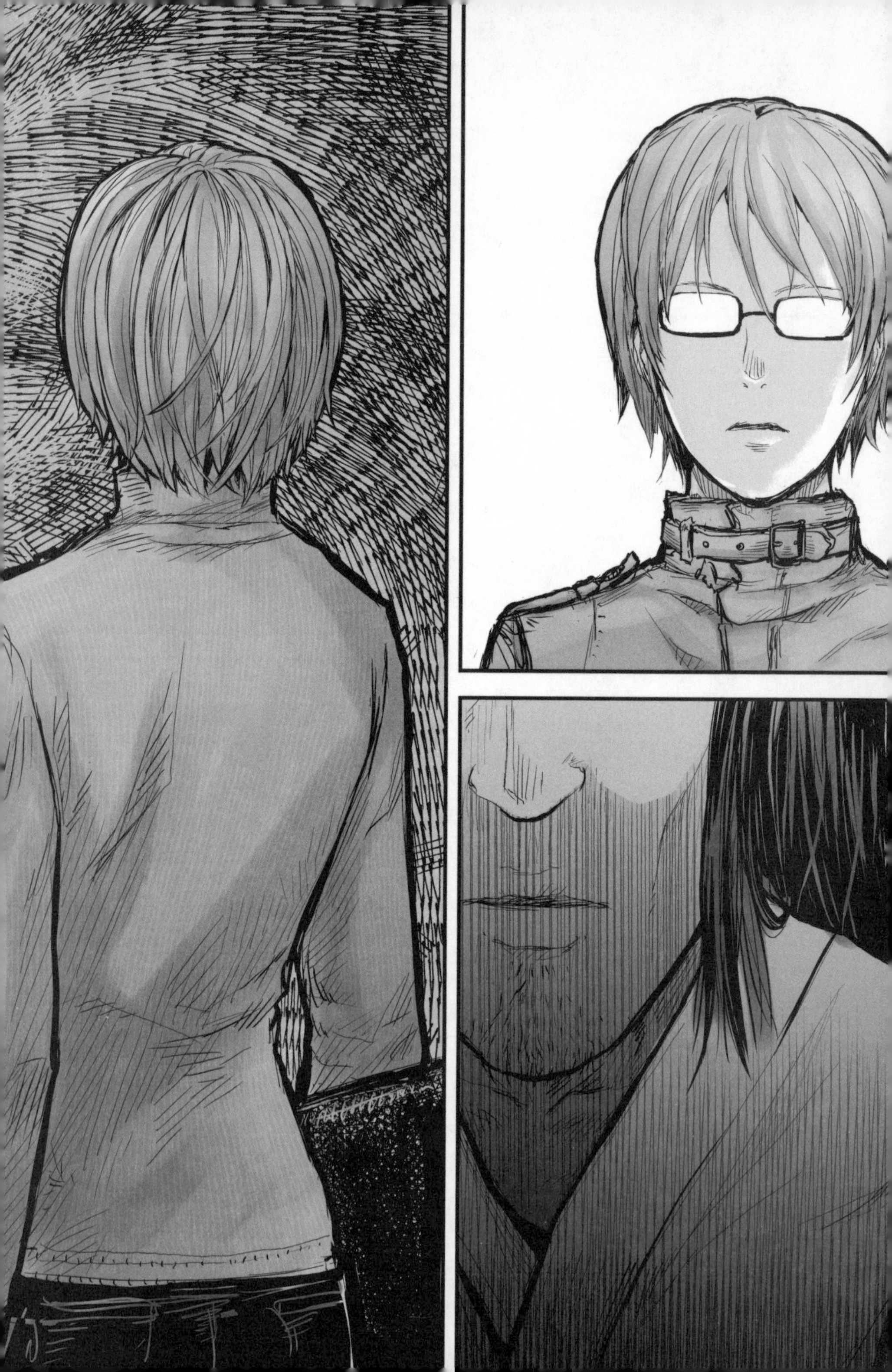

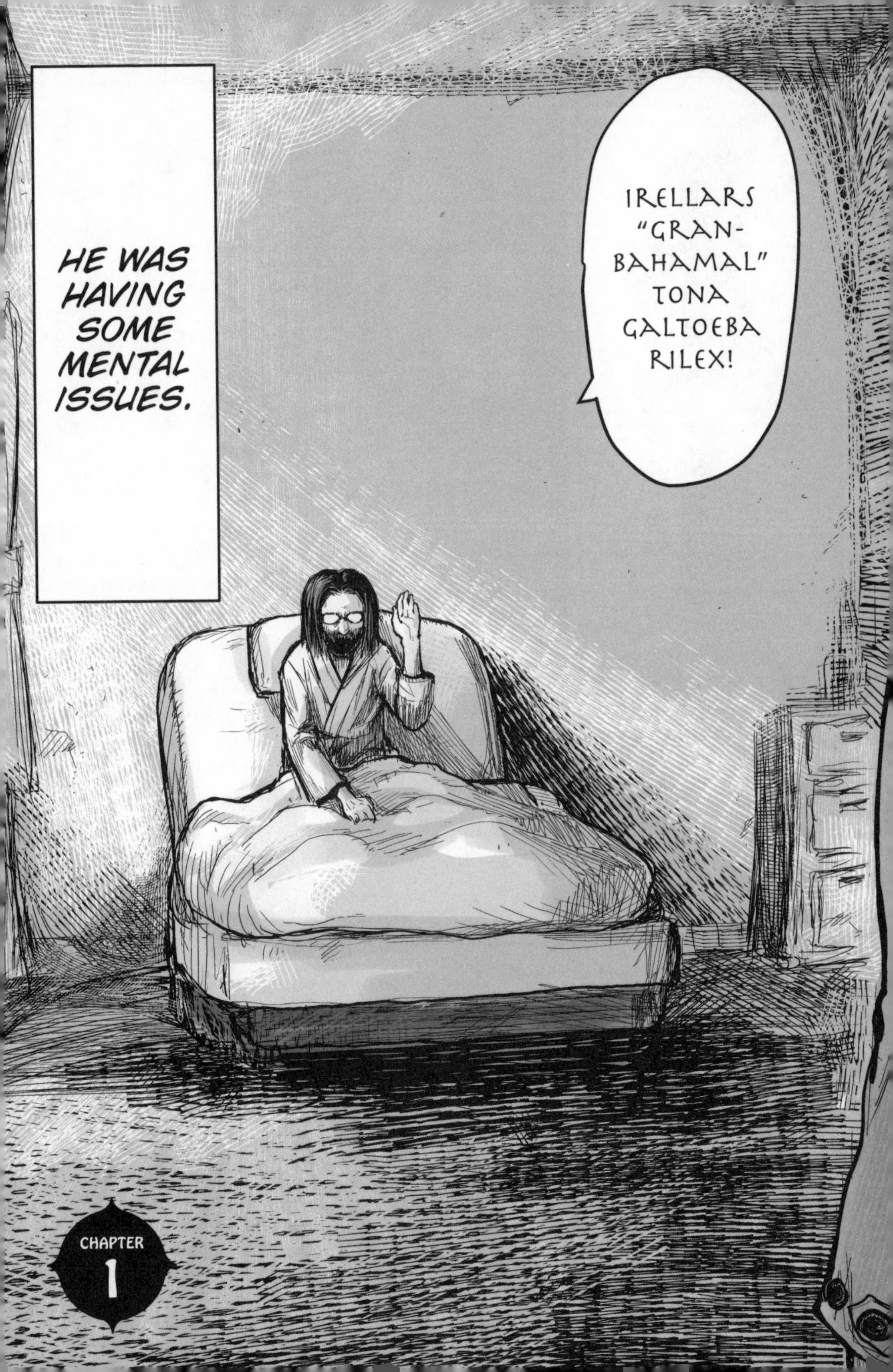
IRELLARS "GRAN-BAHAMAL" TONA GALTOEBA RILEX!
HE WAS HAVING SOME MENTAL ISSUES.
CHAPTER 1

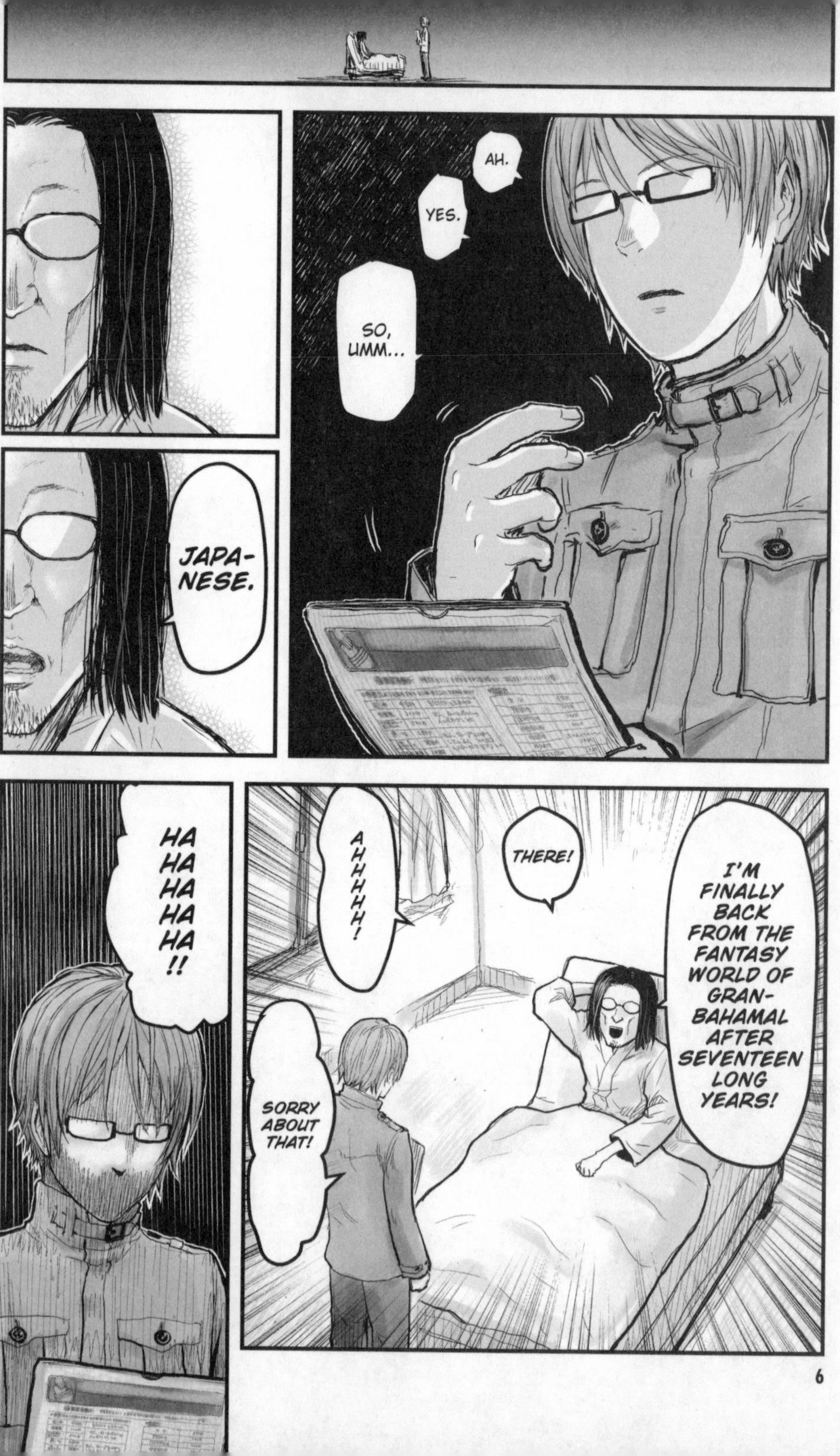
AH.
YES.
SO, UMM...
JAPA-NESE.
I'M FINALLY BACK FROM THE FANTASY WORLD OF GRAN-BAHAMAL AFTER SEVENTEEN LONG YEARS!
THERE!
AHHHHH!
SORRY ABOUT THAT!
HA HA HA HA HA!!

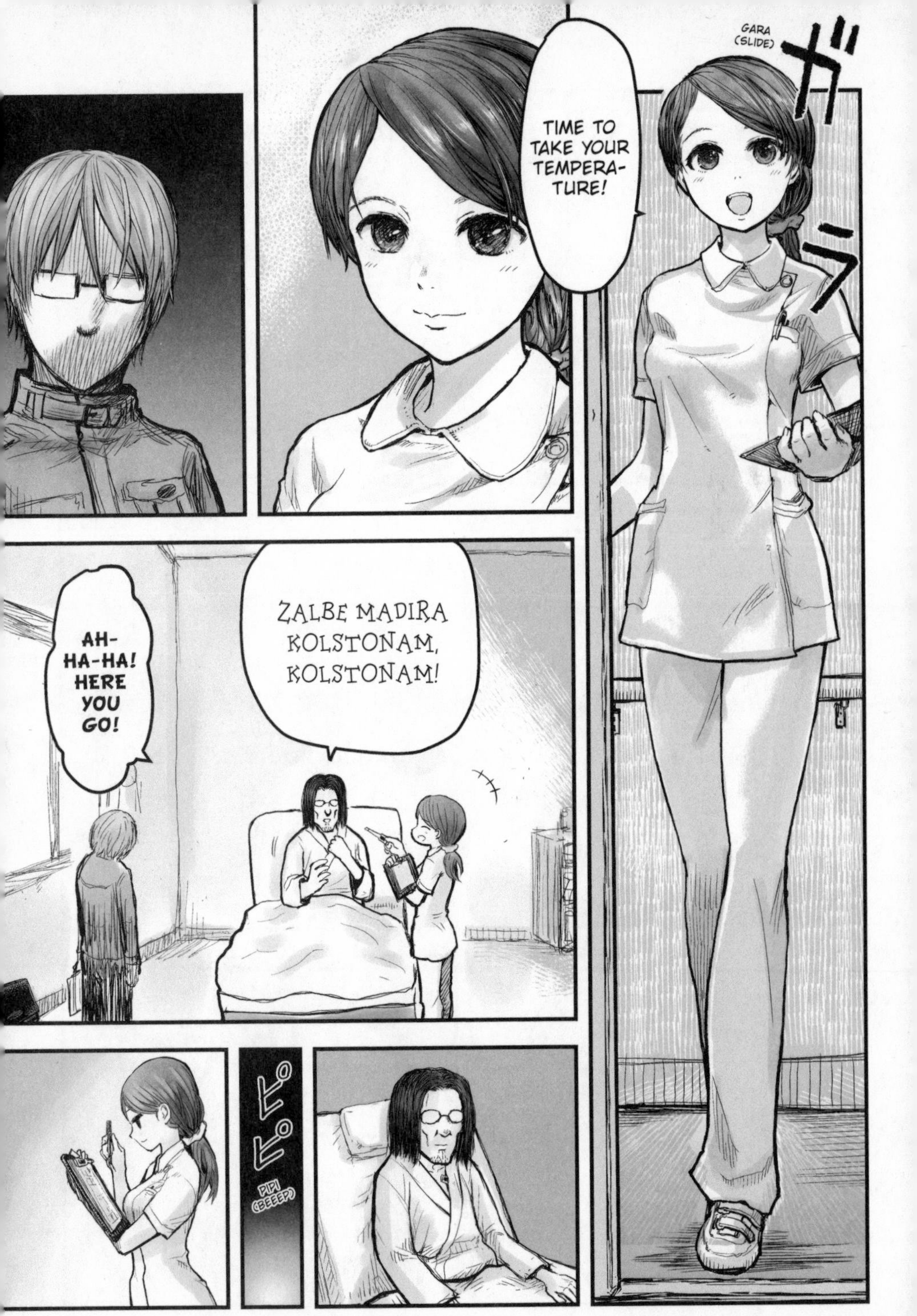
ガラ
GARA (SLIDE)
TIME TO TAKE YOUR TEMPERA-TURE!
ZALBE MADIRA KOLSTONAM, KOLSTONAM!
AH-HA-HA! HERE YOU GO!
ピピ
PIPI (BEEEP)

YES, RIGHT!

DEL STORBA TONA RABELT GAL.

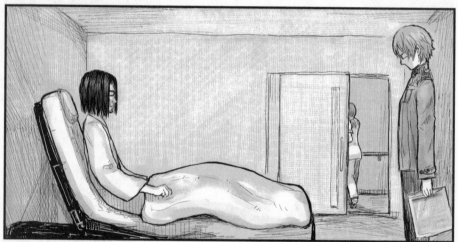

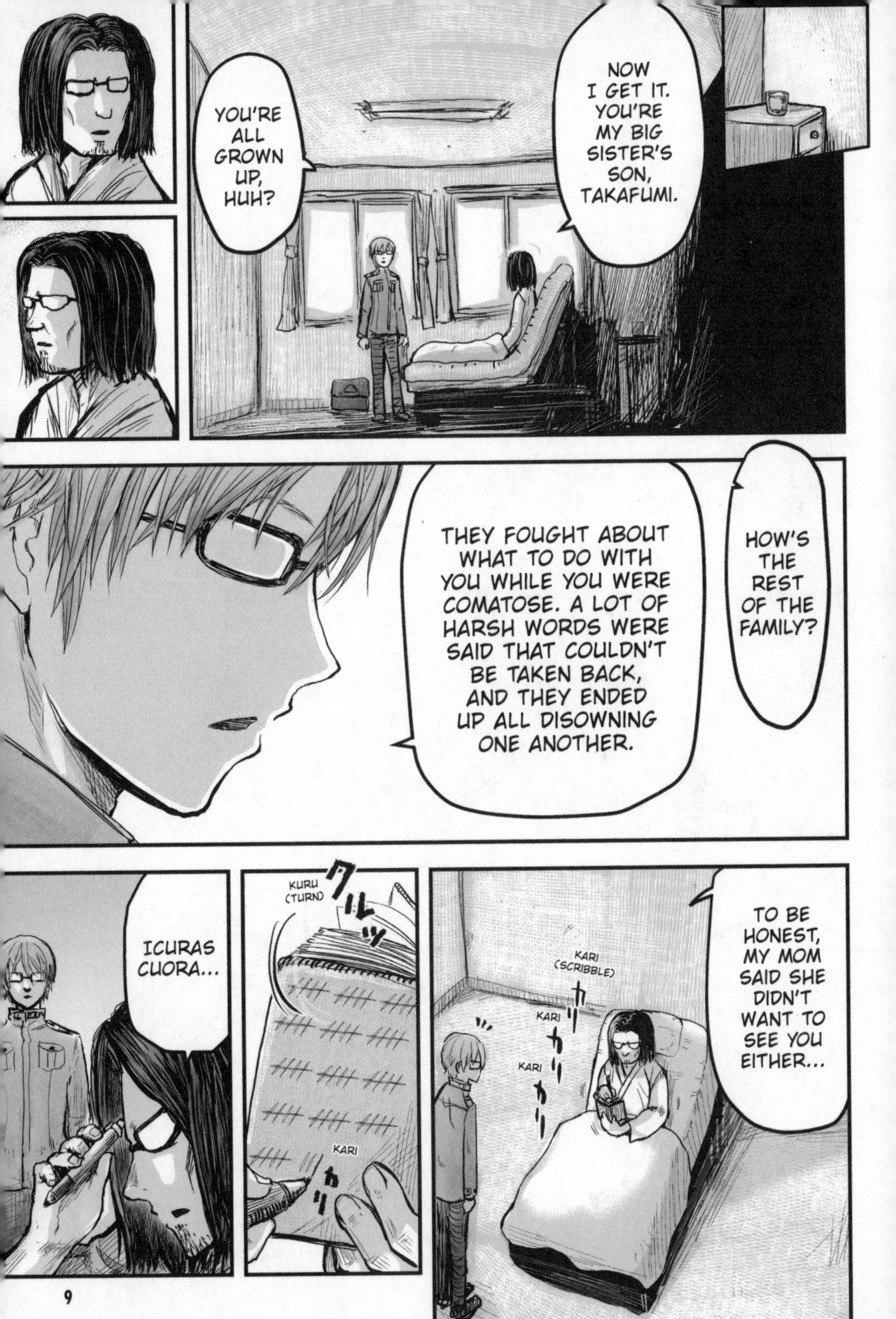

NOW I GET IT. YOU'RE MY BIG SISTER'S SON, TAKAFUMI.
YOU'RE ALL GROWN UP, HUH?
HOW'S THE REST OF THE FAMILY?
THEY FOUGHT ABOUT WHAT TO DO WITH YOU WHILE YOU WERE COMATOSE. A LOT OF HARSH WORDS WERE SAID THAT COULDN'T BE TAKEN BACK, AND THEY ENDED UP ALL DISOWNING ONE ANOTHER.
TO BE HONEST, MY MOM SAID SHE DIDN'T WANT TO SEE YOU EITHER...
KARI (SCRIBBLE)
KARI
KARI
KURU (TURN)
KARI
ICURAS CUORA...

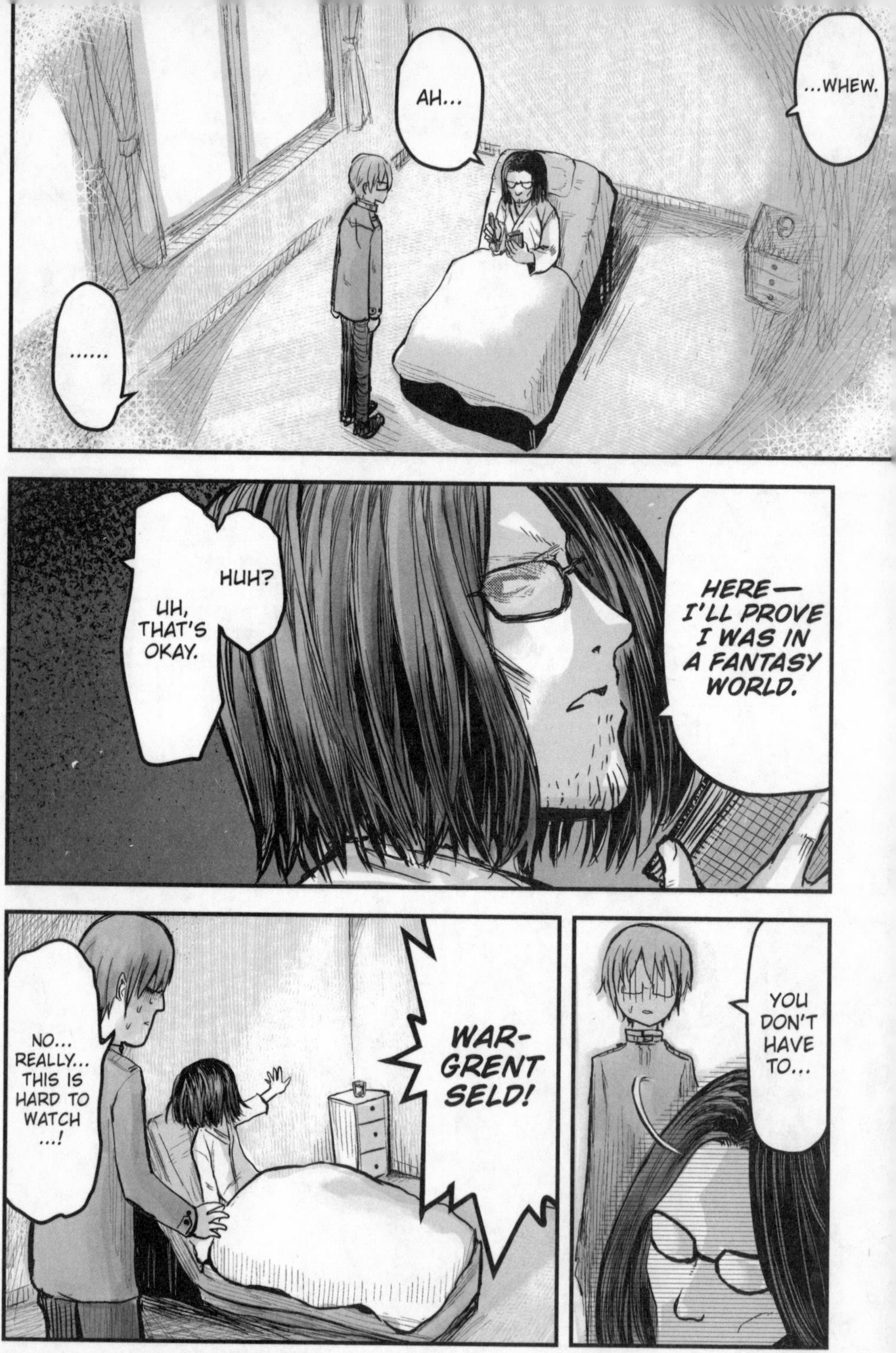
...WHEW.
AH...
......
HERE— I'LL PROVE I WAS IN A FANTASY WORLD.
HUH?
UH, THAT'S OKAY.
YOU DON'T HAVE TO...
WAR-GRENT SELD!
NO... REALLY... THIS IS HARD TO WATCH ...!

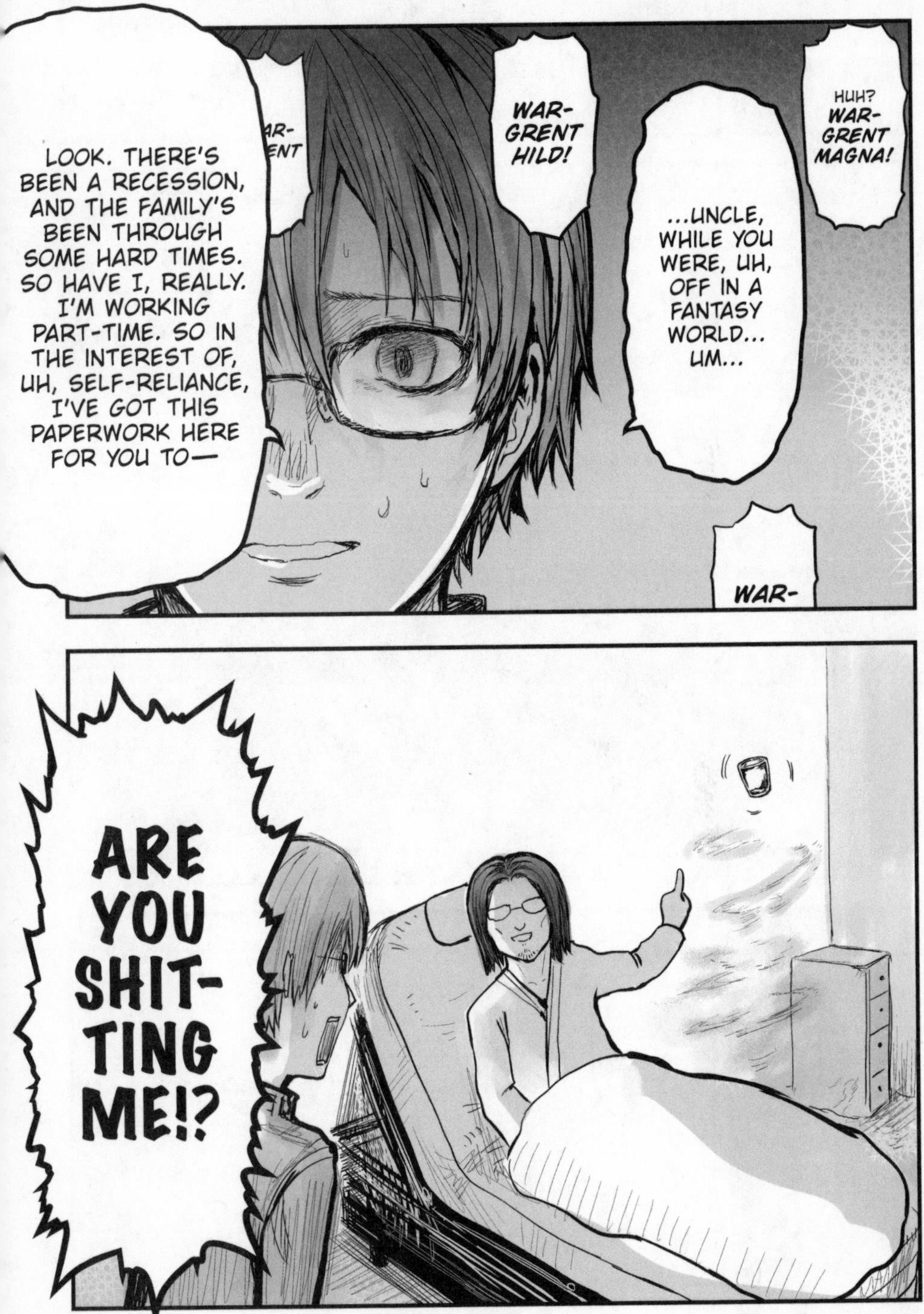
HUH? WAR-GRENT MAGNA!
WAR-GRENT HILD!
...UNCLE, WHILE YOU WERE, UH, OFF IN A FANTASY WORLD... UM...
LOOK. THERE'S BEEN A RECESSION, AND THE FAMILY'S BEEN THROUGH SOME HARD TIMES. SO HAVE I, REALLY. I'M WORKING PART-TIME. SO IN THE INTEREST OF, UH, SELF-RELIANCE, I'VE GOT THIS PAPERWORK HERE FOR YOU TO—
WAR-
ARE YOU SHIT-TING ME!?

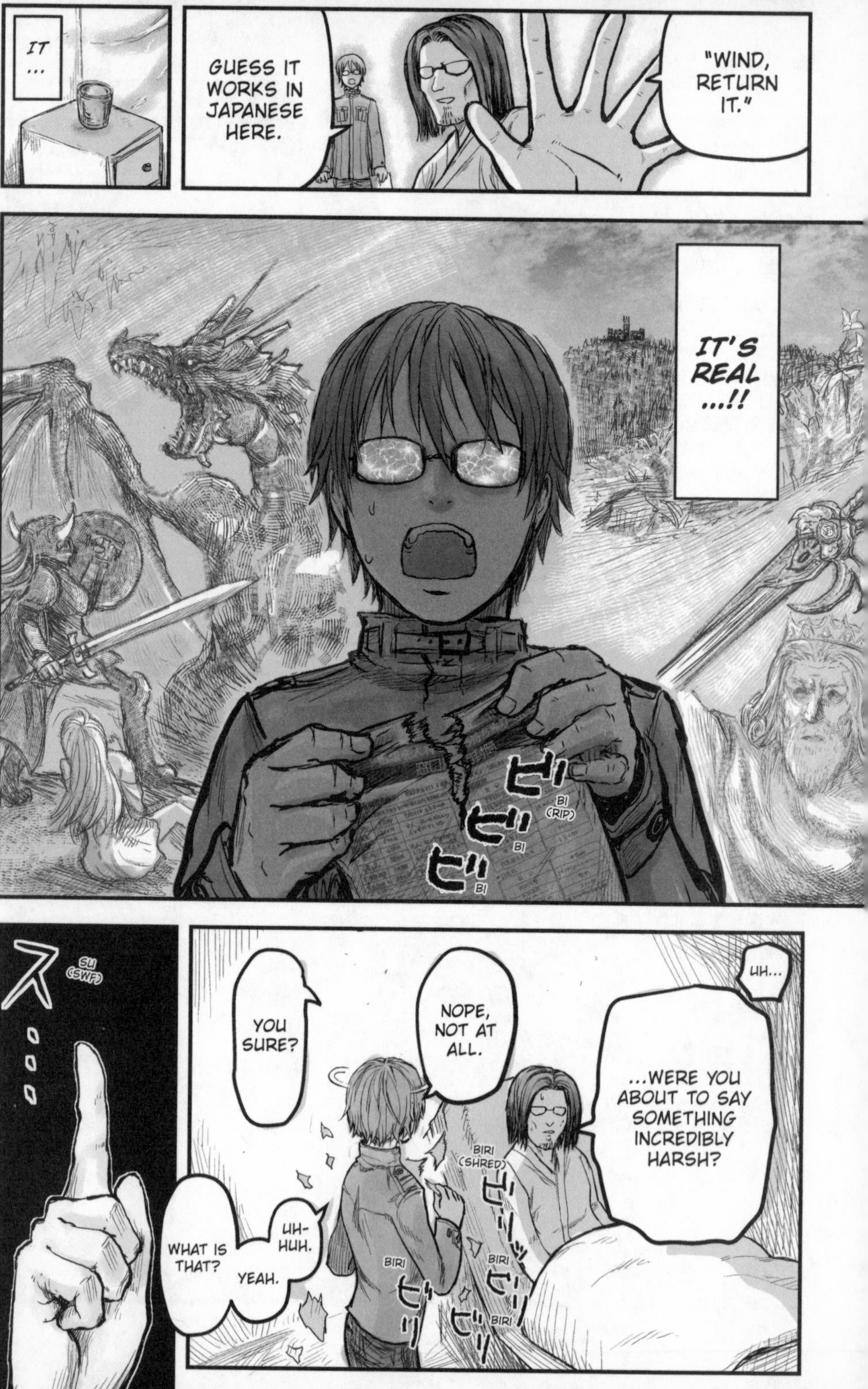
"WIND, RETURN IT."
GUESS IT WORKS IN JAPANESE HERE.
IT ...
IT'S REAL ...!!
ビ BI (RIP)
ビ BI
ビ BI
UH...
...WERE YOU ABOUT TO SAY SOMETHING INCREDIBLY HARSH?
NOPE, NOT AT ALL.
YOU SURE?
ビリッ BIRI (SHRED)
ビリ BIRI
ビリ BIRI
ビリ BIRI
UH-HUH.
YEAH.
WHAT IS THAT?
ス SU (SWF)
...

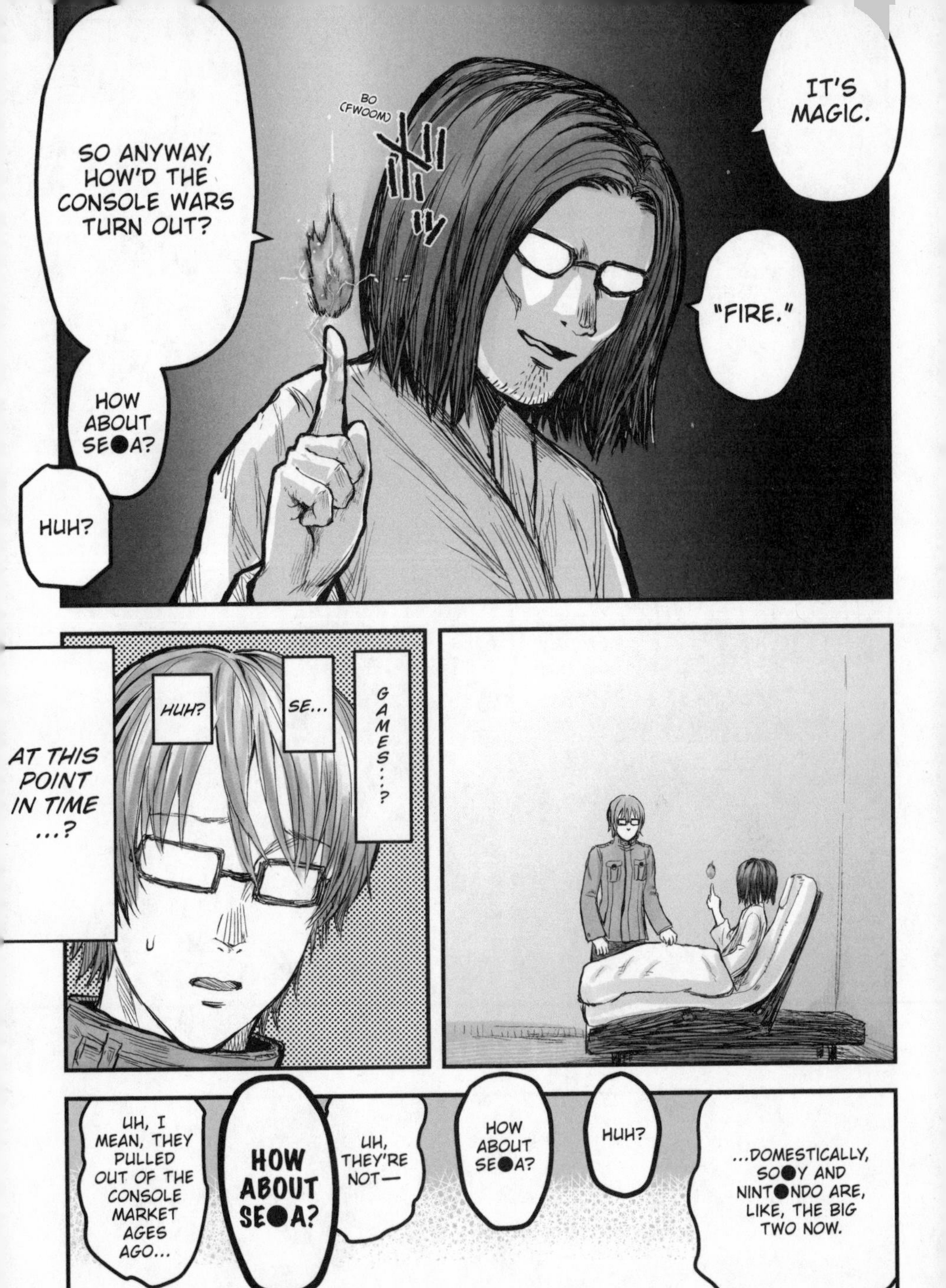
IT'S MAGIC.
BO (FWOOM)
"FIRE."
SO ANYWAY, HOW'D THE CONSOLE WARS TURN OUT?
HOW ABOUT SE●A?
HUH?
GAMES...?
SE...
HUH?
AT THIS POINT IN TIME ...?
...DOMESTICALLY, SO●Y AND NINT●NDO ARE, LIKE, THE BIG TWO NOW.
HUH?
HOW ABOUT SE●A?
UH, THEY'RE NOT—
HOW ABOUT SE●A?
UH, I MEAN, THEY PULLED OUT OF THE CONSOLE MARKET AGES AGO...

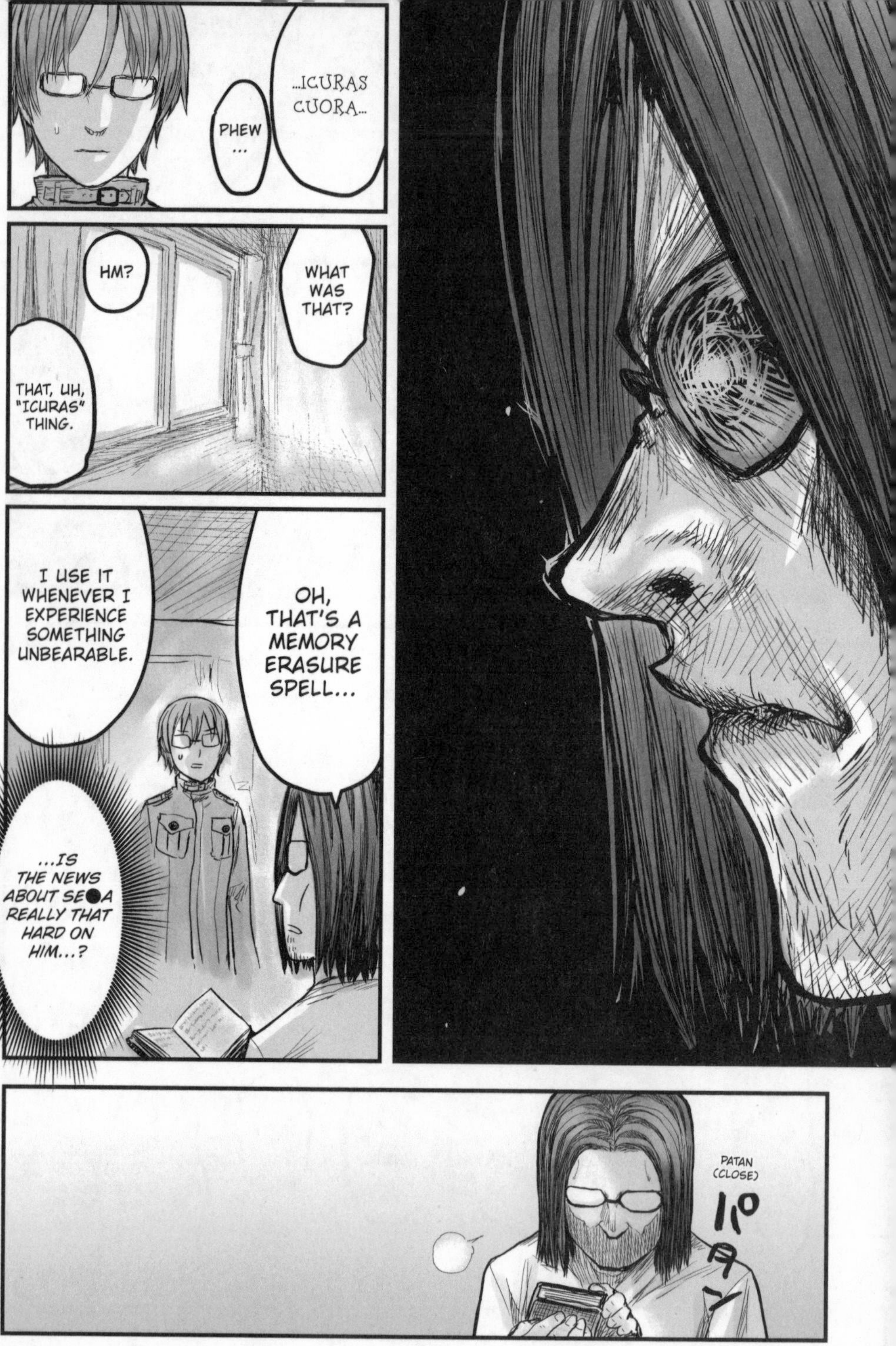
...ICURAS CUORA...
PHEW ...
WHAT WAS THAT?
HM?
THAT, UH, "ICURAS" THING.
OH, THAT'S A MEMORY ERASURE SPELL...
I USE IT WHENEVER I EXPERIENCE SOMETHING UNBEARABLE.
...IS THE NEWS ABOUT SE●A REALLY THAT HARD ON HIM...?
PATAN (CLOSE)
パタン

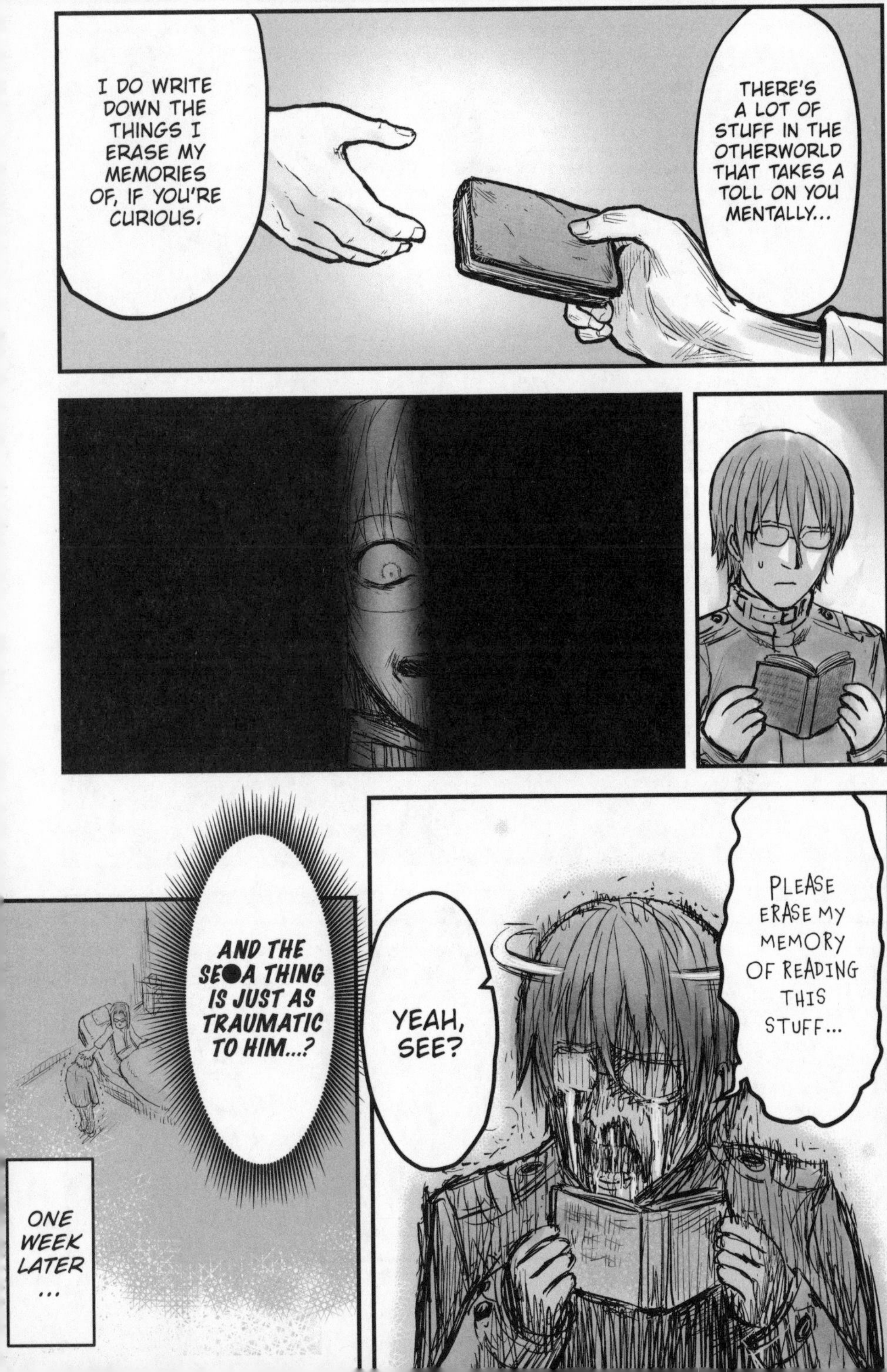
THERE'S A LOT OF STUFF IN THE OTHERWORLD THAT TAKES A TOLL ON YOU MENTALLY...
I DO WRITE DOWN THE THINGS I ERASE MY MEMORIES OF, IF YOU'RE CURIOUS.
PLEASE ERASE MY MEMORY OF READING THIS STUFF...
YEAH, SEE?
AND THE SE●A THING IS JUST AS TRAUMATIC TO HIM...?
ONE WEEK LATER ...

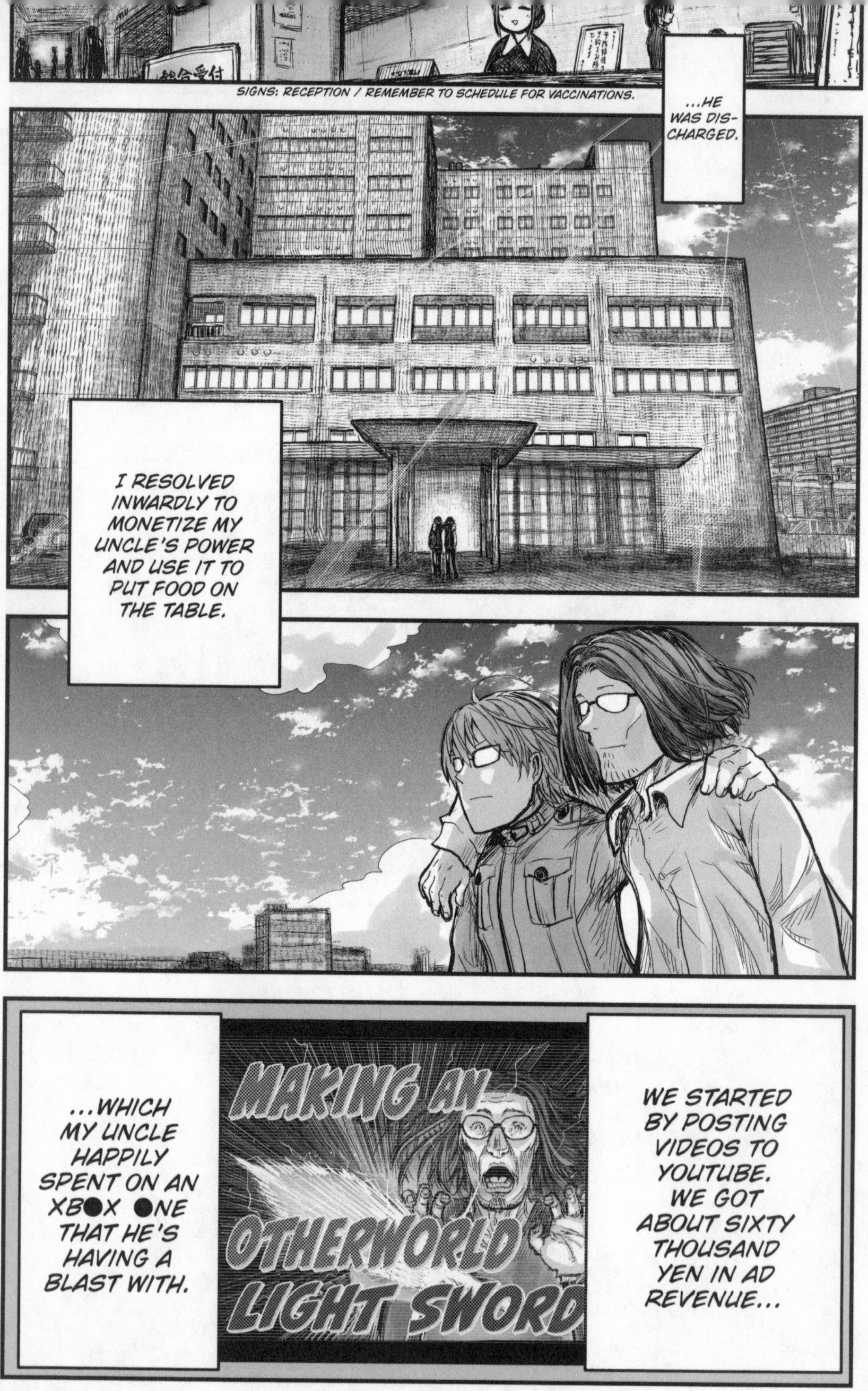
SIGNS: RECEPTION / REMEMBER TO SCHEDULE FOR VACCINATIONS.
...HE WAS DISCHARGED.
I RESOLVED INWARDLY TO MONETIZE MY UNCLE'S POWER AND USE IT TO PUT FOOD ON THE TABLE.
WE STARTED BY POSTING VIDEOS TO YOUTUBE. WE GOT ABOUT SIXTY THOUSAND YEN IN AD REVENUE...
MAKING AN OTHERWORLD LIGHT SWORD
...WHICH MY UNCLE HAPPILY SPENT ON AN XB●X ●NE THAT HE'S HAVING A BLAST WITH.

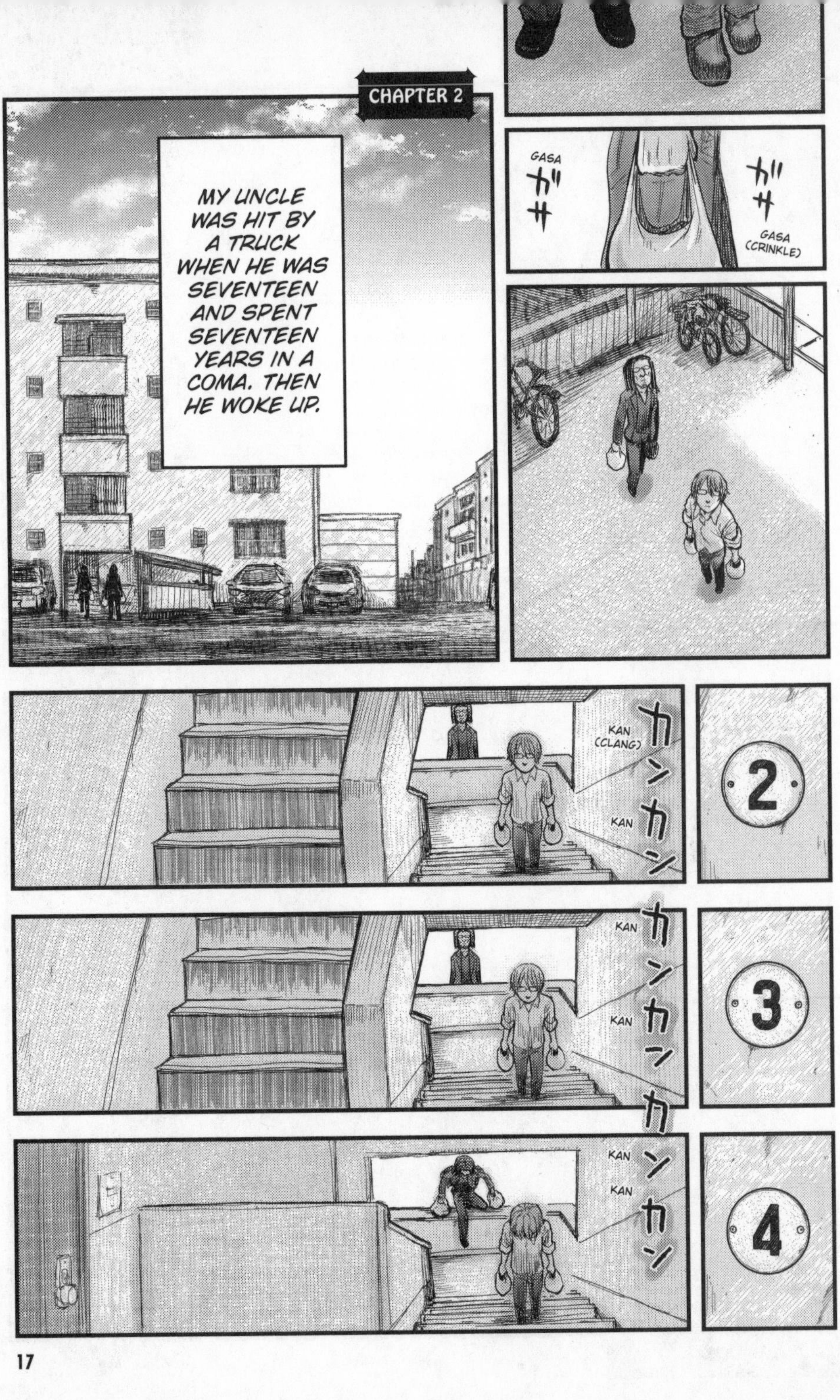
GASA
GASA (CRINKLE)
CHAPTER 2
MY UNCLE WAS HIT BY A TRUCK WHEN HE WAS SEVENTEEN AND SPENT SEVENTEEN YEARS IN A COMA. THEN HE WOKE UP.
2
KAN (CLANG)
KAN
3
KAN
KAN
4
KAN
KAN

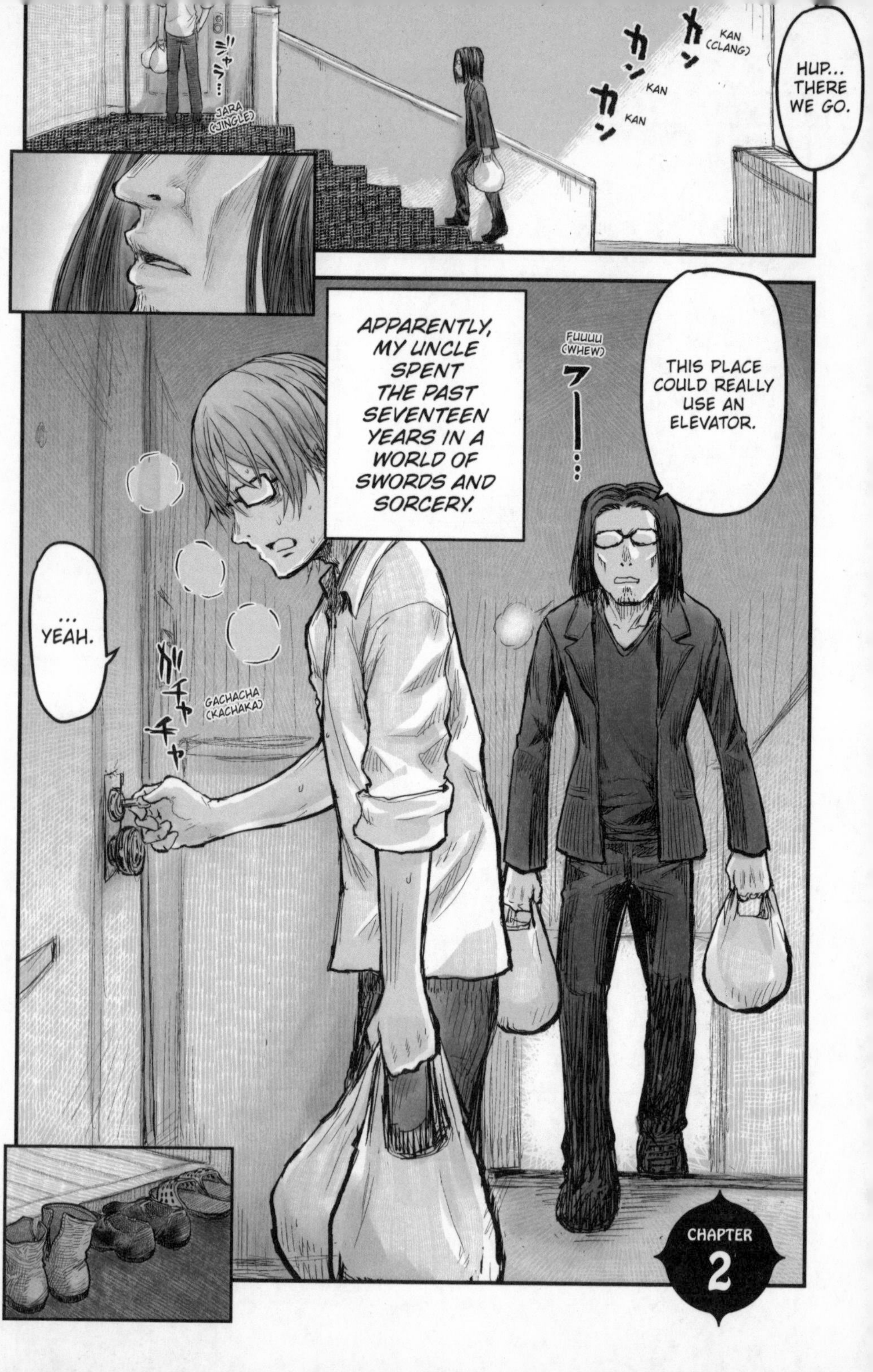
カン
KAN (CLANG)
カン
KAN
カン
KAN
HUP... THERE WE GO.
ジャラ...
JARA (JINGLE)
THIS PLACE COULD REALLY USE AN ELEVATOR.
フー...
FUUUU (WHEW)
APPARENTLY, MY UNCLE SPENT THE PAST SEVENTEEN YEARS IN A WORLD OF SWORDS AND SORCERY.
ガチャチャ
GACHACHA (KACHAKA)
... YEAH.
CHAPTER 2

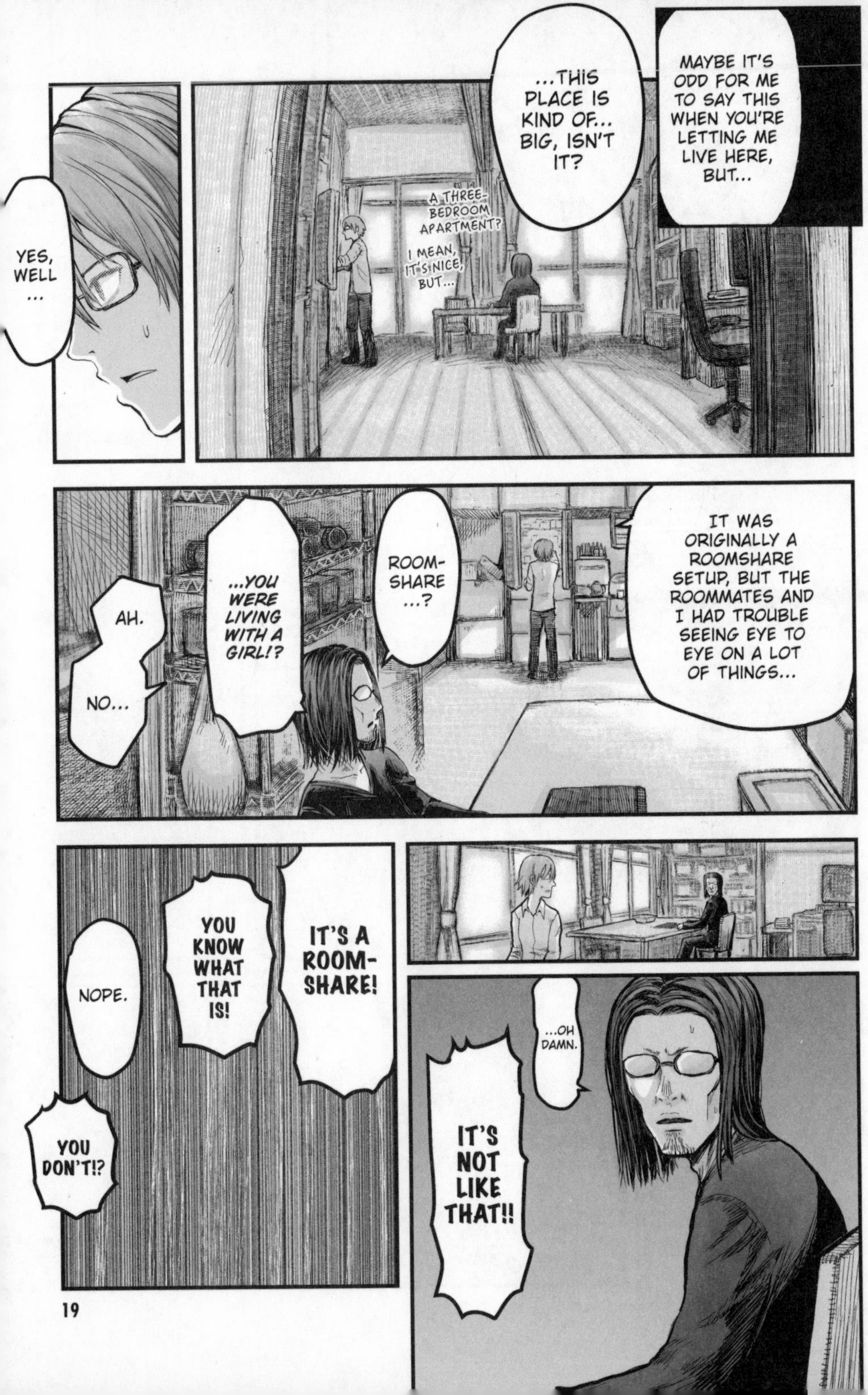
MAYBE IT'S ODD FOR ME TO SAY THIS WHEN YOU'RE LETTING ME LIVE HERE, BUT...
...THIS PLACE IS KIND OF... BIG, ISN'T IT?
A THREE-BEDROOM APARTMENT?
I MEAN, IT'S NICE, BUT...
YES, WELL ...
IT WAS ORIGINALLY A ROOMSHARE SETUP, BUT THE ROOMMATES AND I HAD TROUBLE SEEING EYE TO EYE ON A LOT OF THINGS...
ROOM-SHARE ...?
...YOU WERE LIVING WITH A GIRL!?
AH.
NO...
...OH DAMN.
IT'S NOT LIKE THAT!!
IT'S A ROOM-SHARE!
YOU KNOW WHAT THAT IS!
NOPE.
YOU DON'T!?

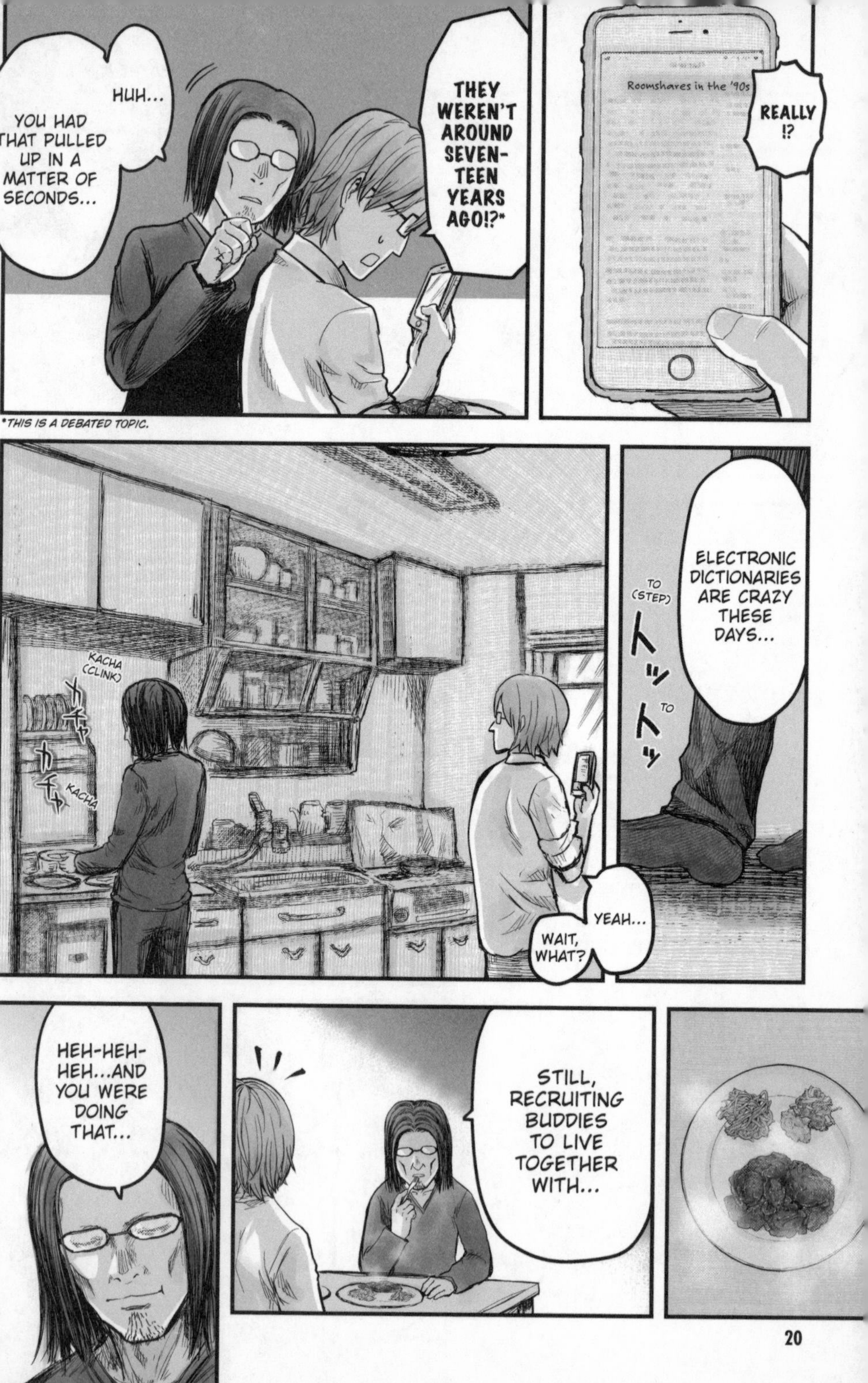
Roomshares in the '90s
REALLY!?
THEY WEREN'T AROUND SEVENTEEN YEARS AGO!?*
HUH...
YOU HAD THAT PULLED UP IN A MATTER OF SECONDS...
ELECTRONIC DICTIONARIES ARE CRAZY THESE DAYS...
TO (STEP)
TO
YEAH...
WAIT, WHAT?
KACHA (CLINK)
KACHA
STILL, RECRUITING BUDDIES TO LIVE TOGETHER WITH...
HEH-HEH-HEH...AND YOU WERE DOING THAT...

*THIS IS A DEBATED TOPIC.

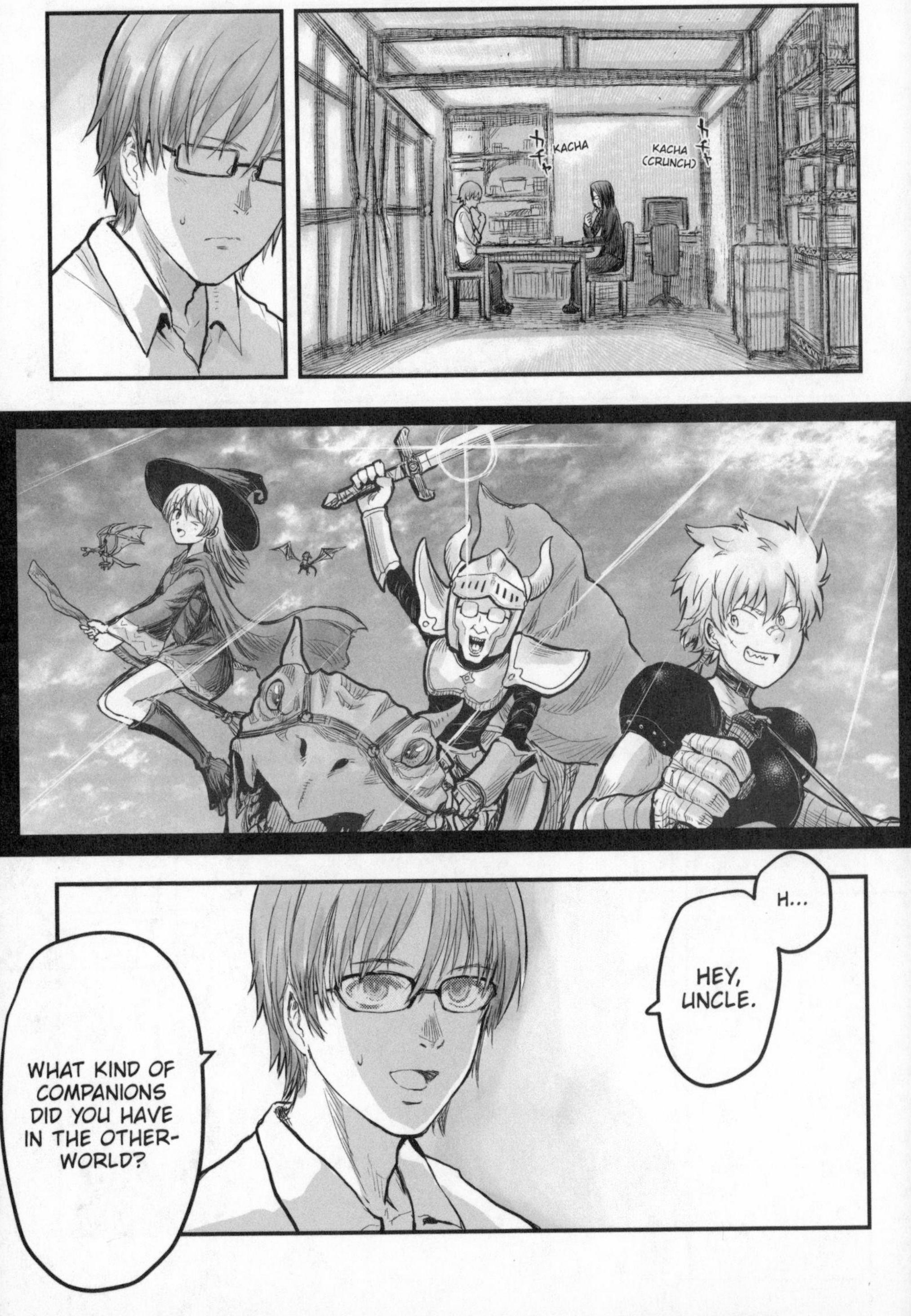
KACHA
KACHA (CRUNCH)
H...
HEY, UNCLE.
WHAT KIND OF COMPANIONS DID YOU HAVE IN THE OTHER-WORLD?

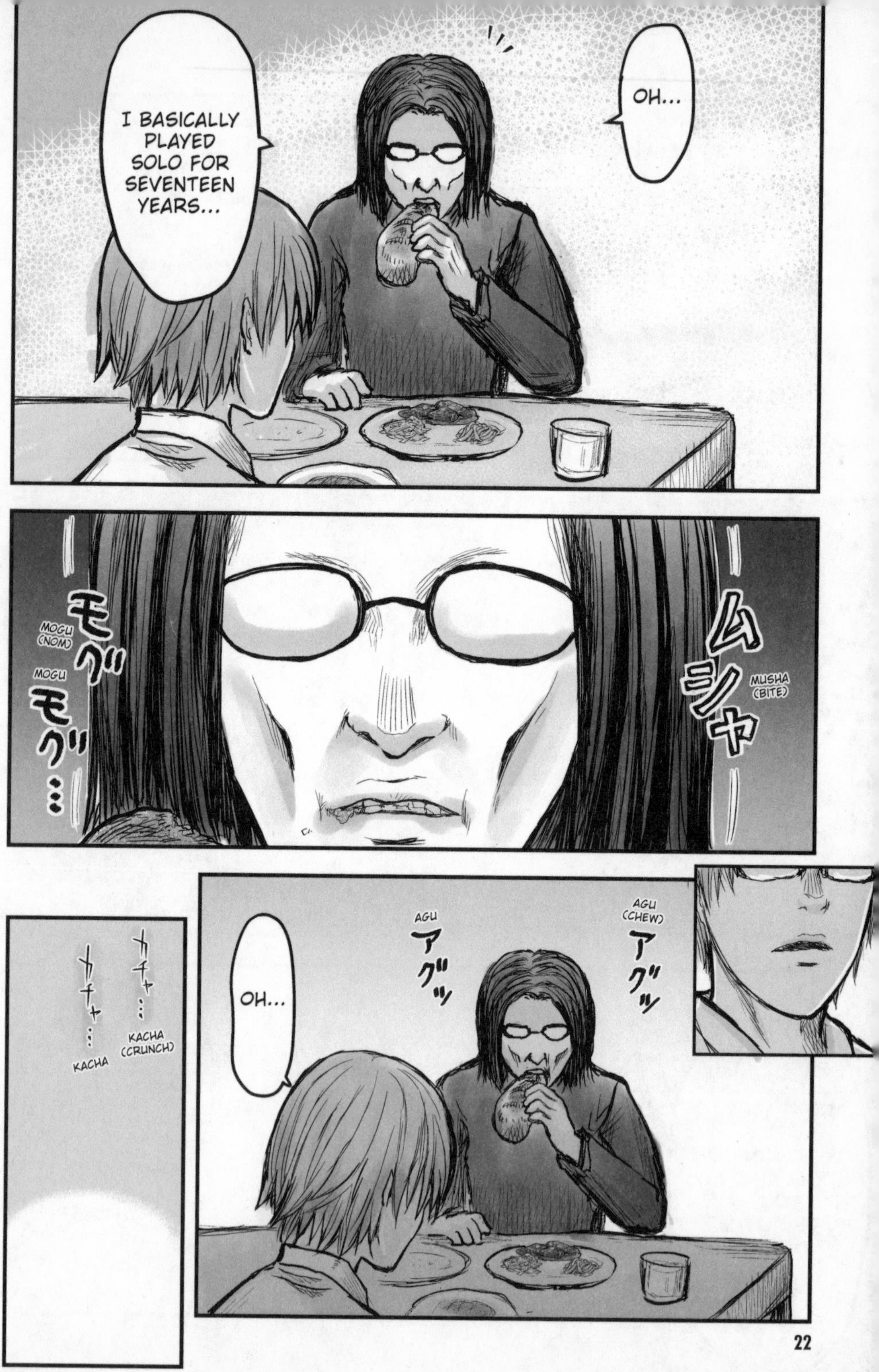
OH...
I BASICALLY PLAYED SOLO FOR SEVENTEEN YEARS...
ムシャー
MUSHA (BITE)
モグ
MOGU (NOM)
モグ…
MOGU
アグッ
AGU (CHEW)
アグッ
AGU
OH...
カチャ…
KACHA (CRUNCH)
カチャ…
KACHA

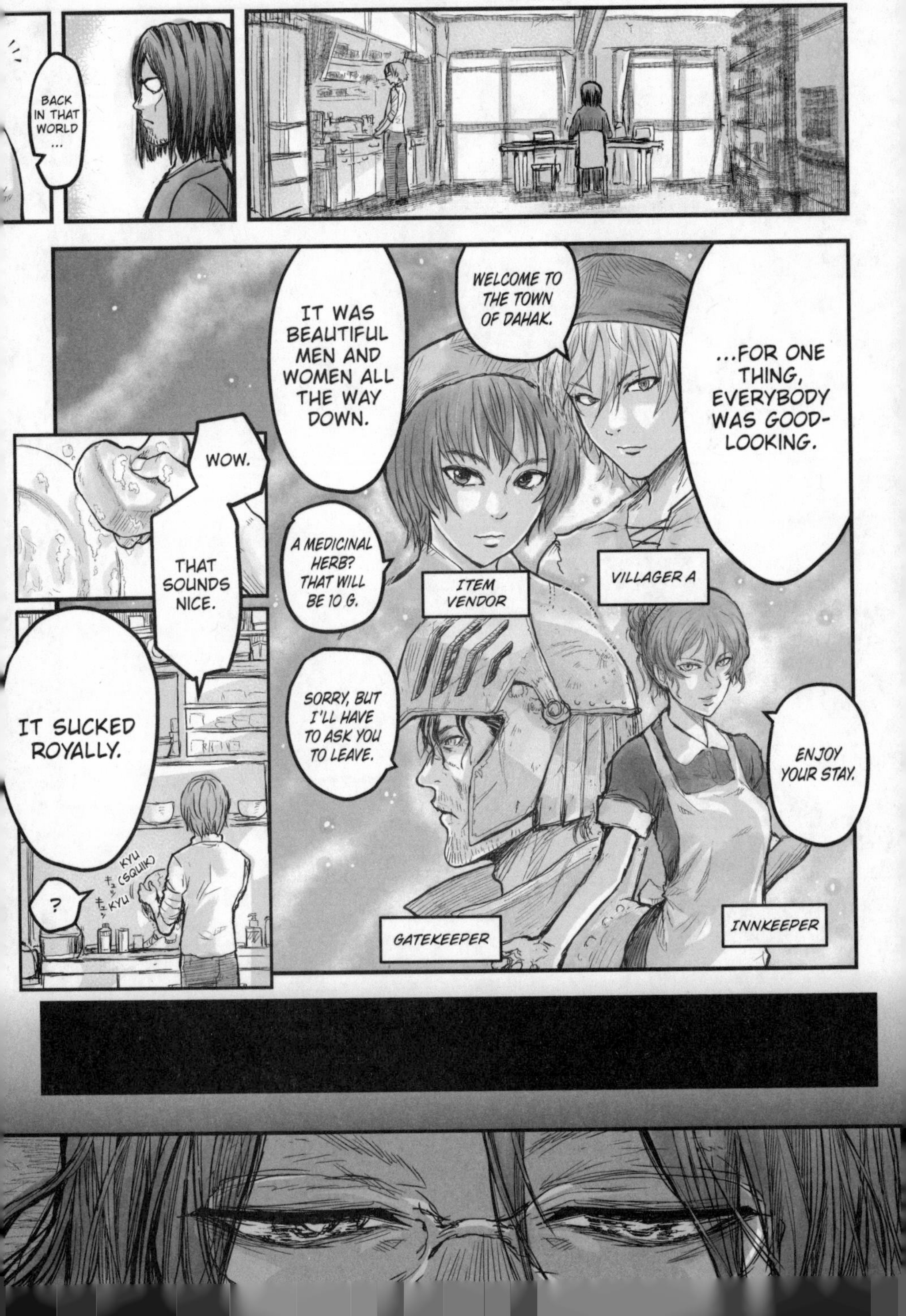
BACK IN THAT WORLD ...
...FOR ONE THING, EVERYBODY WAS GOOD-LOOKING.
WELCOME TO THE TOWN OF DAHAK.
VILLAGER A
IT WAS BEAUTIFUL MEN AND WOMEN ALL THE WAY DOWN.
A MEDICINAL HERB? THAT WILL BE 10 G.
ITEM VENDOR
ENJOY YOUR STAY.
INNKEEPER
SORRY, BUT I'LL HAVE TO ASK YOU TO LEAVE.
GATEKEEPER
WOW.
THAT SOUNDS NICE.
IT SUCKED ROYALLY.
KYU (SQUIK)
KYU
?

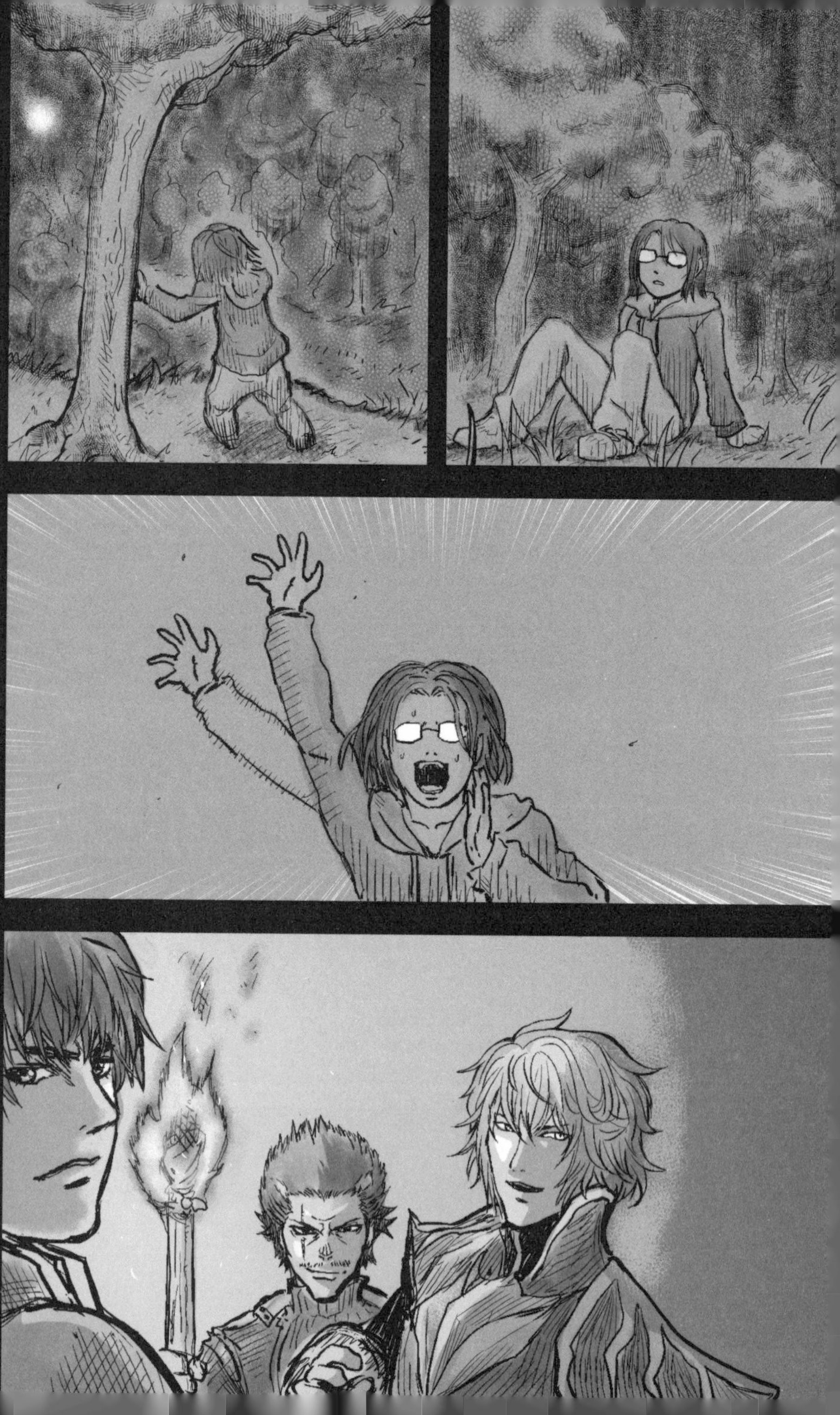

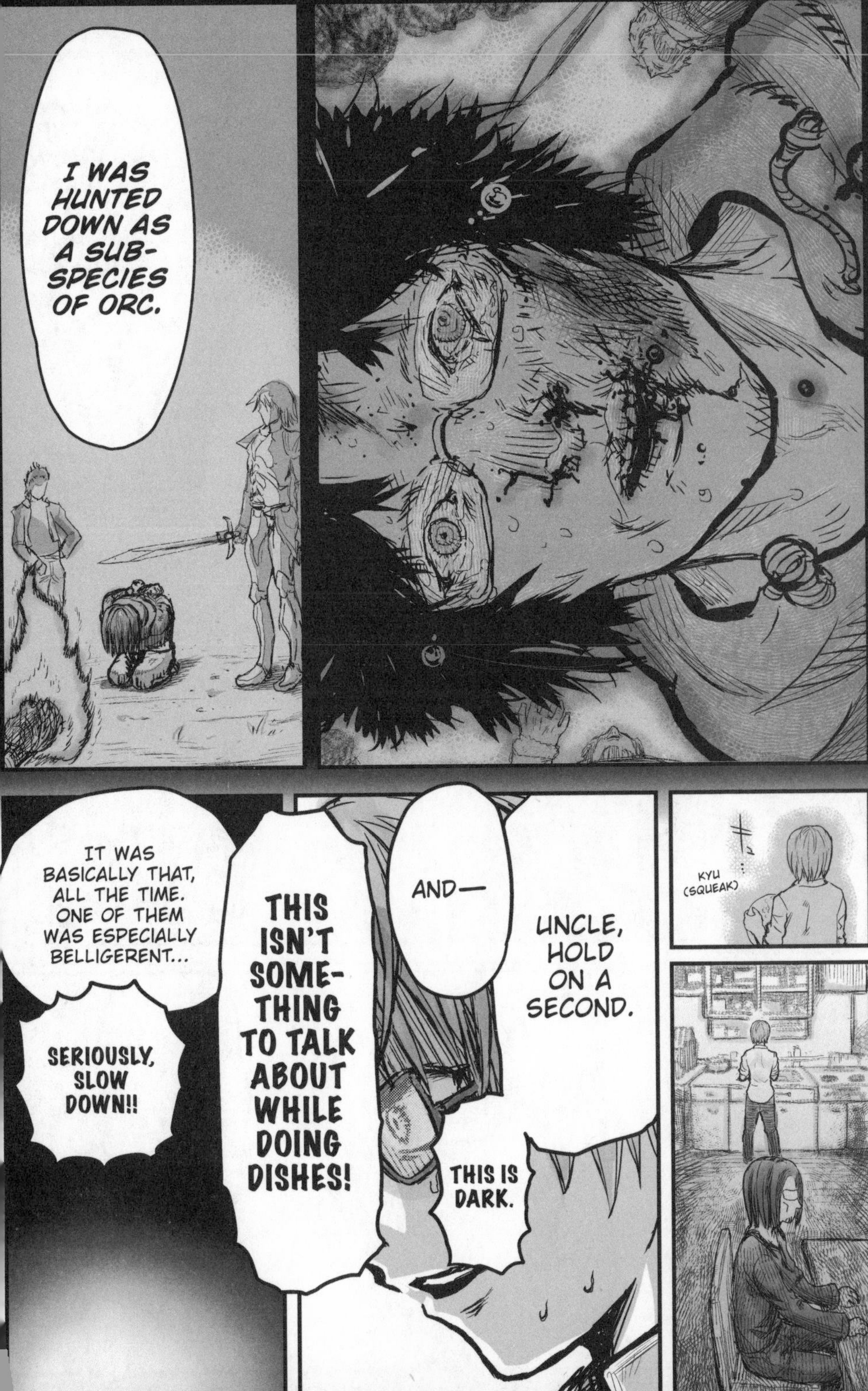
I WAS HUNTED DOWN AS A SUB-SPECIES OF ORC.
KYU (SQUEAK)
AND—
UNCLE, HOLD ON A SECOND.
THIS ISN'T SOMETHING TO TALK ABOUT WHILE DOING DISHES!
THIS IS DARK.
IT WAS BASICALLY THAT, ALL THE TIME. ONE OF THEM WAS ESPECIALLY BELLIGERENT...
SERIOUSLY, SLOW DOWN!!

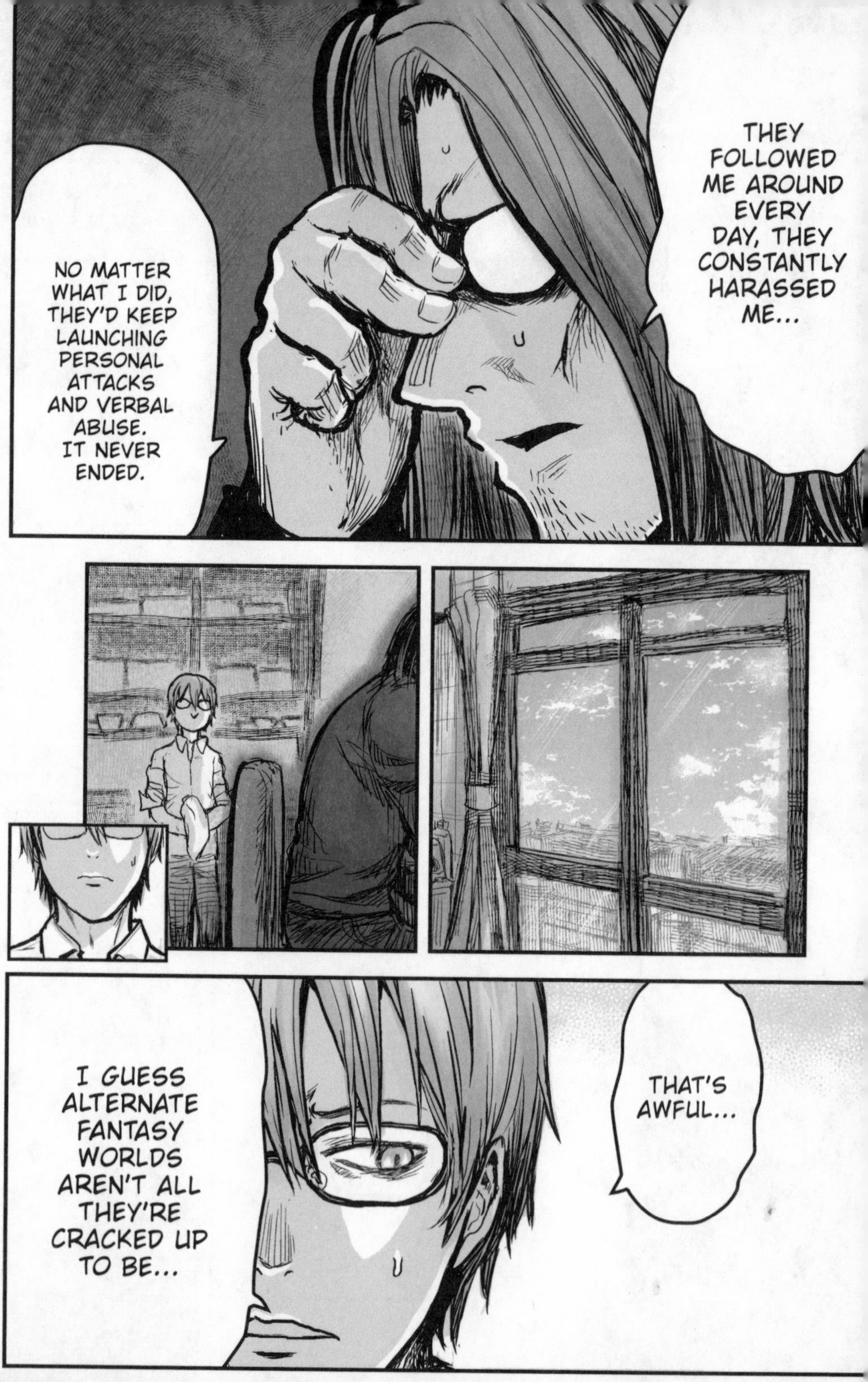
THEY FOLLOWED ME AROUND EVERY DAY, THEY CONSTANTLY HARASSED ME...
NO MATTER WHAT I DID, THEY'D KEEP LAUNCHING PERSONAL ATTACKS AND VERBAL ABUSE. IT NEVER ENDED.
THAT'S AWFUL...
I GUESS ALTERNATE FANTASY WORLDS AREN'T ALL THEY'RE CRACKED UP TO BE...

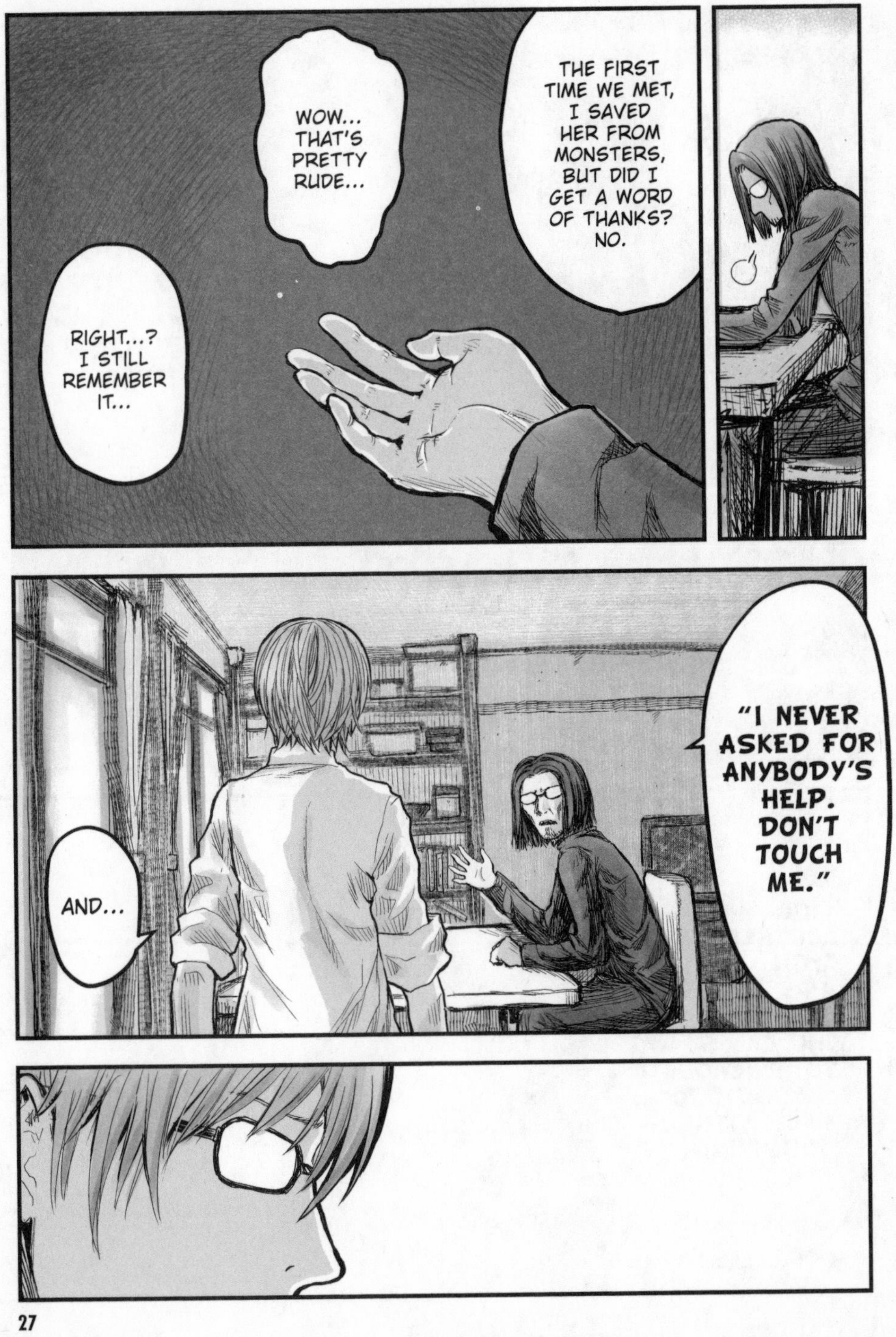
THE FIRST TIME WE MET, I SAVED HER FROM MONSTERS, BUT DID I GET A WORD OF THANKS? NO.
WOW... THAT'S PRETTY RUDE...
RIGHT...? I STILL REMEMBER IT...
"I NEVER ASKED FOR ANYBODY'S HELP. DON'T TOUCH ME."
AND...

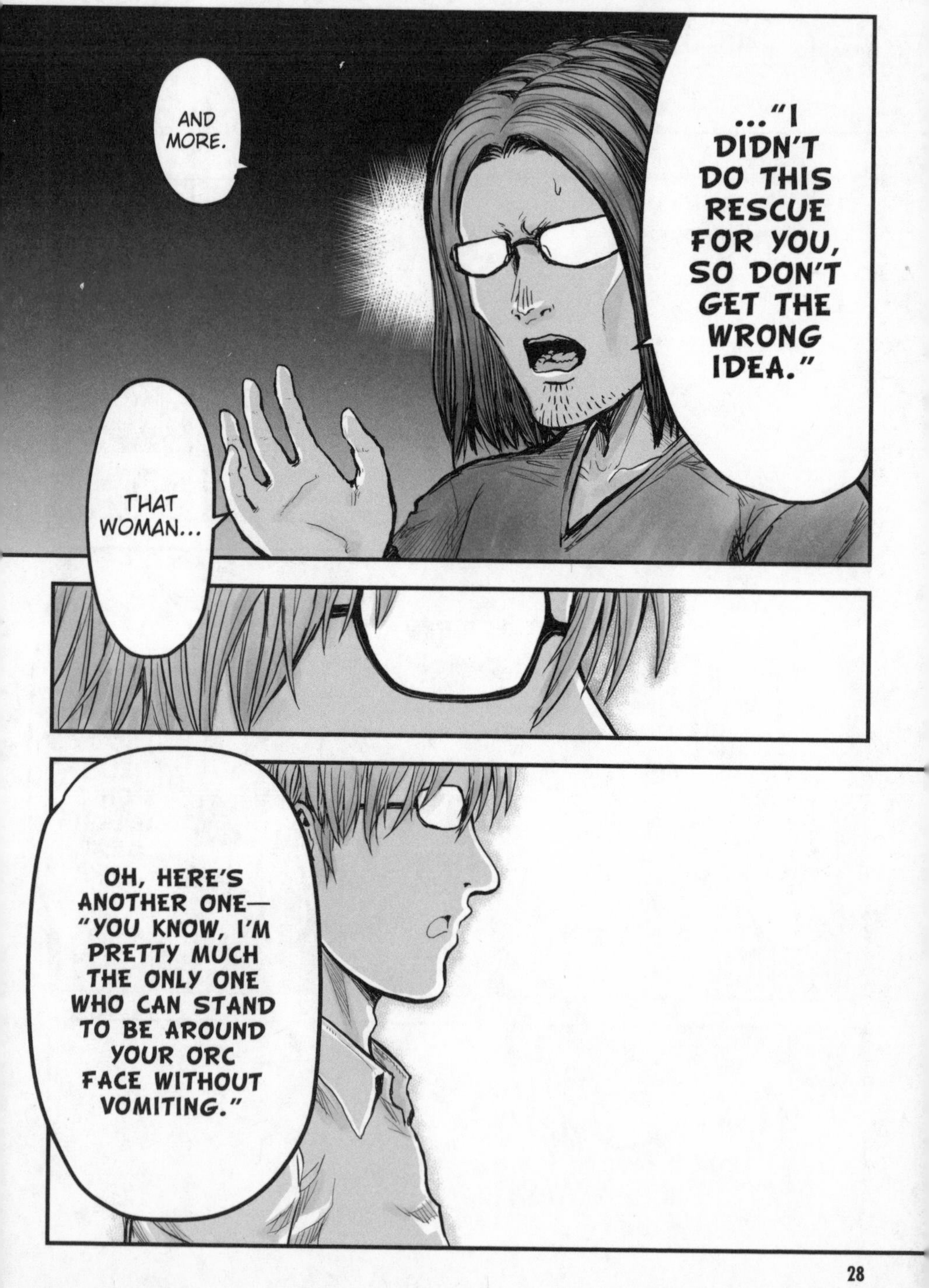
..."I DIDN'T DO THIS RESCUE FOR YOU, SO DON'T GET THE WRONG IDEA."
AND MORE.
THAT WOMAN...
OH, HERE'S ANOTHER ONE— "YOU KNOW, I'M PRETTY MUCH THE ONLY ONE WHO CAN STAND TO BE AROUND YOUR ORC FACE WITHOUT VOMITING."

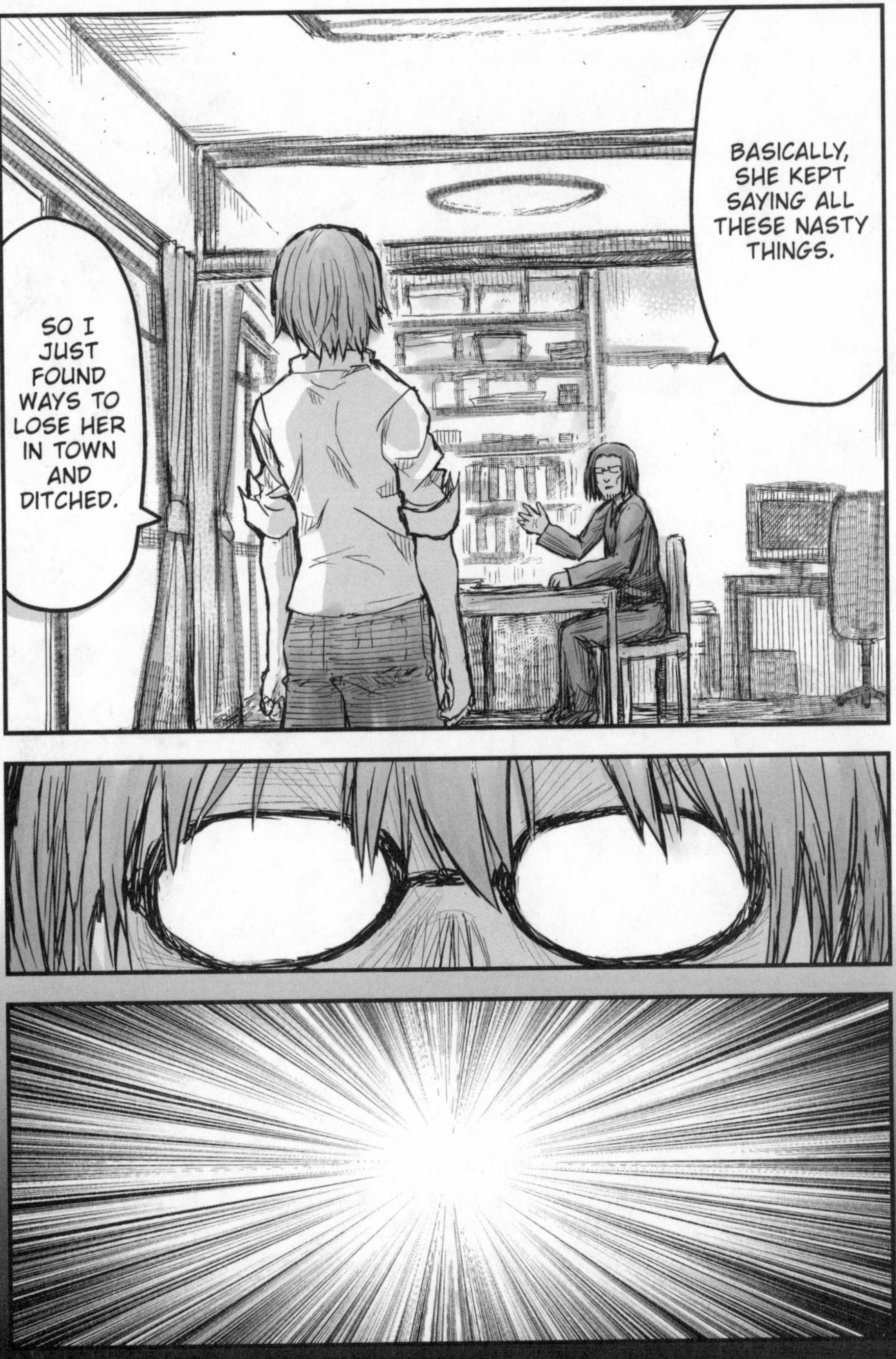
BASICALLY, SHE KEPT SAYING ALL THESE NASTY THINGS.
SO I JUST FOUND WAYS TO LOSE HER IN TOWN AND DITCHED.

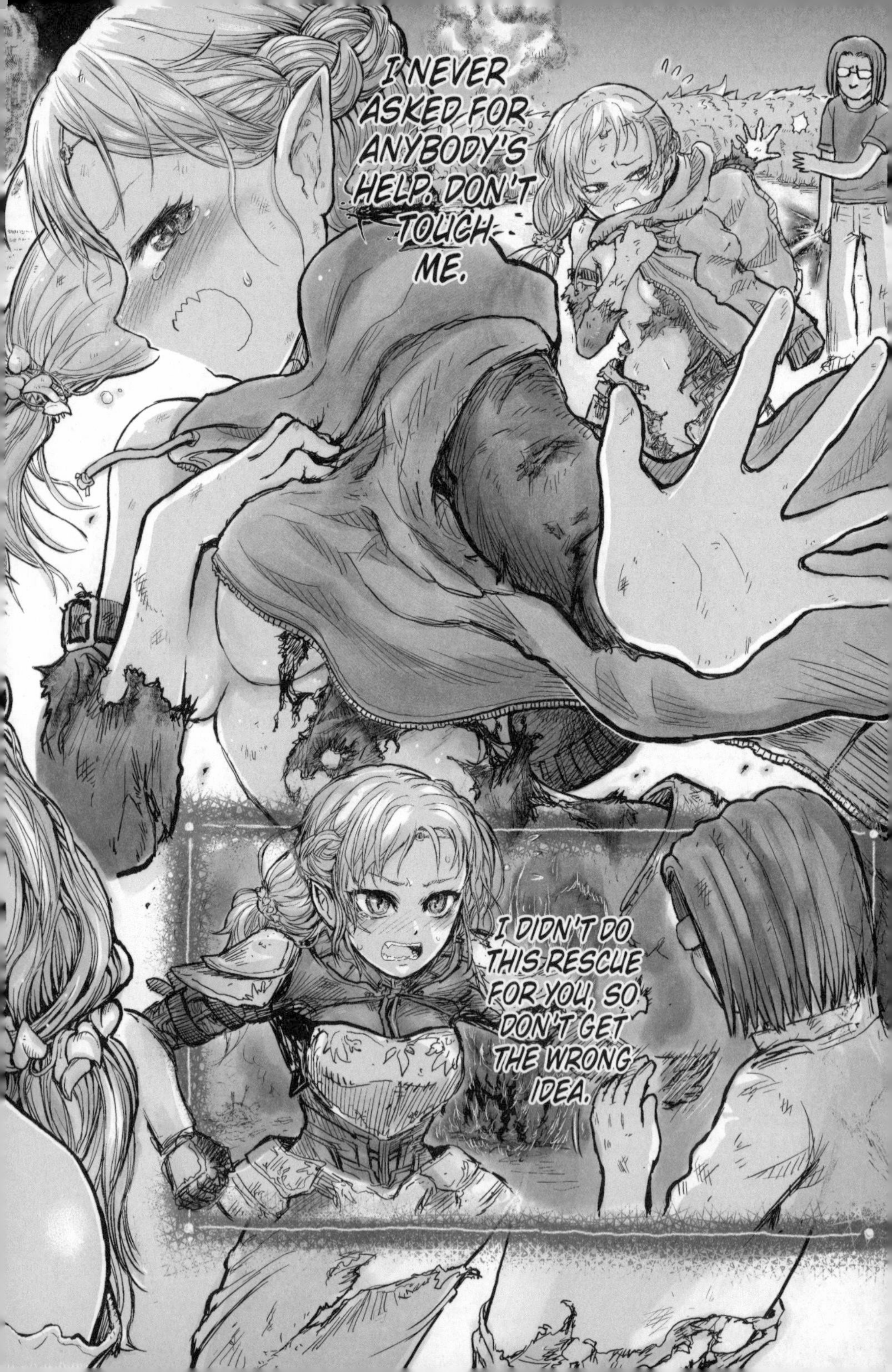
I NEVER ASKED FOR ANYBODY'S HELP. DON'T TOUCH ME.
I DIDN'T DO THIS RESCUE FOR YOU, SO DON'T GET THE WRONG IDEA.

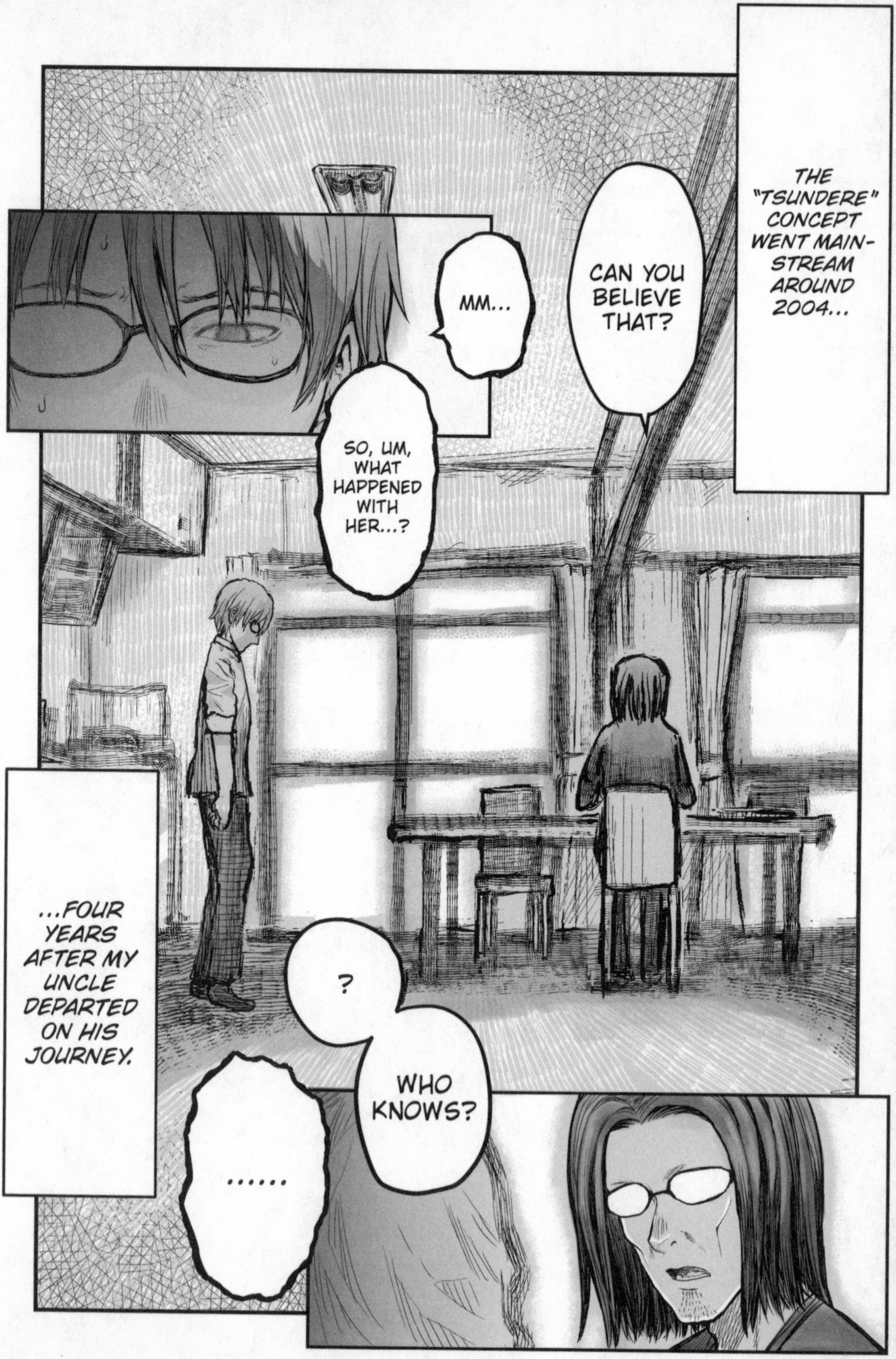
THE "TSUNDERE" CONCEPT WENT MAIN-STREAM AROUND 2004...
CAN YOU BELIEVE THAT?
MM...
SO, UM, WHAT HAPPENED WITH HER...?
?
WHO KNOWS?
......
...FOUR YEARS AFTER MY UNCLE DEPARTED ON HIS JOURNEY.

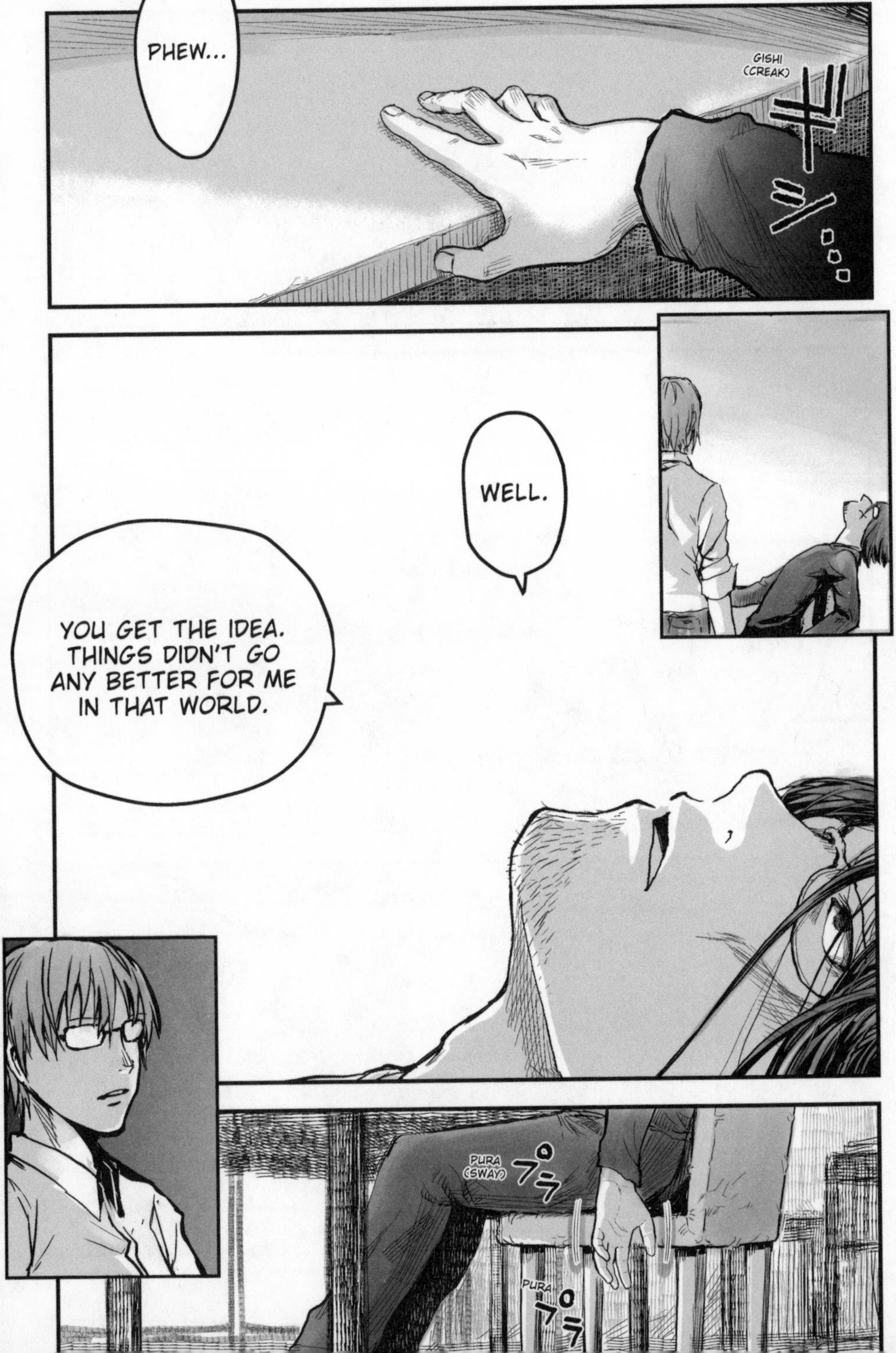
GISHI (CREAK)
PHEW...
WELL.
YOU GET THE IDEA. THINGS DIDN'T GO ANY BETTER FOR ME IN THAT WORLD.
PURA (SWAY)
PURA

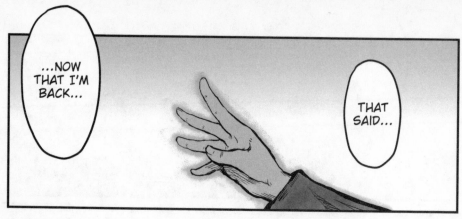

...NOW THAT I'M BACK...

THAT SAID...

WEB TIME!

THIS IS NICE!

KACHI

KACHI
(CLICK)

34

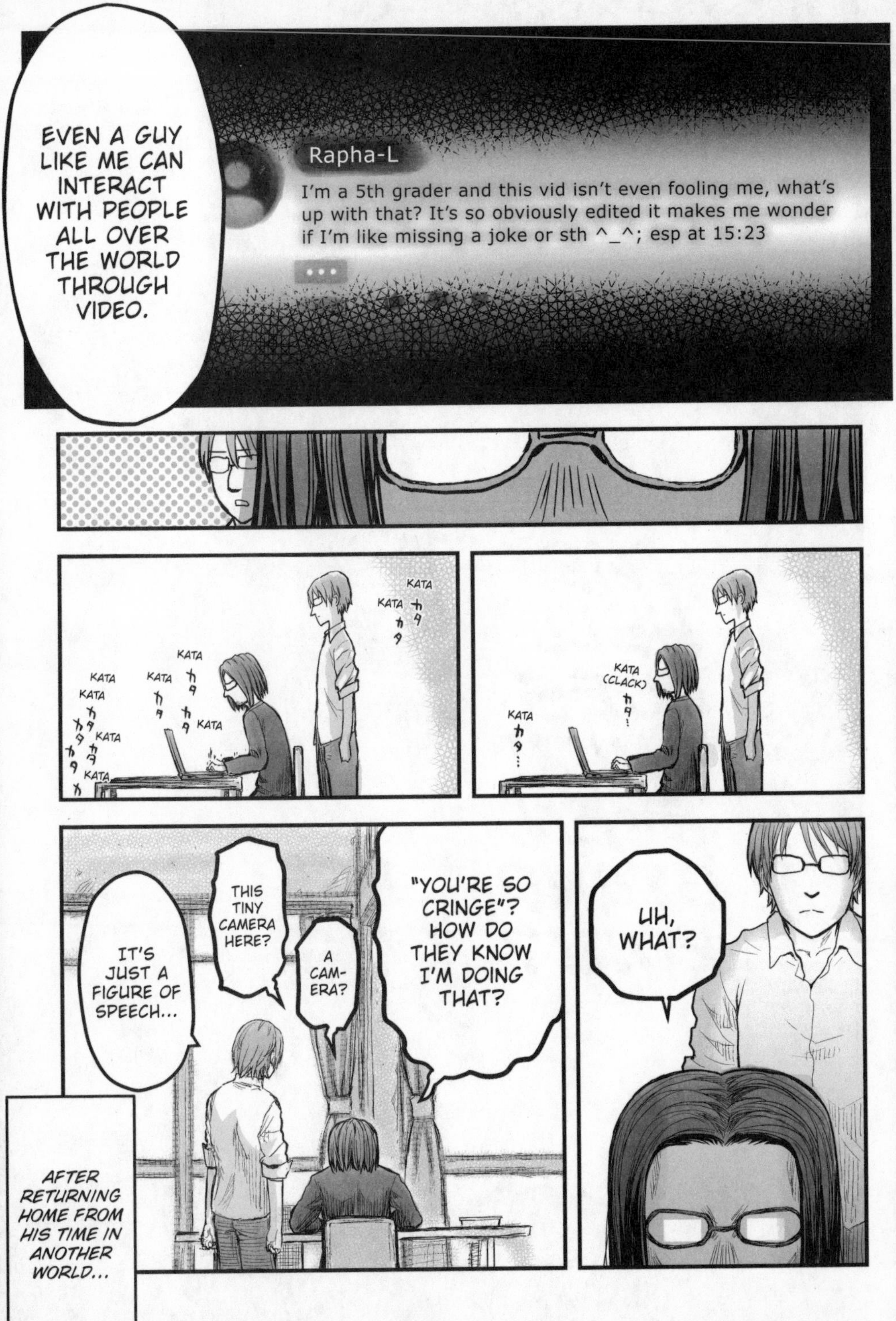

Rapha-L
I'm a 5th grader and this vid isn't even fooling me, what's up with that? It's so obviously edited it makes me wonder if I'm like missing a joke or sth ^_^; esp at 15:23
...
EVEN A GUY LIKE ME CAN INTERACT WITH PEOPLE ALL OVER THE WORLD THROUGH VIDEO.
KATA (CLACK) カタ…
KATA カタ…
KATA KATA カタカタ
KATA KATA カタカタ
KATA KATA カタカタ
KATA KATA KATA KATA カタカタカタカタ
UH, WHAT?
"YOU'RE SO CRINGE"? HOW DO THEY KNOW I'M DOING THAT?
A CAM-ERA?
THIS TINY CAMERA HERE?
IT'S JUST A FIGURE OF SPEECH...
AFTER RETURNING HOME FROM HIS TIME IN ANOTHER WORLD...

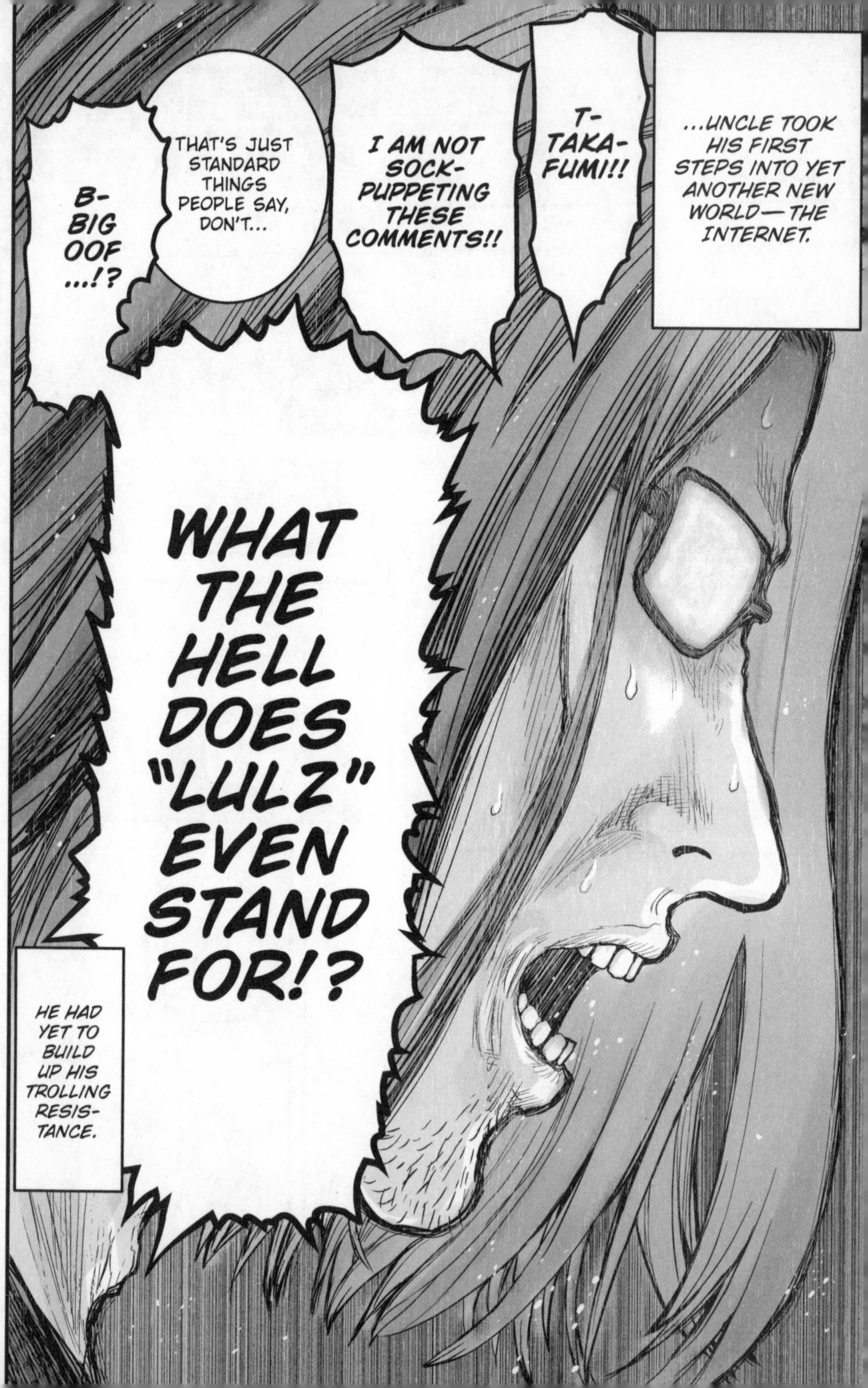
...UNCLE TOOK HIS FIRST STEPS INTO YET ANOTHER NEW WORLD—THE INTERNET.
T-TAKA-FUMI!!
I AM NOT SOCK-PUPPETING THESE COMMENTS!!
THAT'S JUST STANDARD THINGS PEOPLE SAY, DON'T...
B-BIG OOF ...!?
WHAT THE HELL DOES "LULZ" EVEN STAND FOR!?
HE HAD YET TO BUILD UP HIS TROLLING RESIS-TANCE.

Tsundere

The concept known as "tsundere" first appeared as Net slang in late 2002. The generally accepted timeframe during which the concept grew widespread enough to be accepted in the mainstream is 2004-2005.

Works cited:
Tagashi, Junichi. "Tsundere Expression Case Study: The Relationship Between Tsundere Attributes and Linguistic Representation." Paper presented at Symposium: Role, Character, Language, Kobe University Centennial Hall, March 28-29, 2009.

TIPS

UNCLE from ANOTHER WORLD

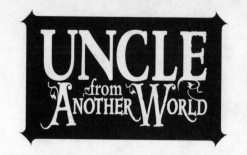

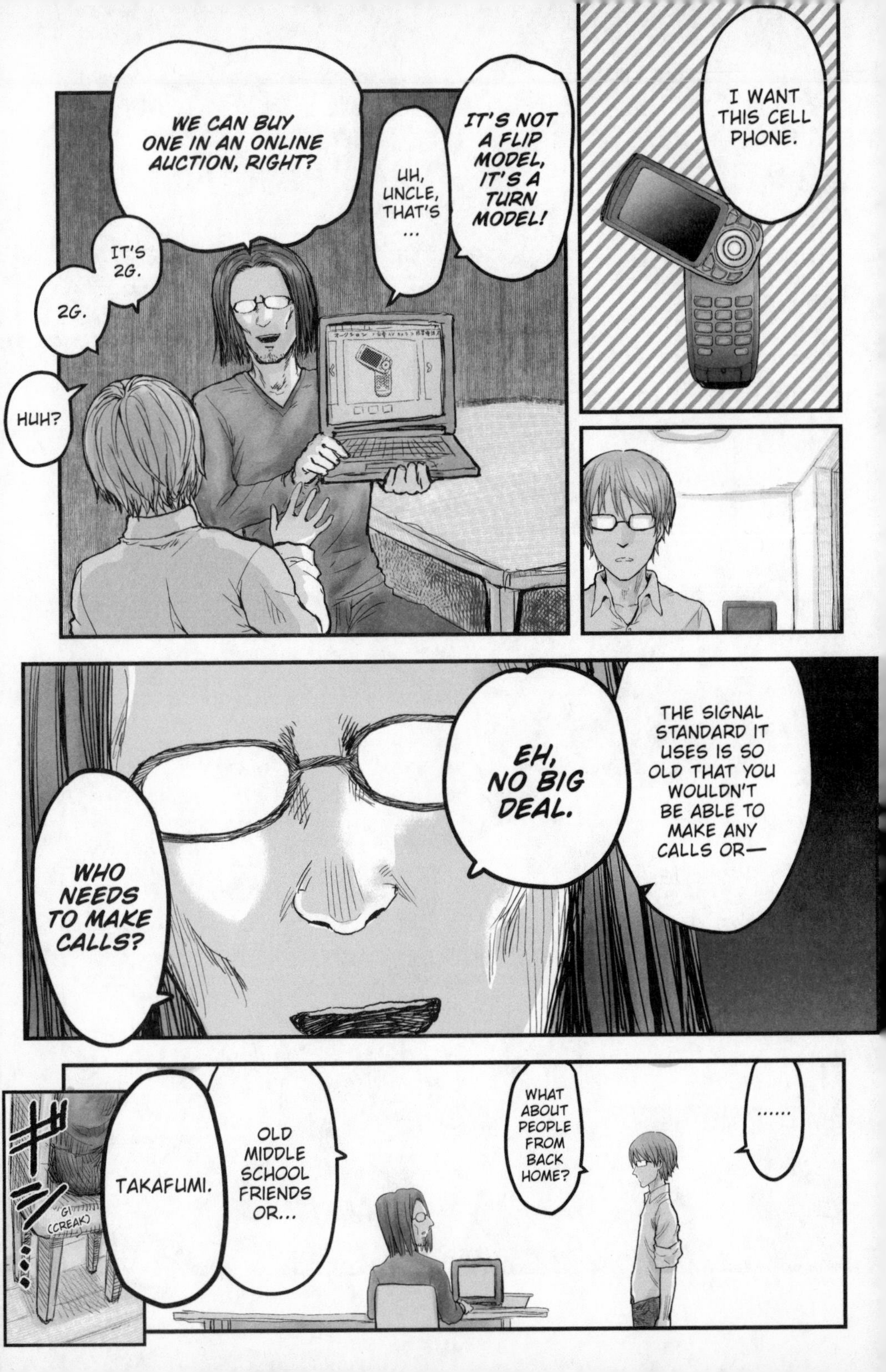
I WANT THIS CELL PHONE.
IT'S NOT A FLIP MODEL, IT'S A TURN MODEL!
UH, UNCLE, THAT'S ...
WE CAN BUY ONE IN AN ONLINE AUCTION, RIGHT?
IT'S 2G.
2G.
HUH?
THE SIGNAL STANDARD IT USES IS SO OLD THAT YOU WOULDN'T BE ABLE TO MAKE ANY CALLS OR—
EH, NO BIG DEAL.
WHO NEEDS TO MAKE CALLS?
......
WHAT ABOUT PEOPLE FROM BACK HOME?
OLD MIDDLE SCHOOL FRIENDS OR...
TAKAFUMI.
GI (CREAK)

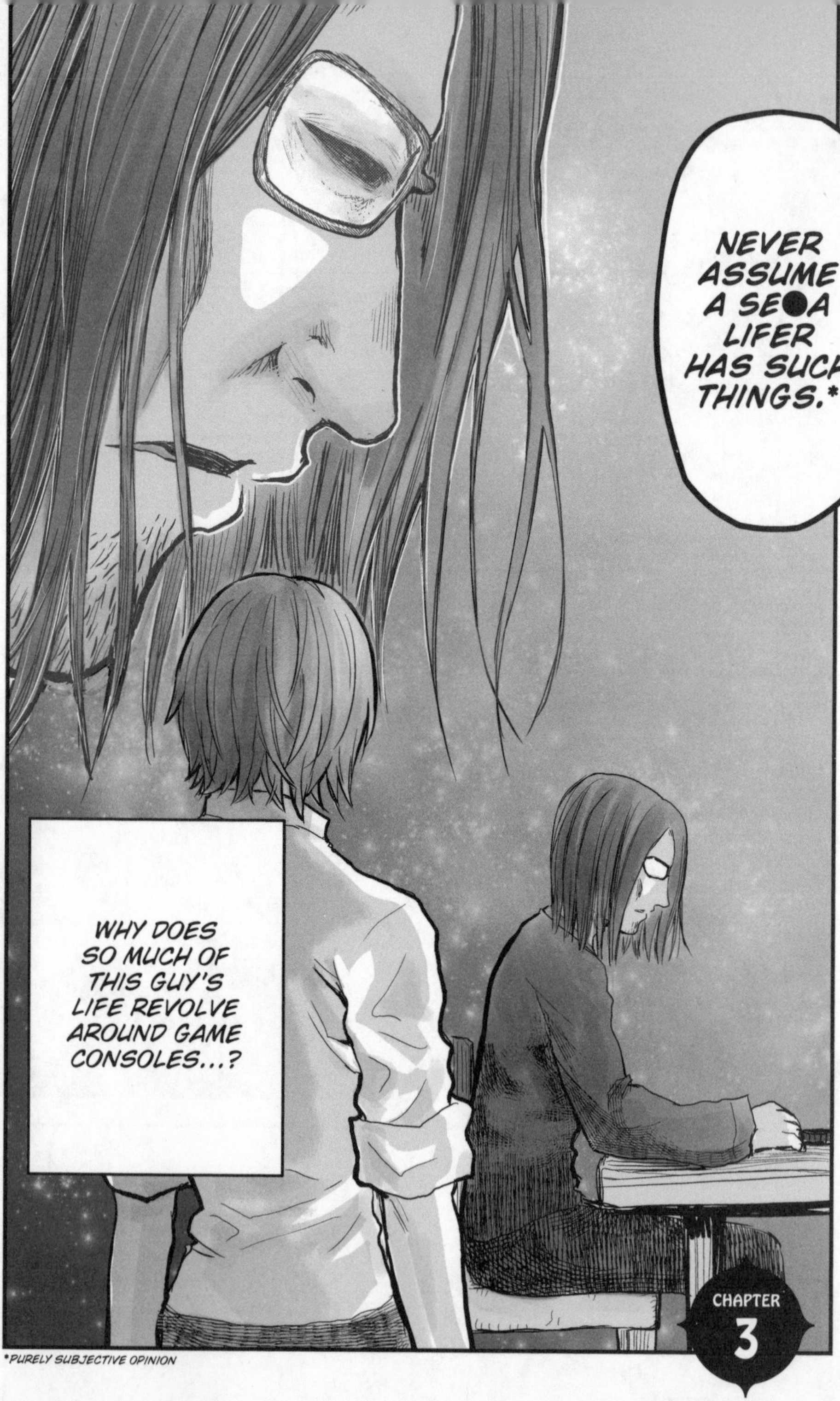
NEVER ASSUME A SE●A LIFER HAS SUCH THINGS.*
WHY DOES SO MUCH OF THIS GUY'S LIFE REVOLVE AROUND GAME CONSOLES...?
CHAPTER 3

*PURELY SUBJECTIVE OPINION

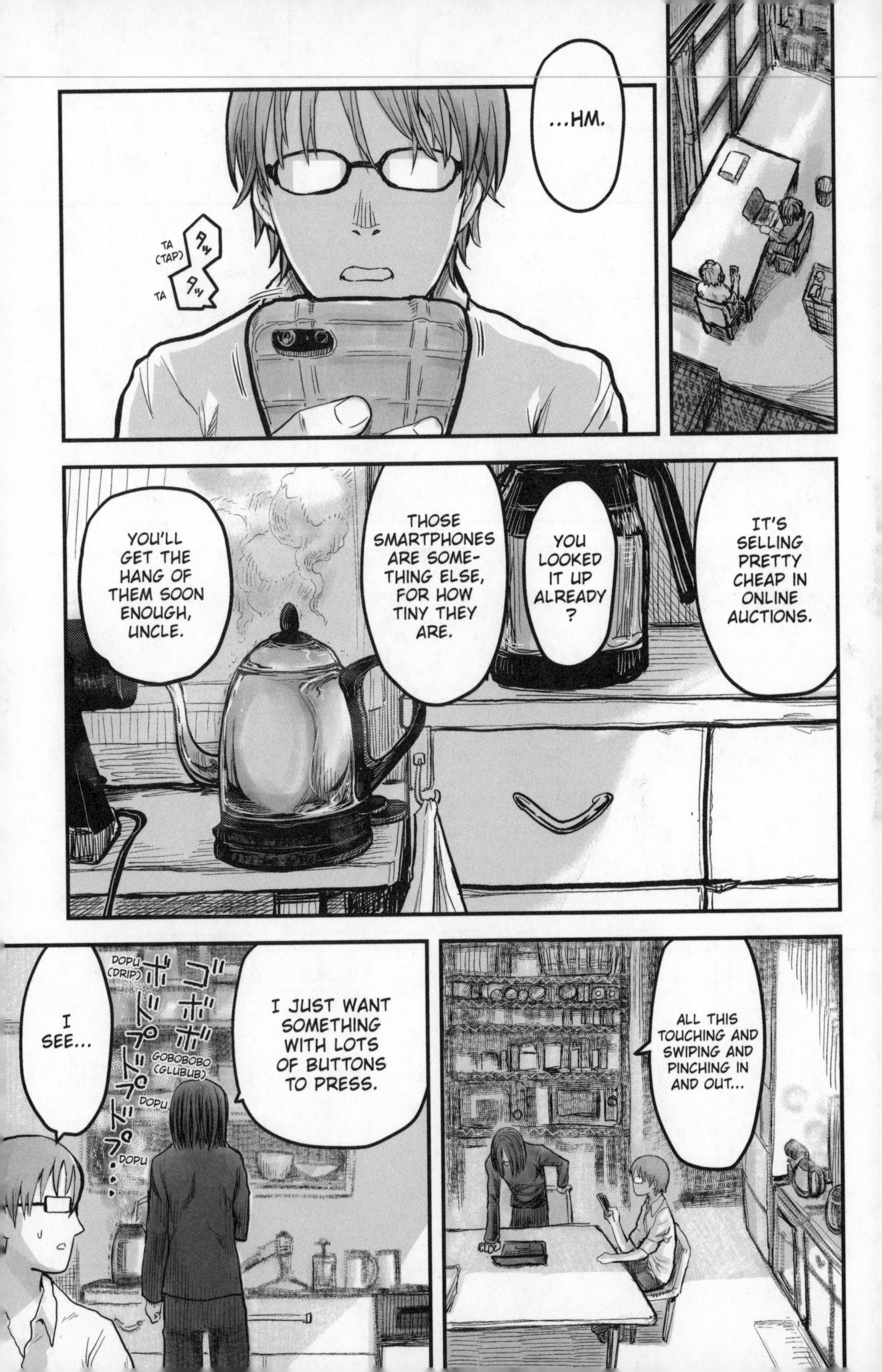
...HM.
TA (TAP)
TA
IT'S SELLING PRETTY CHEAP IN ONLINE AUCTIONS.
YOU LOOKED IT UP ALREADY?
THOSE SMARTPHONES ARE SOME-THING ELSE, FOR HOW TINY THEY ARE.
YOU'LL GET THE HANG OF THEM SOON ENOUGH, UNCLE.
ALL THIS TOUCHING AND SWIPING AND PINCHING IN AND OUT...
I JUST WANT SOMETHING WITH LOTS OF BUTTONS TO PRESS.
DOPU (DRIP)
GOBOBOBO (GLUBUB)
DOPU
DOPU
I SEE...

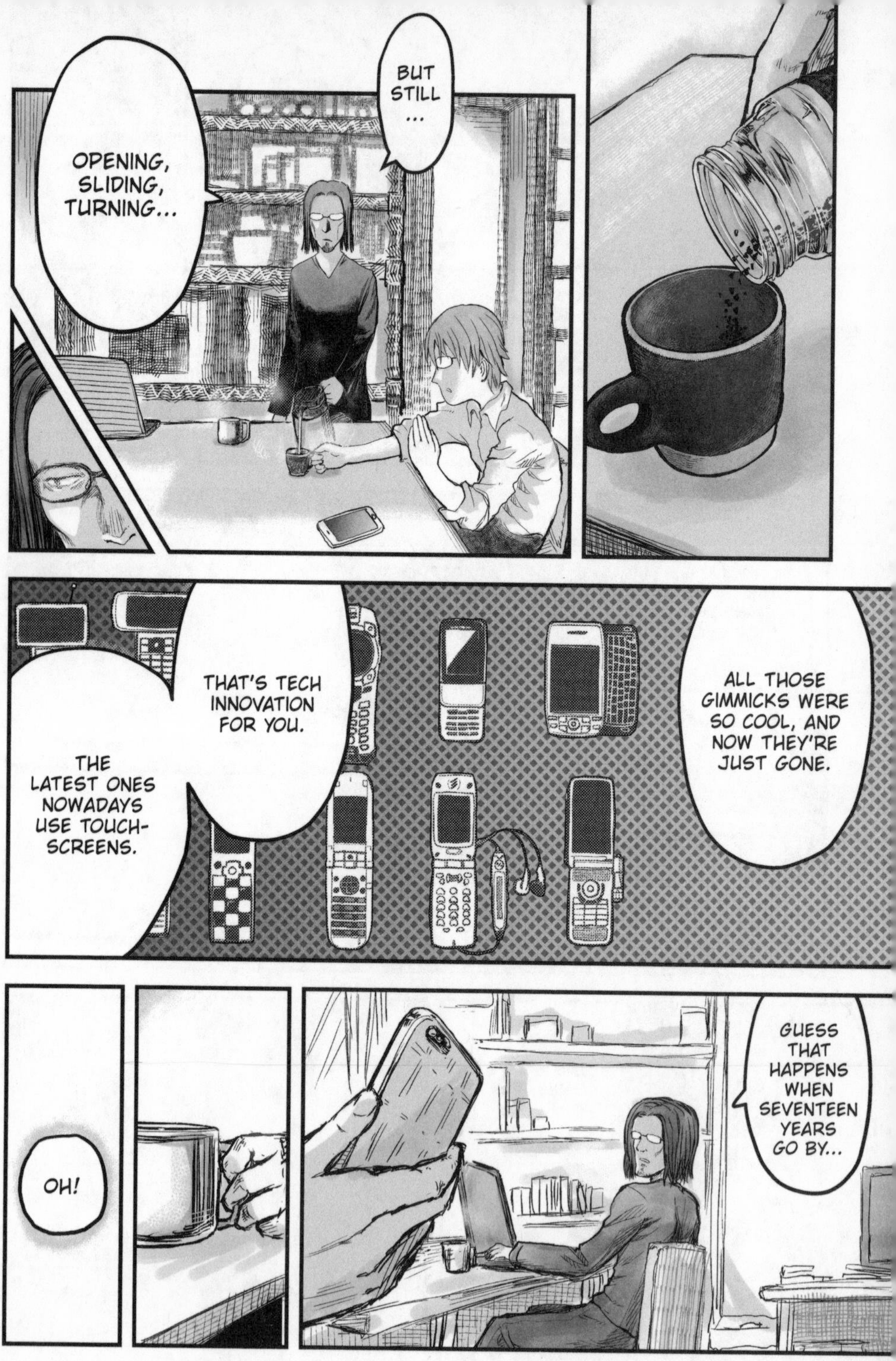
BUT STILL...
OPENING, SLIDING, TURNING...
ALL THOSE GIMMICKS WERE SO COOL, AND NOW THEY'RE JUST GONE.
THAT'S TECH INNOVATION FOR YOU.
THE LATEST ONES NOWADAYS USE TOUCH-SCREENS.
GUESS THAT HAPPENS WHEN SEVENTEEN YEARS GO BY...
OH!

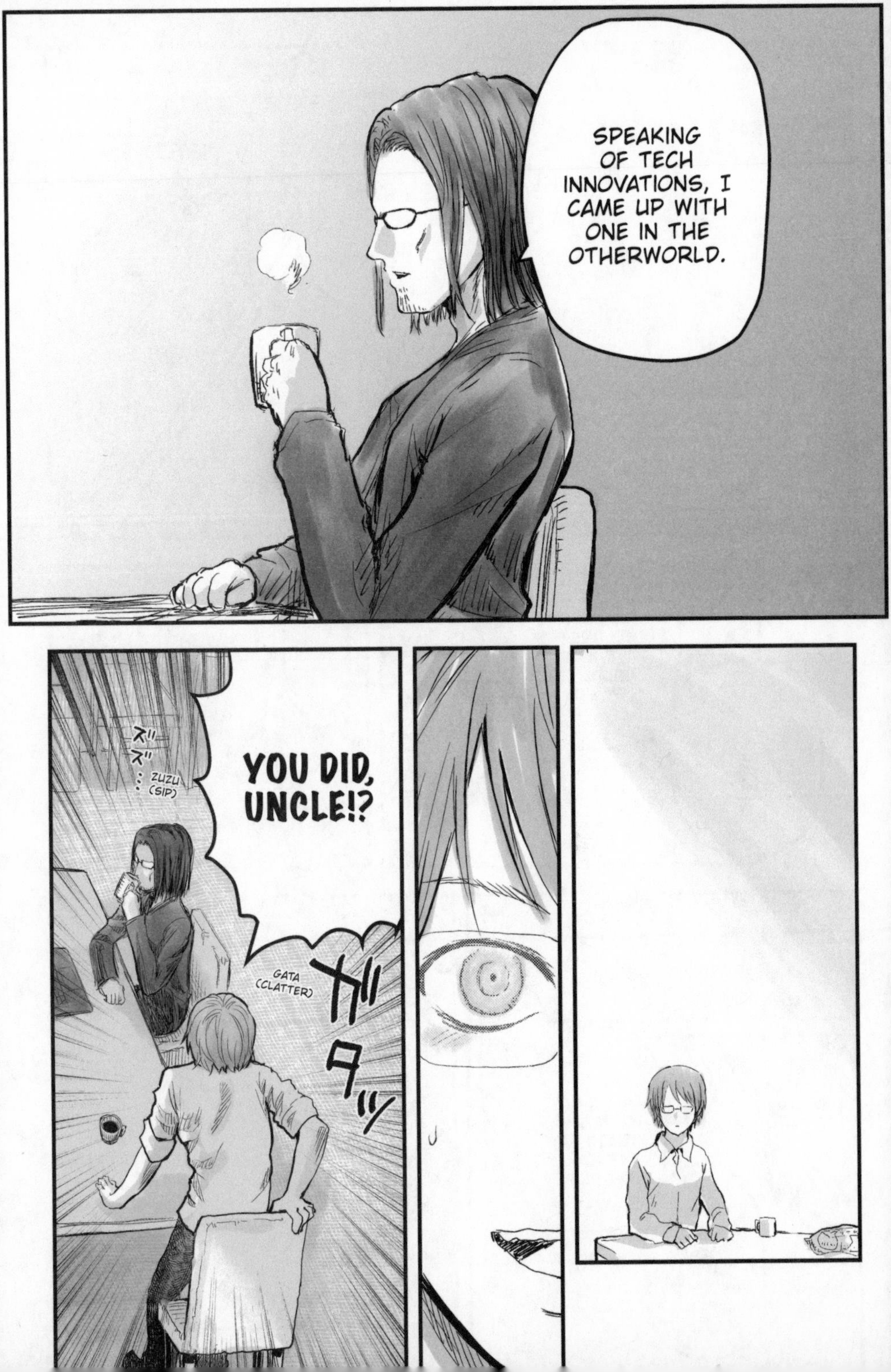
SPEAKING OF TECH INNOVATIONS, I CAME UP WITH ONE IN THE OTHERWORLD.
YOU DID, UNCLE!?
ズズ…
ZUZU (SIP)
ガタッ
GATA (CLATTER)

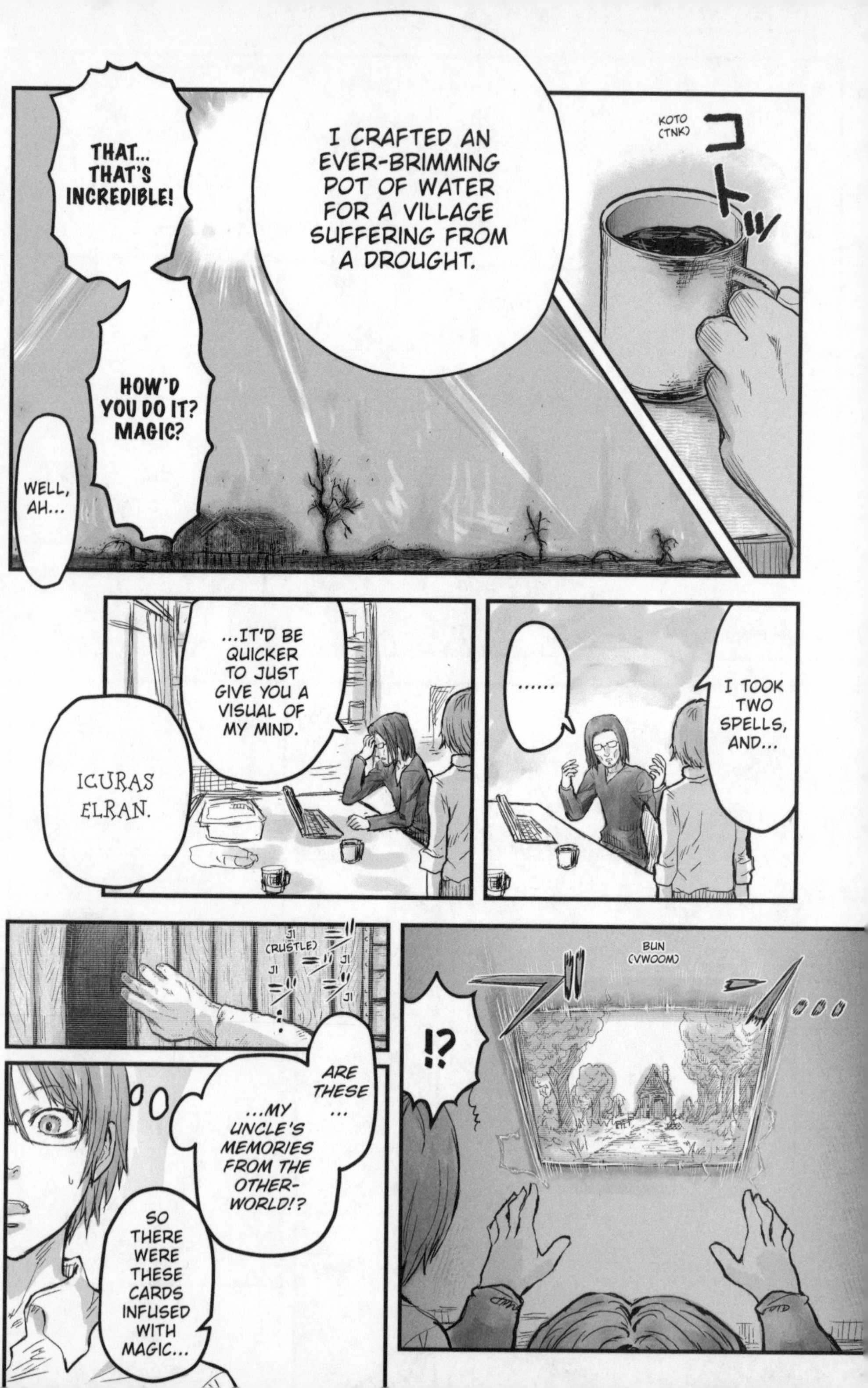
KOTO (TNK)
I CRAFTED AN EVER-BRIMMING POT OF WATER FOR A VILLAGE SUFFERING FROM A DROUGHT.
THAT... THAT'S INCREDIBLE!
HOW'D YOU DO IT? MAGIC?
WELL, AH...
I TOOK TWO SPELLS, AND...
......
...IT'D BE QUICKER TO JUST GIVE YOU A VISUAL OF MY MIND.
ICURAS ELRAN.
BUN (VWOOM)
!?
JI (RUSTLE) JI JI JI
ARE THESE ...
...MY UNCLE'S MEMORIES FROM THE OTHER-WORLD!?
SO THERE WERE THESE CARDS INFUSED WITH MAGIC...

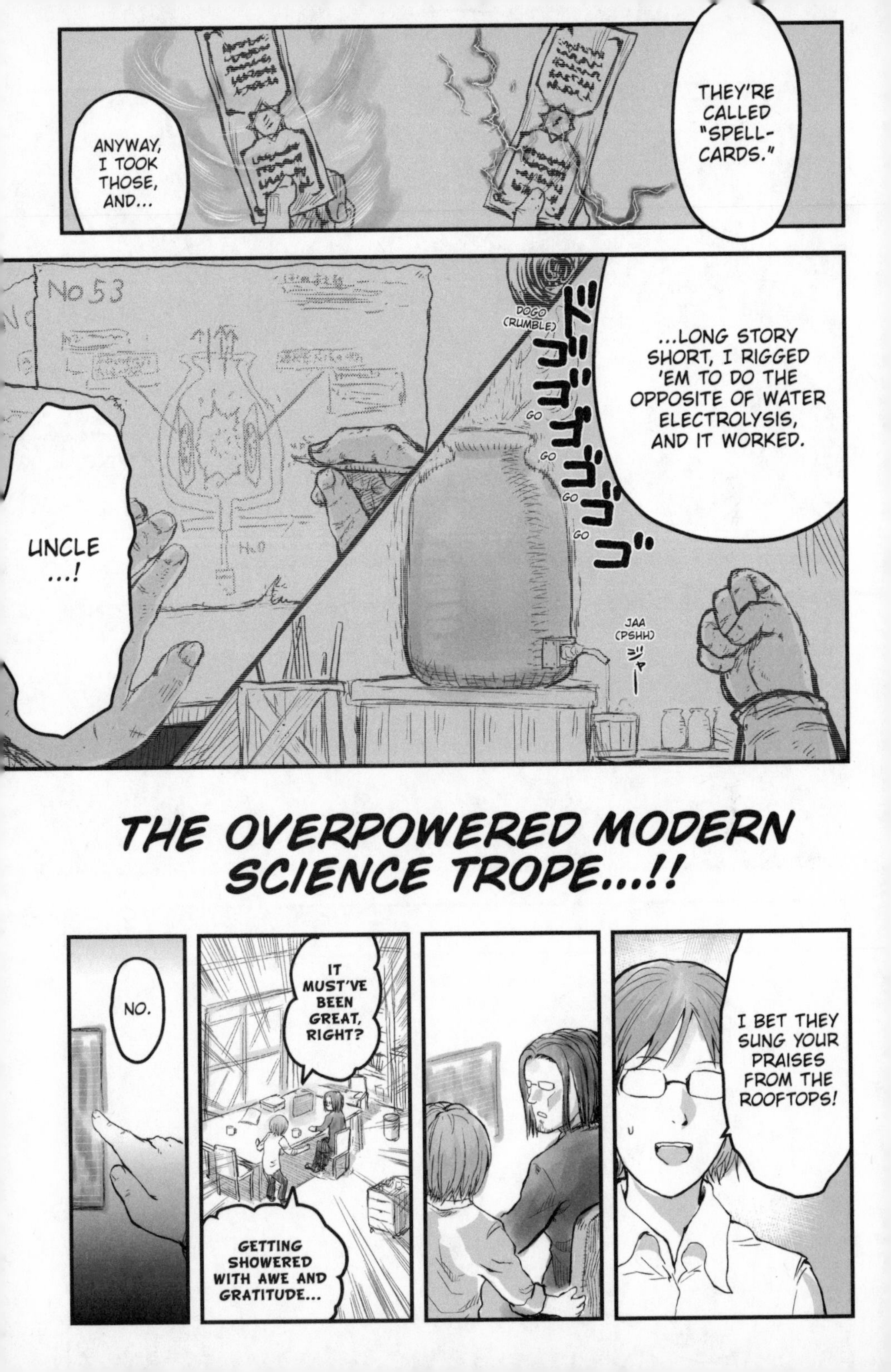
THEY'RE CALLED "SPELL-CARDS."
ANYWAY, I TOOK THOSE, AND...
No 53
...LONG STORY SHORT, I RIGGED 'EM TO DO THE OPPOSITE OF WATER ELECTROLYSIS, AND IT WORKED.
DOGO (RUMBLE)
GO
GO
GO
GO
JAA (PSHH)
ジャー
UNCLE...!
THE OVERPOWERED MODERN SCIENCE TROPE...!!
I BET THEY SUNG YOUR PRAISES FROM THE ROOFTOPS!
IT MUST'VE BEEN GREAT, RIGHT?
GETTING SHOWERED WITH AWE AND GRATITUDE...
NO.

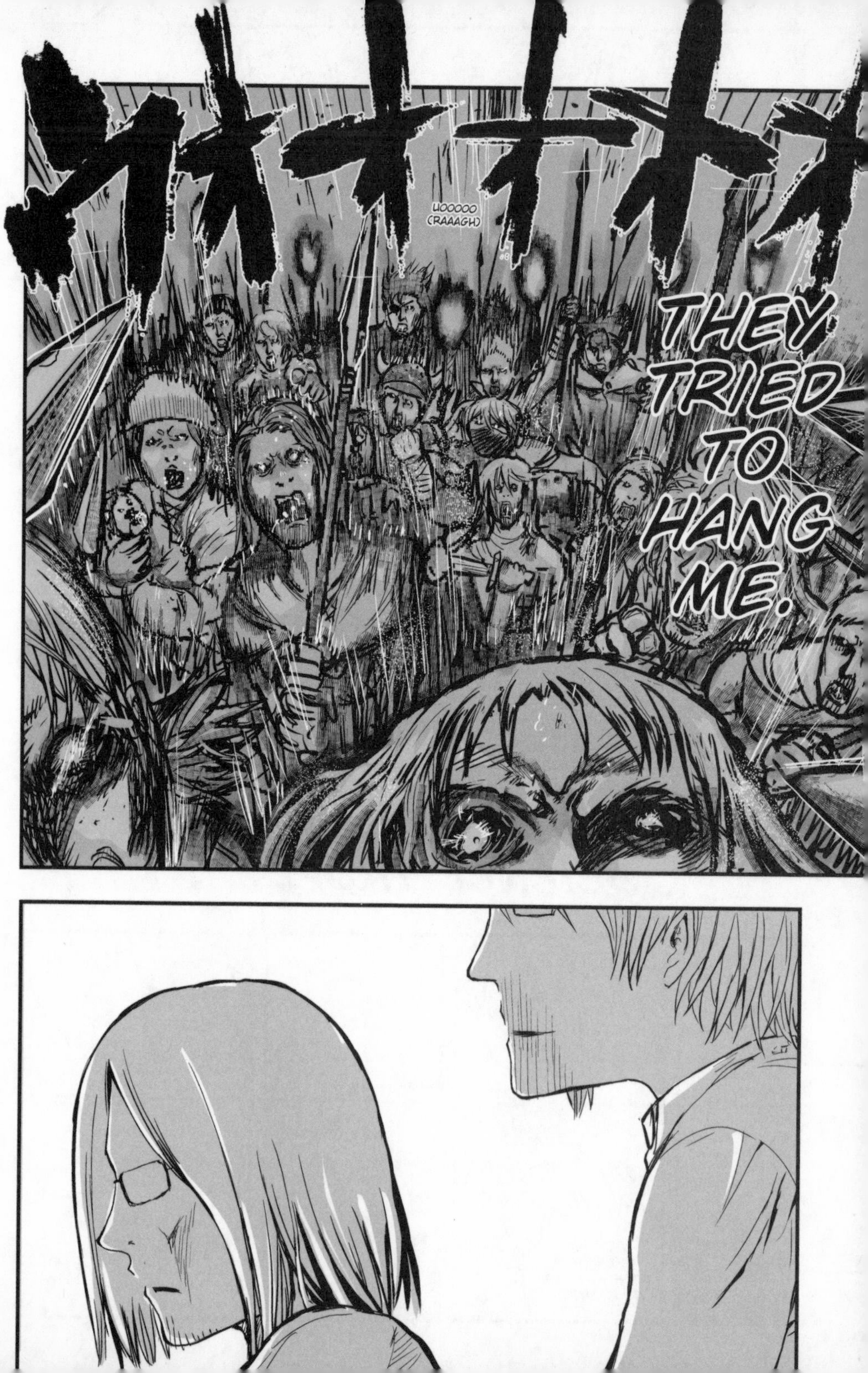
UOOOOO
(RAAAGH)
THEY TRIED TO HANG ME.

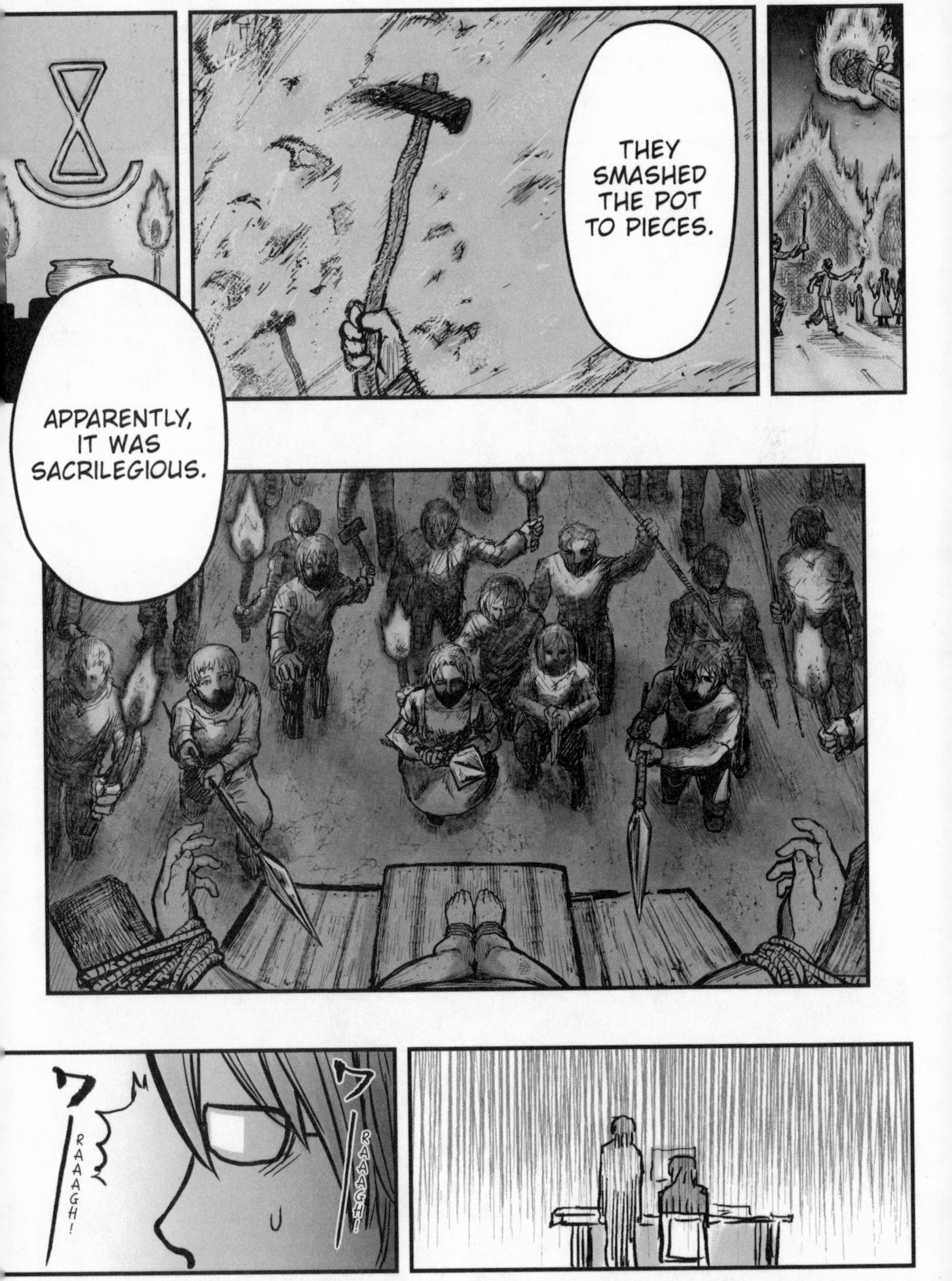
THEY SMASHED THE POT TO PIECES.
APPARENTLY, IT WAS SACRILEGIOUS.
RAAAGH!
RAAAGH!

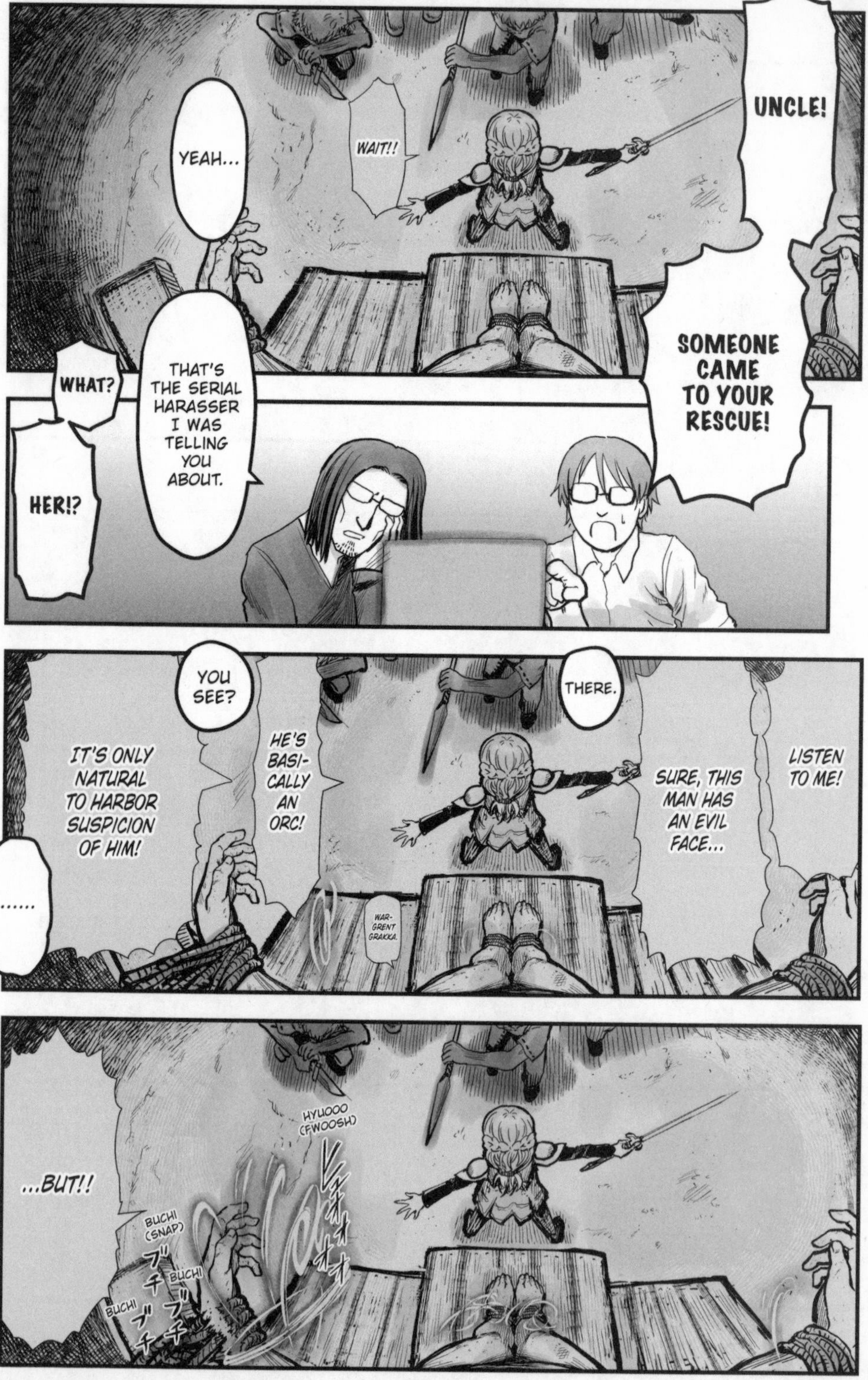
UNCLE!
SOMEONE CAME TO YOUR RESCUE!
WAIT!!
YEAH...
THAT'S THE SERIAL HARASSER I WAS TELLING YOU ABOUT.
WHAT?
HER!?
THERE.
YOU SEE?
LISTEN TO ME!
SURE, THIS MAN HAS AN EVIL FACE...
HE'S BASICALLY AN ORC!
IT'S ONLY NATURAL TO HARBOR SUSPICION OF HIM!
WAR-GRENT GRAKKA.
......
HYUOOO (FWOOSH)
...BUT!!
BUCHI (SNAP)
ブチ
BUCHI
ブチ
BUCHI
ブチ

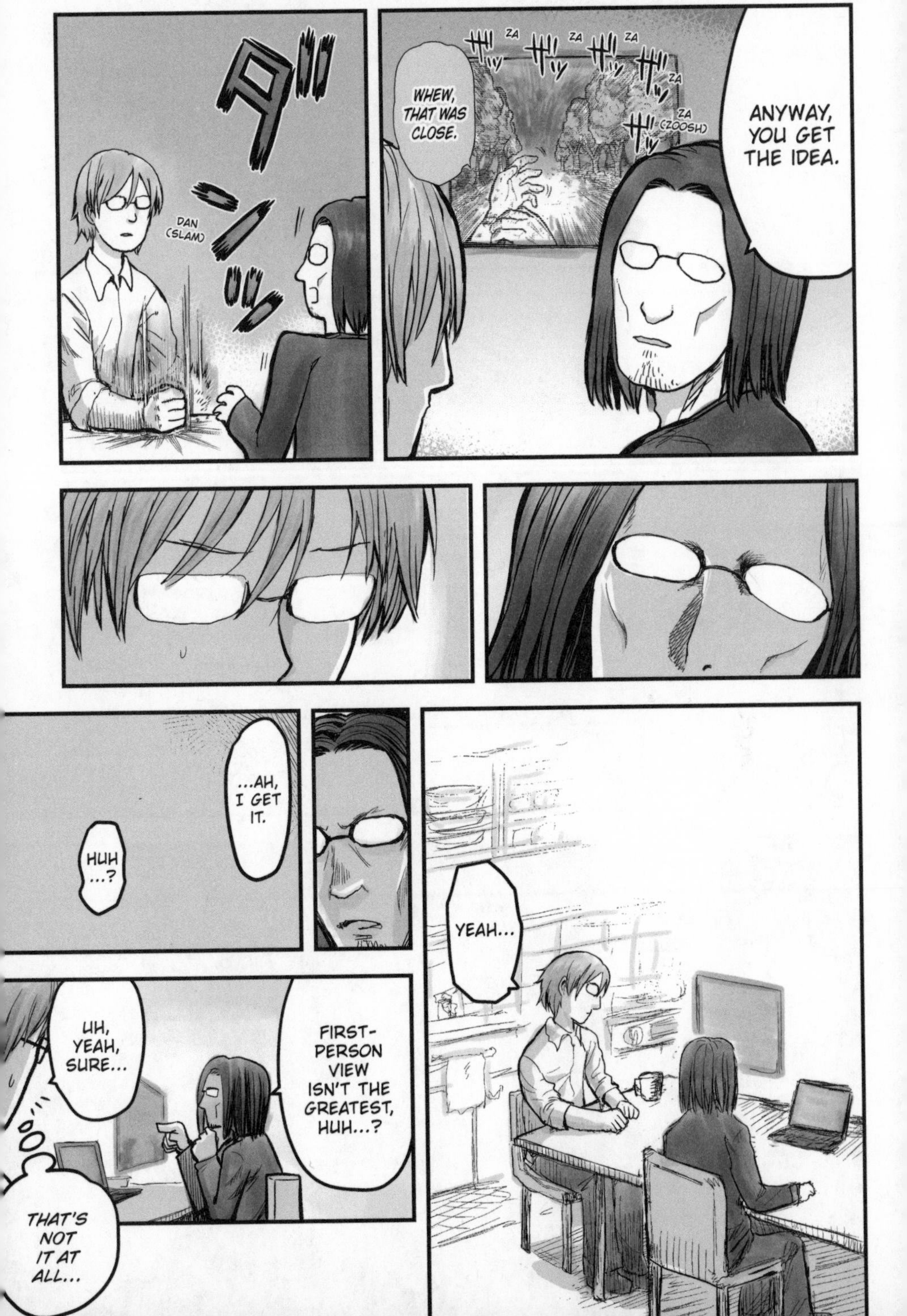
ZA
ZA
ZA
ZA
ZA (ZOOSH)
ANYWAY, YOU GET THE IDEA.
WHEW, THAT WAS CLOSE.
DAN (SLAM)
YEAH...
...AH, I GET IT.
HUH...?
FIRST-PERSON VIEW ISN'T THE GREATEST, HUH...?
UH, YEAH, SURE...
THAT'S NOT IT AT ALL...

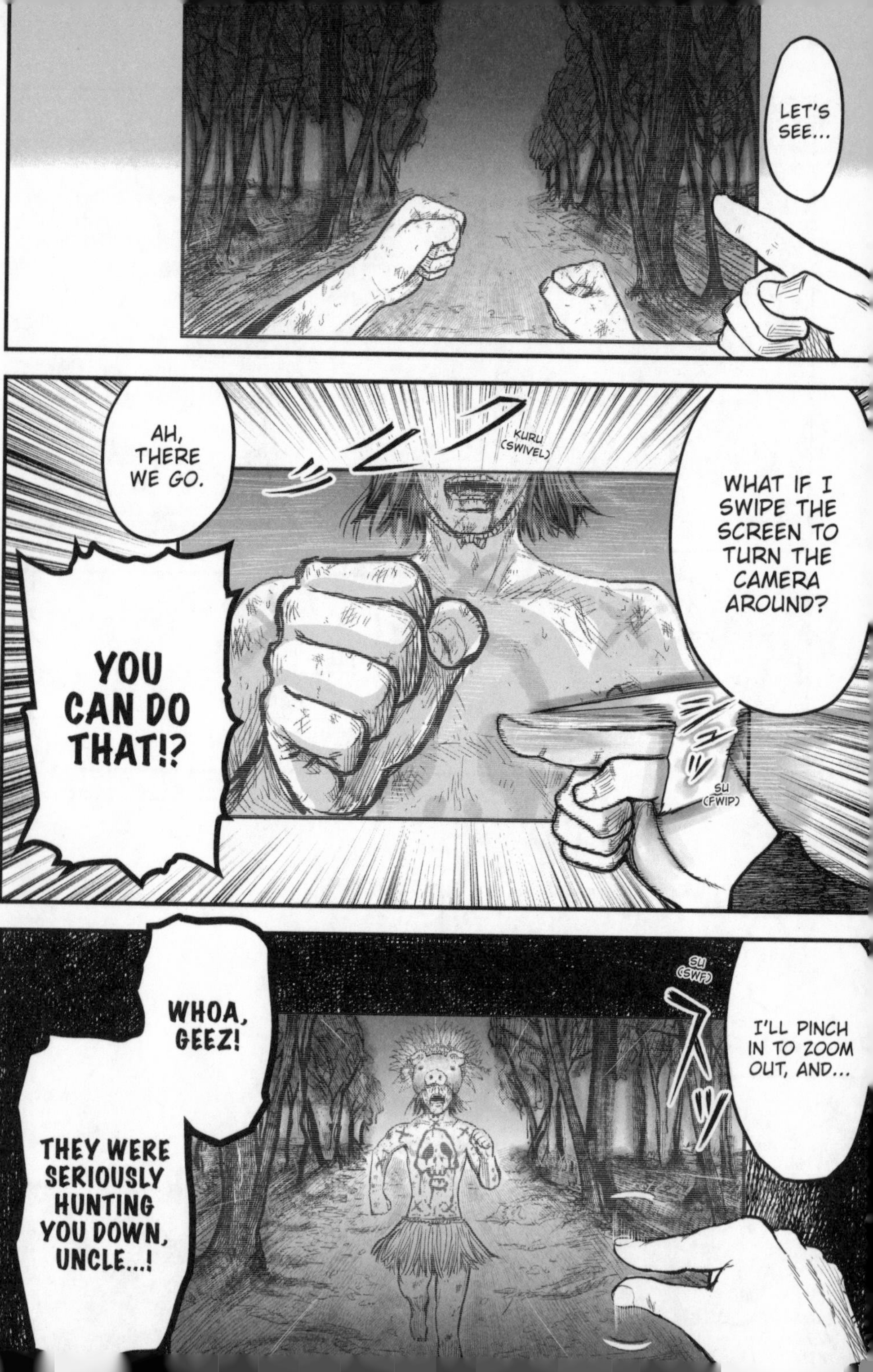
LET'S SEE...
WHAT IF I SWIPE THE SCREEN TO TURN THE CAMERA AROUND?
KURU (SWIVEL)
AH, THERE WE GO.
SU (FWIP)
YOU CAN DO THAT!?
I'LL PINCH IN TO ZOOM OUT, AND...
SU (SWF)
WHOA, GEEZ!
THEY WERE SERIOUSLY HUNTING YOU DOWN, UNCLE...!

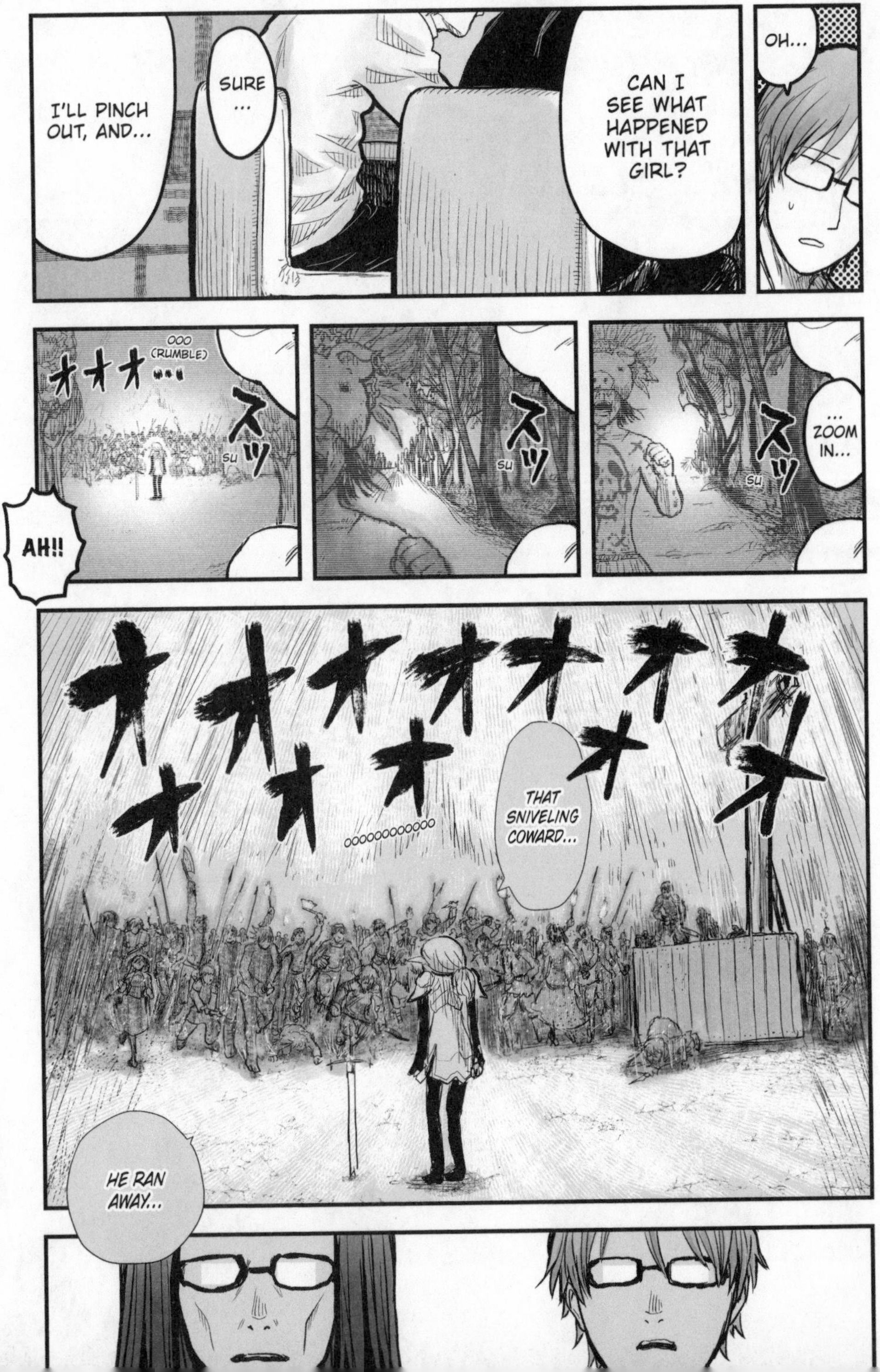
OH...
CAN I SEE WHAT HAPPENED WITH THAT GIRL?
SURE ...
I'LL PINCH OUT, AND...
... ZOOM IN...
スッ
SU
スッ
SU
オオオ
OOO (RUMBLE)
スッ
SU
AH!!
オオオオオオオオオオオオ
OOOOOOOOOOOO
THAT SNIVELING COWARD...
HE RAN AWAY...

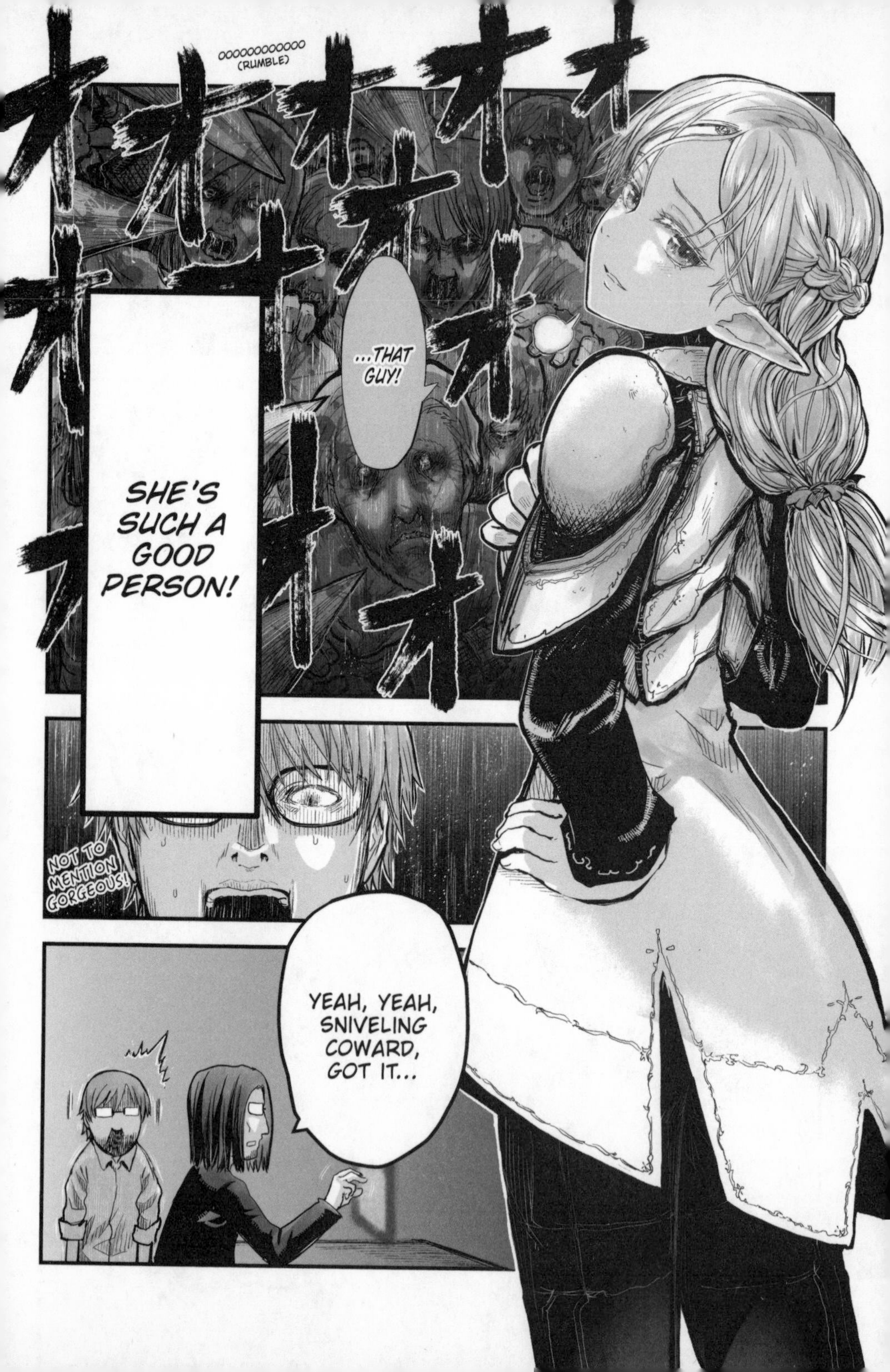

OOOOOOOOOOOO
(RUMBLE)
...THAT GUY!
SHE'S SUCH A GOOD PERSON!
NOT TO MENTION GORGEOUS!
YEAH, YEAH, SNIVELING COWARD, GOT IT...

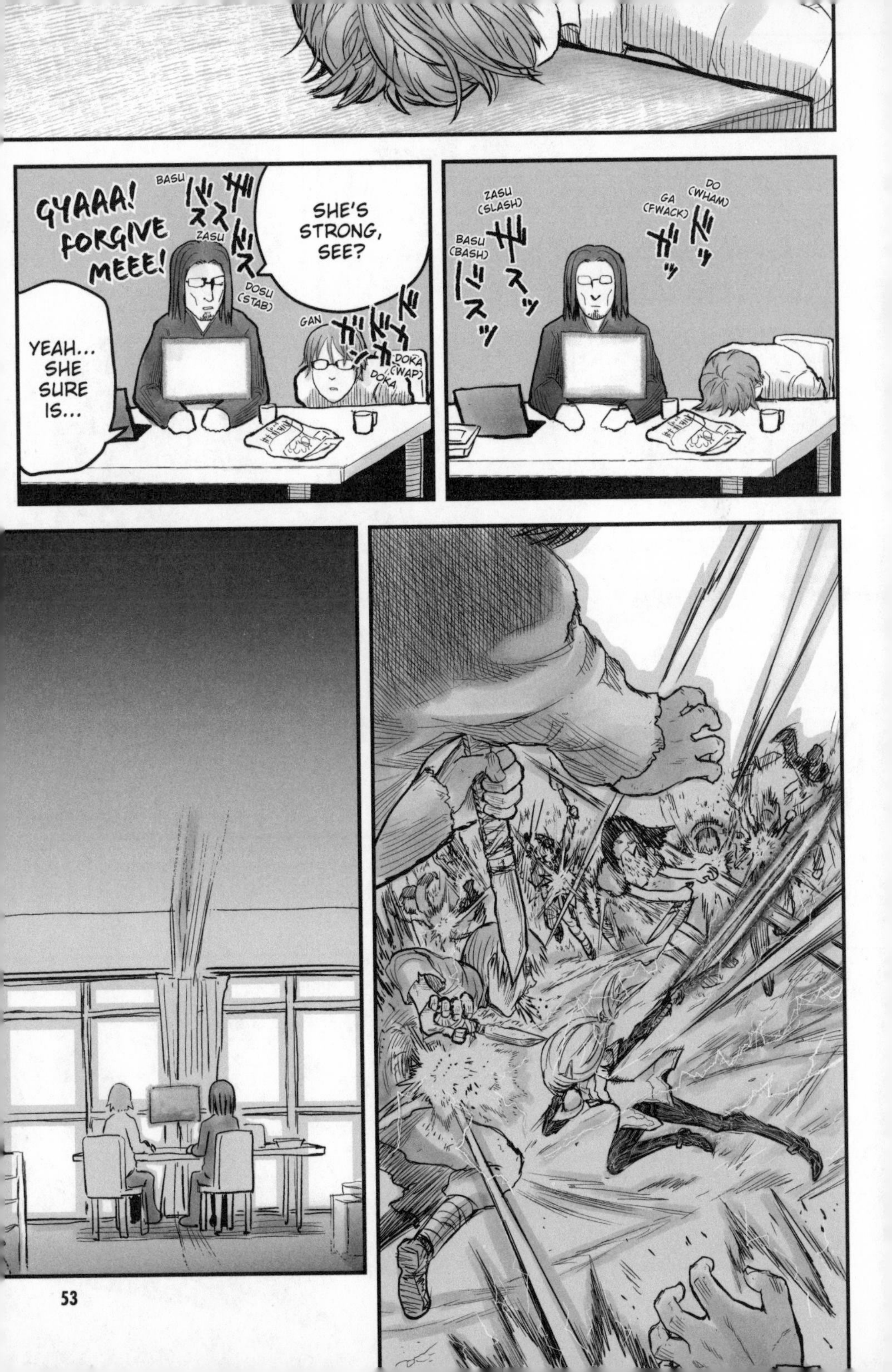
DO (WHAM)
GA (FWACK)
ZASU (SLASH)
BASU (BASH)
SHE'S STRONG, SEE?
ZASU
BASU
GYAAA! FORGIVE MEEE!
DOSU (STAB)
GAN
DOKA (WAP)
DOKA
YEAH... SHE SURE IS...

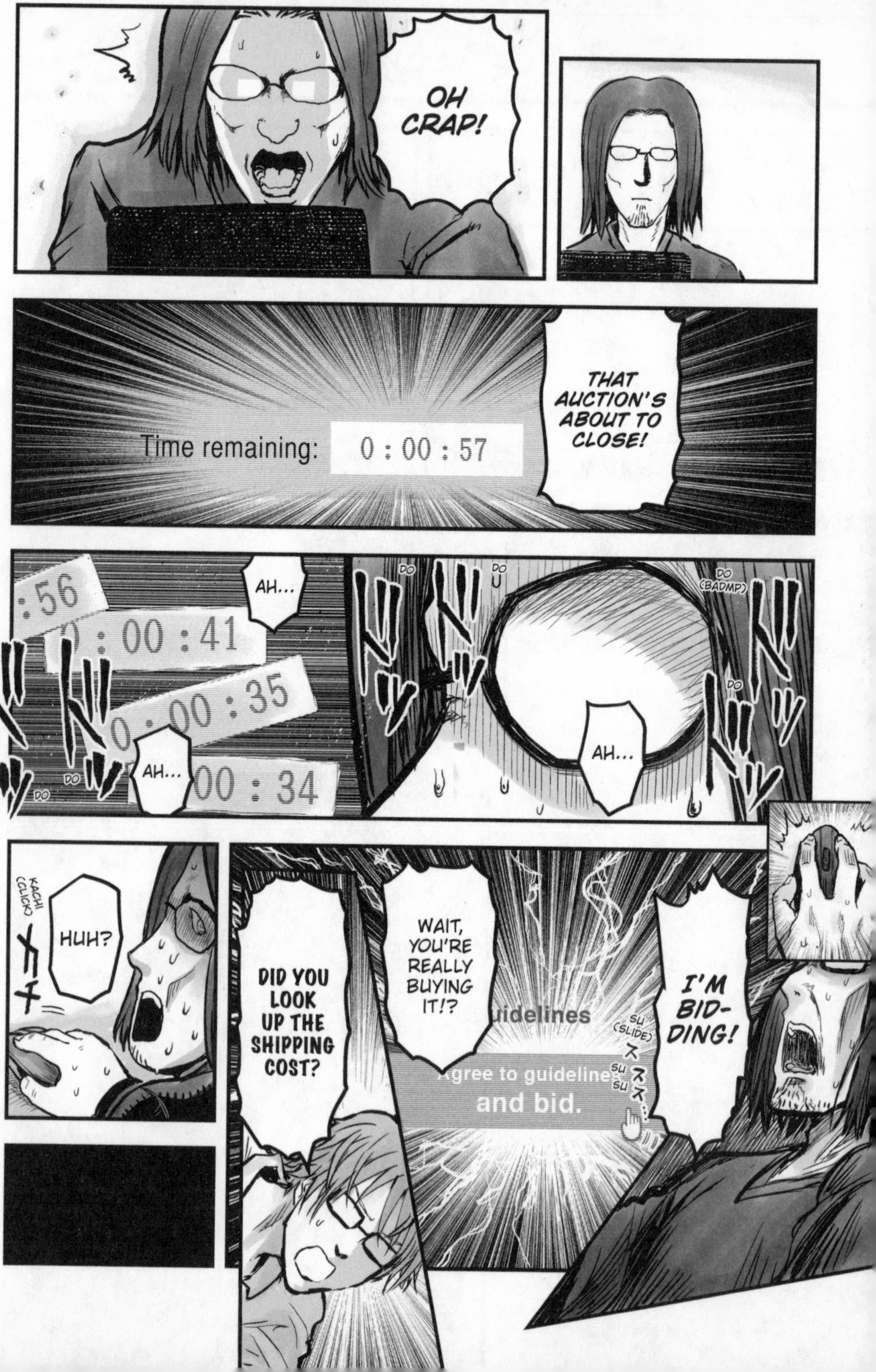
OH CRAP!
THAT AUCTION'S ABOUT TO CLOSE!
Time remaining: 0 : 00 : 57
DO
DO
DO (BADMP)
DO
AH...
AH...
:56
0 : 00 : 41
0 : 00 : 35
00 : 34
AH...
DO
DO
I'M BID-DING!
SU (SLIDE)
SU
SU
and bid.
WAIT, YOU'RE REALLY BUYING IT!?
DID YOU LOOK UP THE SHIPPING COST?
KACHI (CLICK)
HUH?

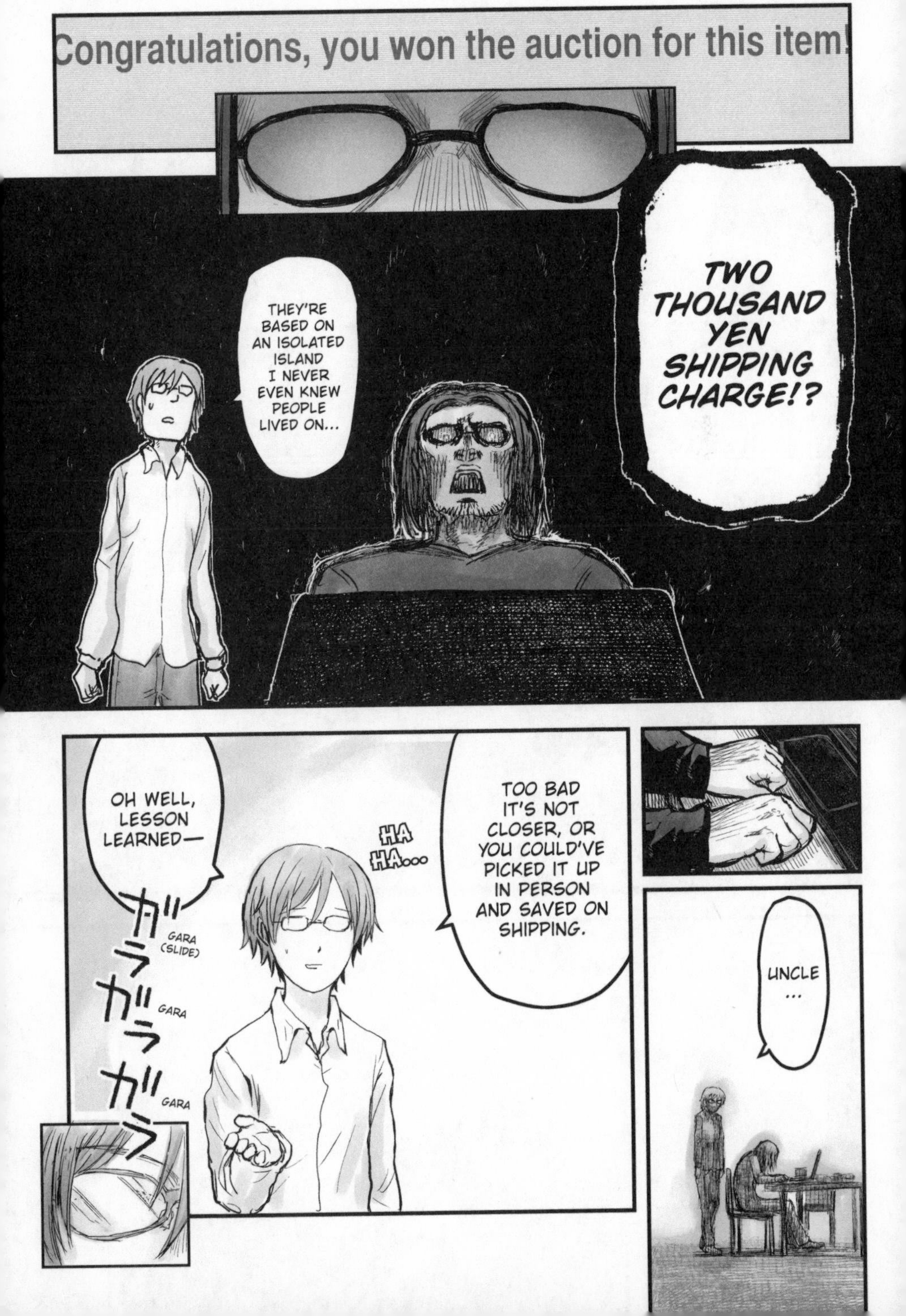
Congratulations, you won the auction for this item!
TWO THOUSAND YEN SHIPPING CHARGE!?
THEY'RE BASED ON AN ISOLATED ISLAND I NEVER EVEN KNEW PEOPLE LIVED ON...
UNCLE...
TOO BAD IT'S NOT CLOSER, OR YOU COULD'VE PICKED IT UP IN PERSON AND SAVED ON SHIPPING.
HA HA...
OH WELL, LESSON LEARNED—
ガラ GARA (SLIDE)
ガラ GARA
ガラ GARA

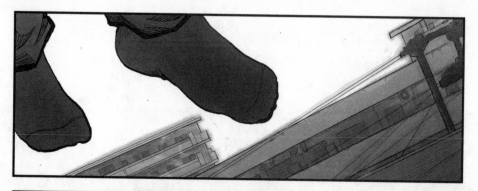

BE
RIGHT
BACK.

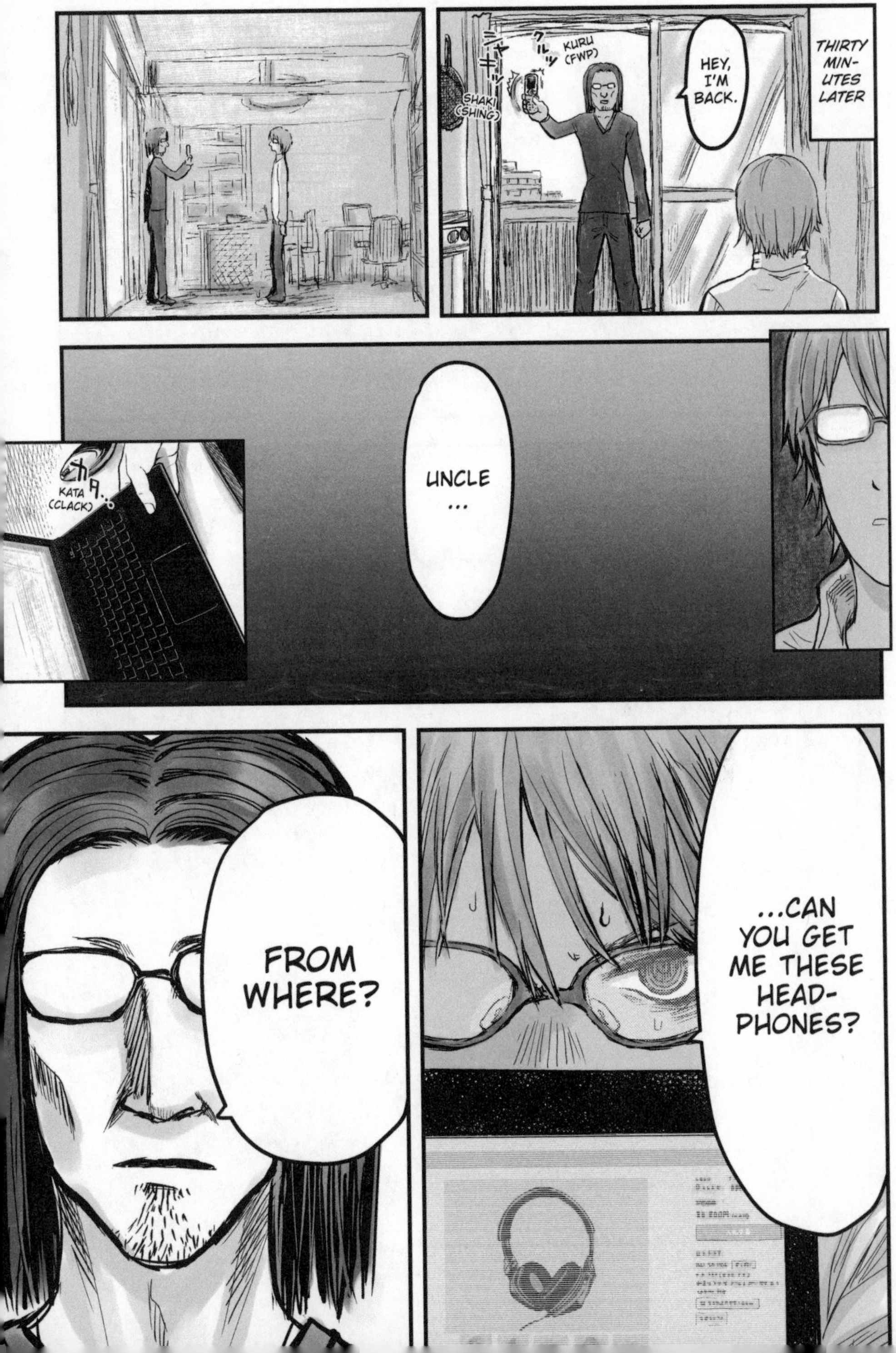
THIRTY MIN-UTES LATER
KURU (FWP)
SHAKI (SHING)
HEY, I'M BACK.
UNCLE ...
KATA (CLACK)
...CAN YOU GET ME THESE HEAD-PHONES?
FROM WHERE?

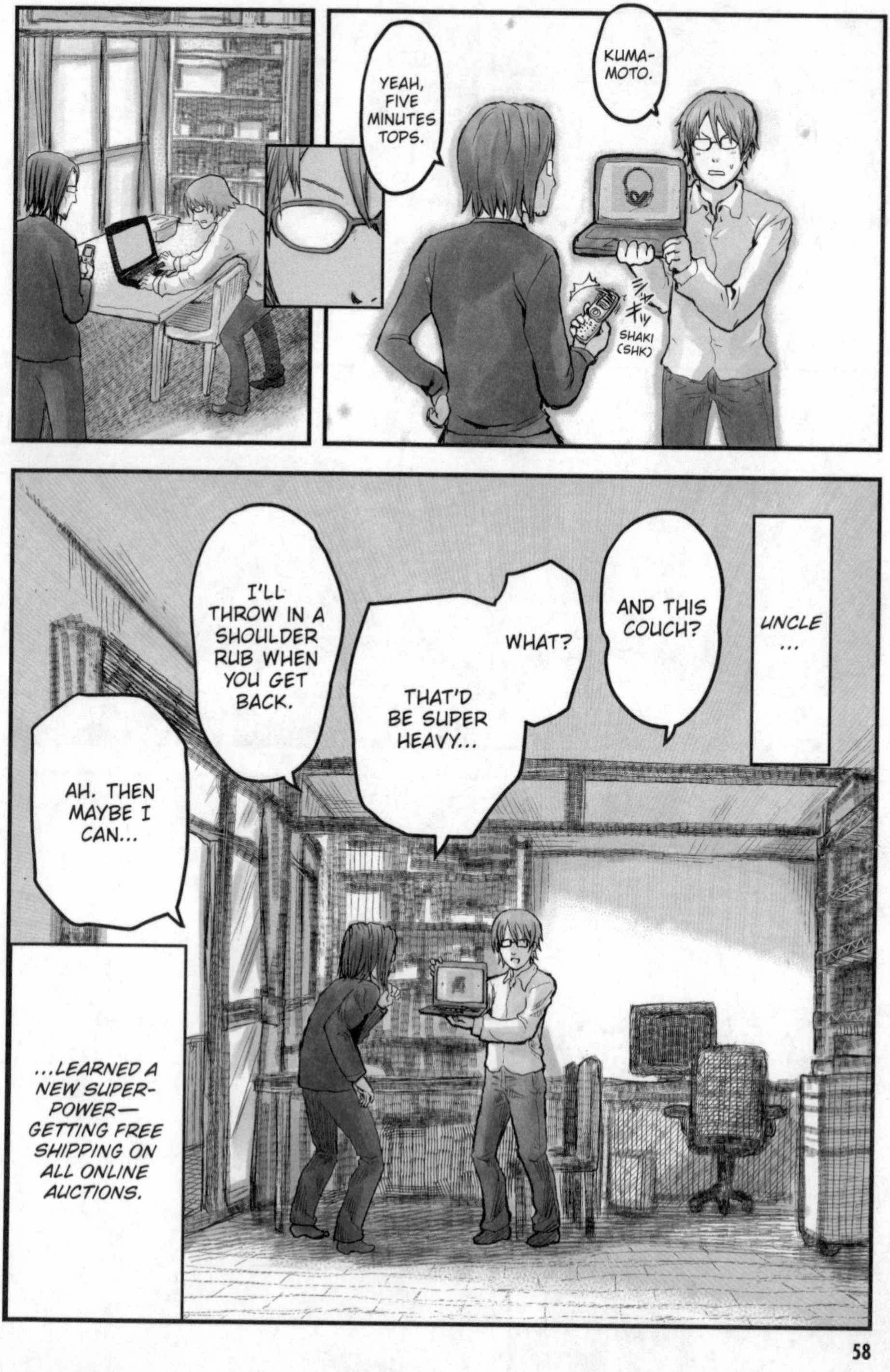

KUMA-MOTO.
YEAH, FIVE MINUTES TOPS.
SHAKI (SHK)
UNCLE ...
AND THIS COUCH?
WHAT?
THAT'D BE SUPER HEAVY...
I'LL THROW IN A SHOULDER RUB WHEN YOU GET BACK.
AH. THEN MAYBE I CAN...
...LEARNED A NEW SUPER-POWER—GETTING FREE SHIPPING ON ALL ONLINE AUCTIONS.

Feature Phone

A type of cellular phone device developed in the 2000s.
They made great advances until the emergence of smartphones in
2010, especially in Japan, where they are sometimes referred to
as "Gala-phones," a name stemming from Galápagos syndrome,
in which the flora and fauna of the Galápagos Islands evolved
independently due to lack of contact with other islands.

TIPS

UNCLE from ANOTHER WORLD

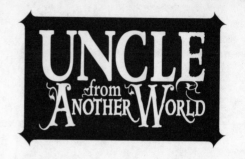

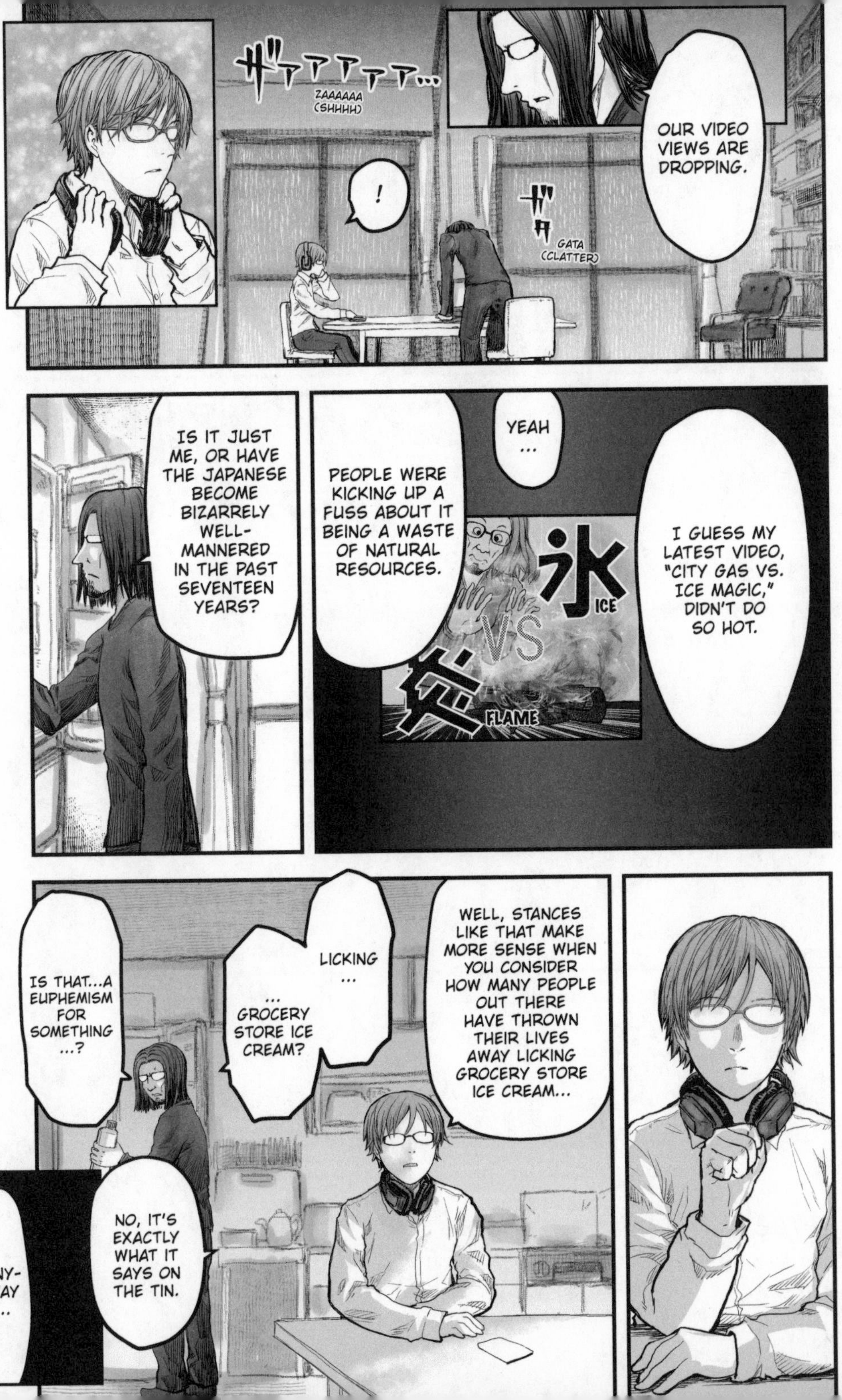
OUR VIDEO VIEWS ARE DROPPING.
ガタ
GATA (CLATTER)
!
ザァァァァァ…
ZAAAAAA (SHHHH)
YEAH ...
I GUESS MY LATEST VIDEO, "CITY GAS VS. ICE MAGIC," DIDN'T DO SO HOT.
氷 ICE
VS
炎 FLAME
PEOPLE WERE KICKING UP A FUSS ABOUT IT BEING A WASTE OF NATURAL RESOURCES.
IS IT JUST ME, OR HAVE THE JAPANESE BECOME BIZARRELY WELL-MANNERED IN THE PAST SEVENTEEN YEARS?
WELL, STANCES LIKE THAT MAKE MORE SENSE WHEN YOU CONSIDER HOW MANY PEOPLE OUT THERE HAVE THROWN THEIR LIVES AWAY LICKING GROCERY STORE ICE CREAM...
LICKING ...
... GROCERY STORE ICE CREAM?
IS THAT...A EUPHEMISM FOR SOMETHING ...?
NO, IT'S EXACTLY WHAT IT SAYS ON THE TIN.
ANY-WAY ...

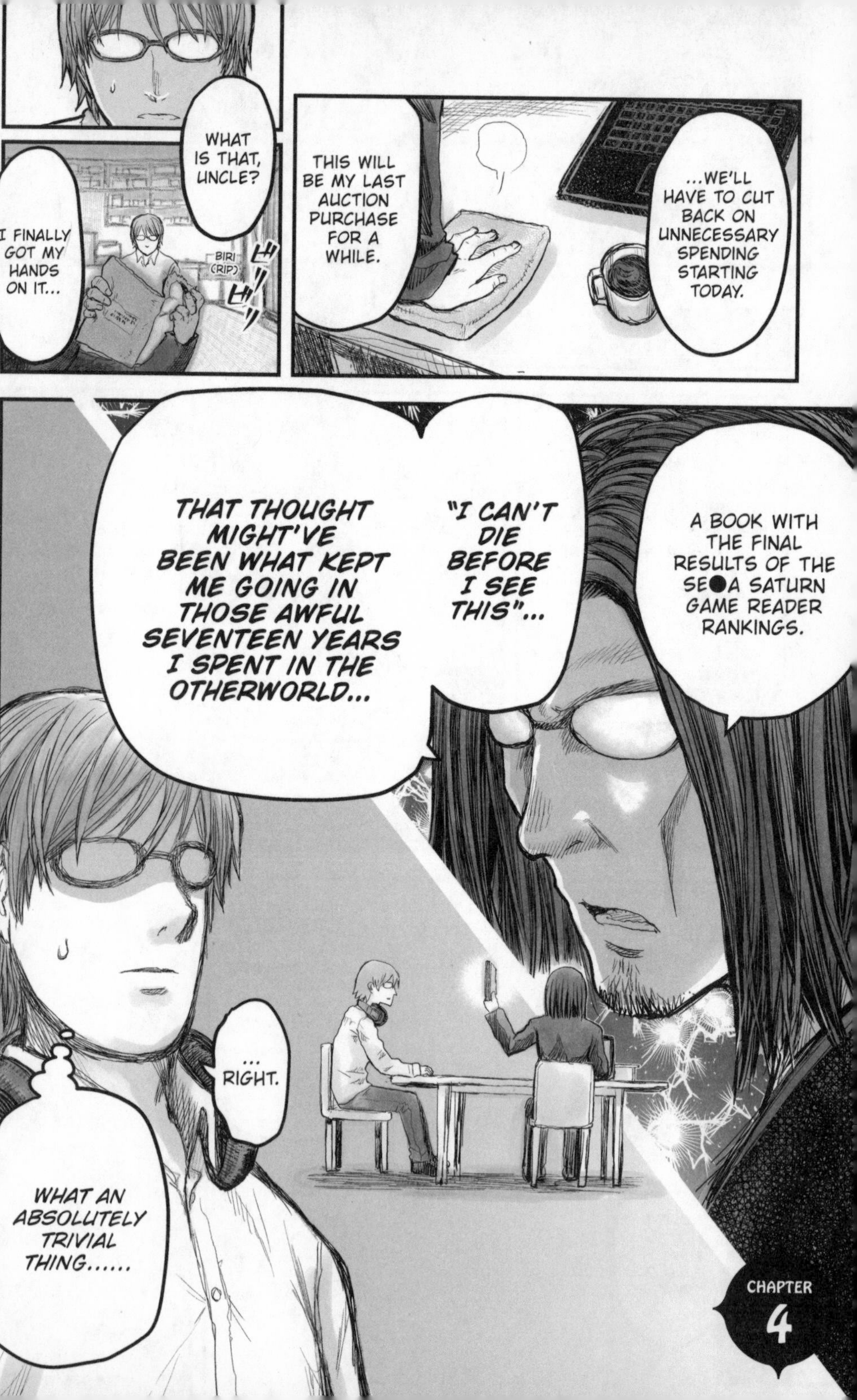
...WE'LL HAVE TO CUT BACK ON UNNECESSARY SPENDING STARTING TODAY.
THIS WILL BE MY LAST AUCTION PURCHASE FOR A WHILE.
WHAT IS THAT, UNCLE?
BIRI (RIP)
I FINALLY GOT MY HANDS ON IT...
A BOOK WITH THE FINAL RESULTS OF THE SE●A SATURN GAME READER RANKINGS.
"I CAN'T DIE BEFORE I SEE THIS"...
THAT THOUGHT MIGHT'VE BEEN WHAT KEPT ME GOING IN THOSE AWFUL SEVENTEEN YEARS I SPENT IN THE OTHERWORLD...
... RIGHT.
WHAT AN ABSOLUTELY TRIVIAL THING......
CHAPTER 4

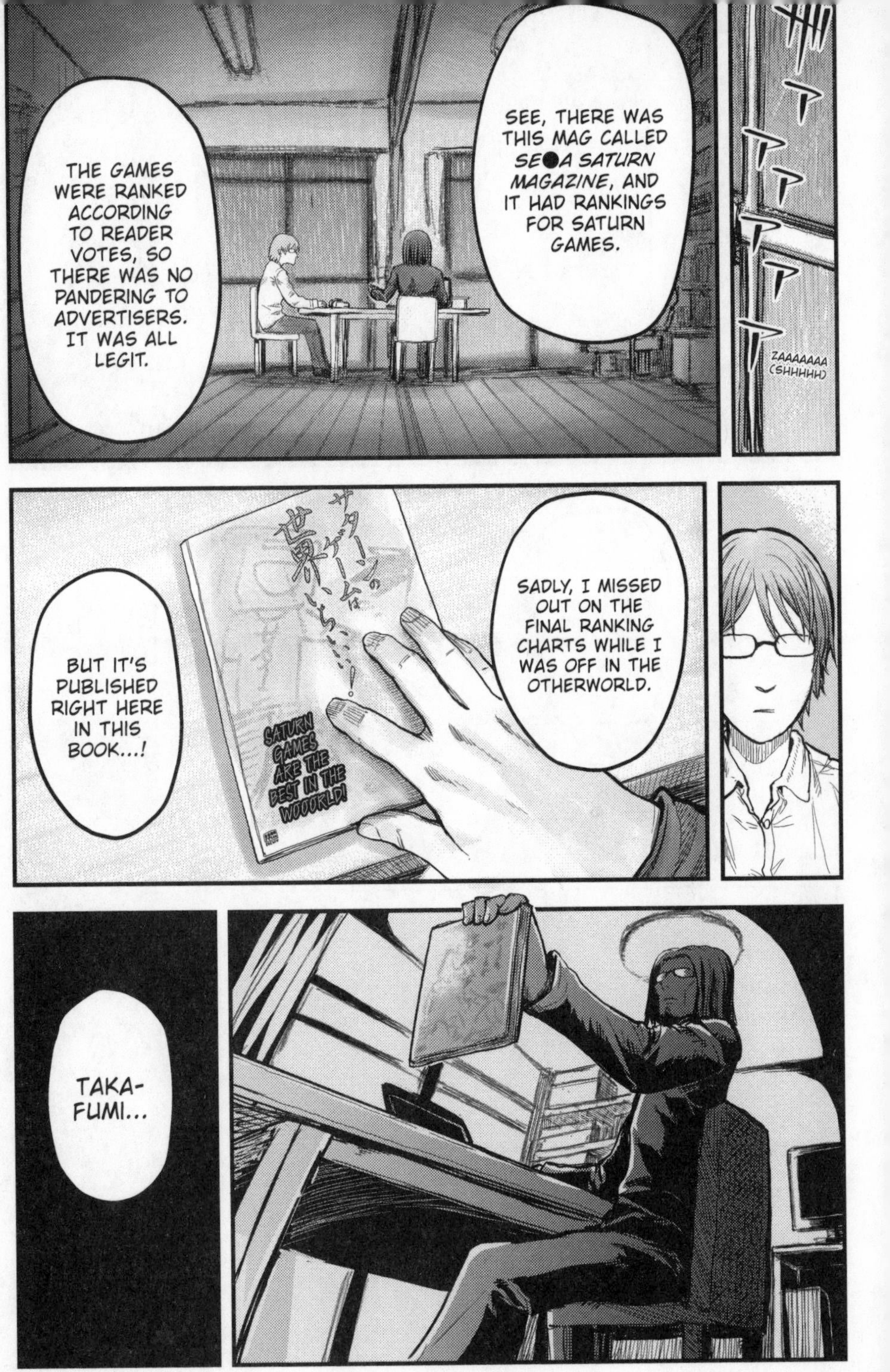
ZAAAAAAA (SHHHHH)
SEE, THERE WAS THIS MAG CALLED SE●A SATURN *MAGAZINE*, AND IT HAD RANKINGS FOR SATURN GAMES.
THE GAMES WERE RANKED ACCORDING TO READER VOTES, SO THERE WAS NO PANDERING TO ADVERTISERS. IT WAS ALL LEGIT.
SADLY, I MISSED OUT ON THE FINAL RANKING CHARTS WHILE I WAS OFF IN THE OTHERWORLD.
SATURN GAMES ARE THE BEST IN THE WOOORLD!
BUT IT'S PUBLISHED RIGHT HERE IN THIS BOOK...!
TAKA-FUMI...

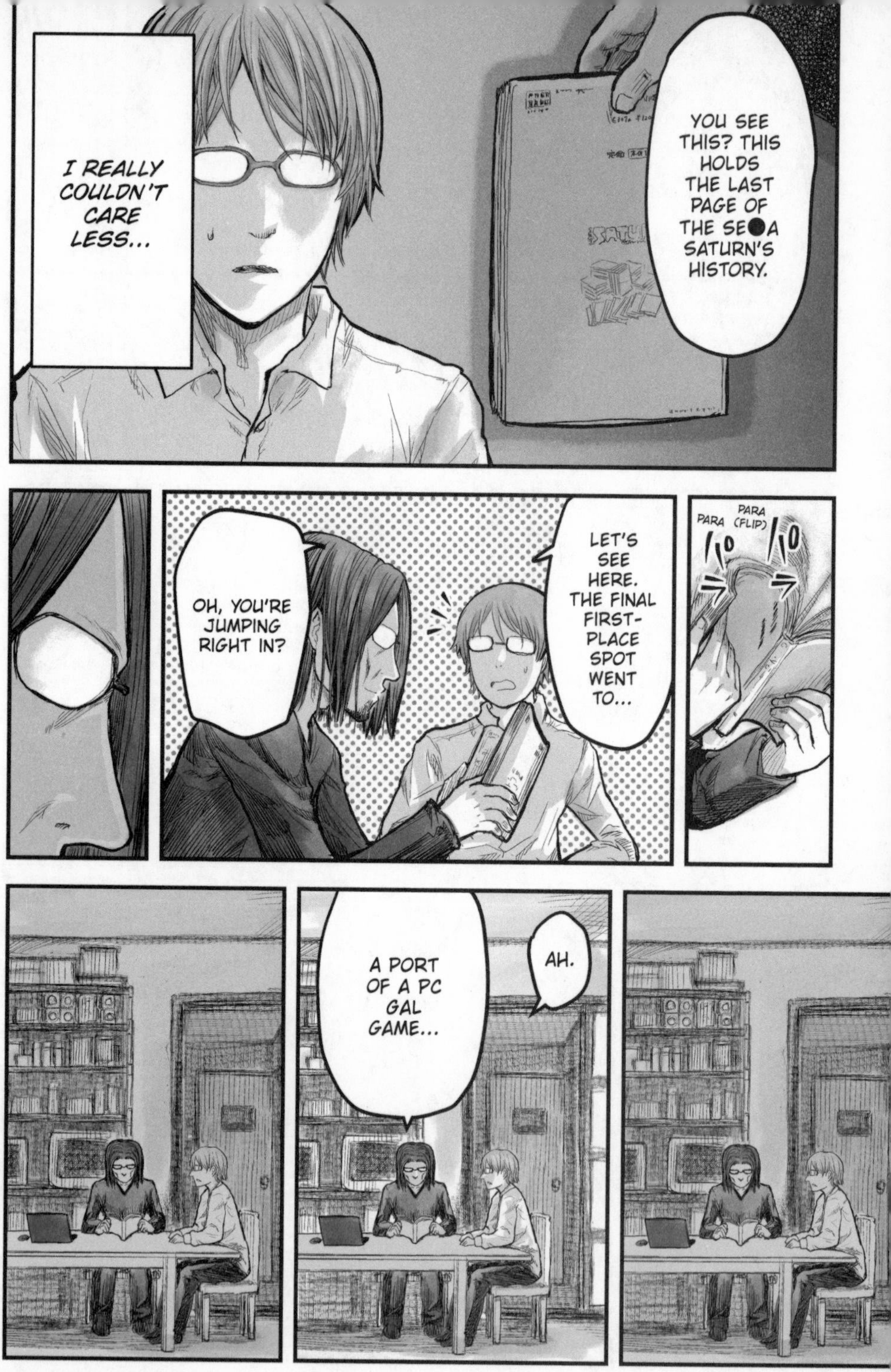
YOU SEE THIS? THIS HOLDS THE LAST PAGE OF THE SE●A SATURN'S HISTORY.
I REALLY COULDN'T CARE LESS...
PARA (FLIP)
PARA
LET'S SEE HERE. THE FINAL FIRST-PLACE SPOT WENT TO...
OH, YOU'RE JUMPING RIGHT IN?
A PORT OF A PC GAL GAME...
AH.

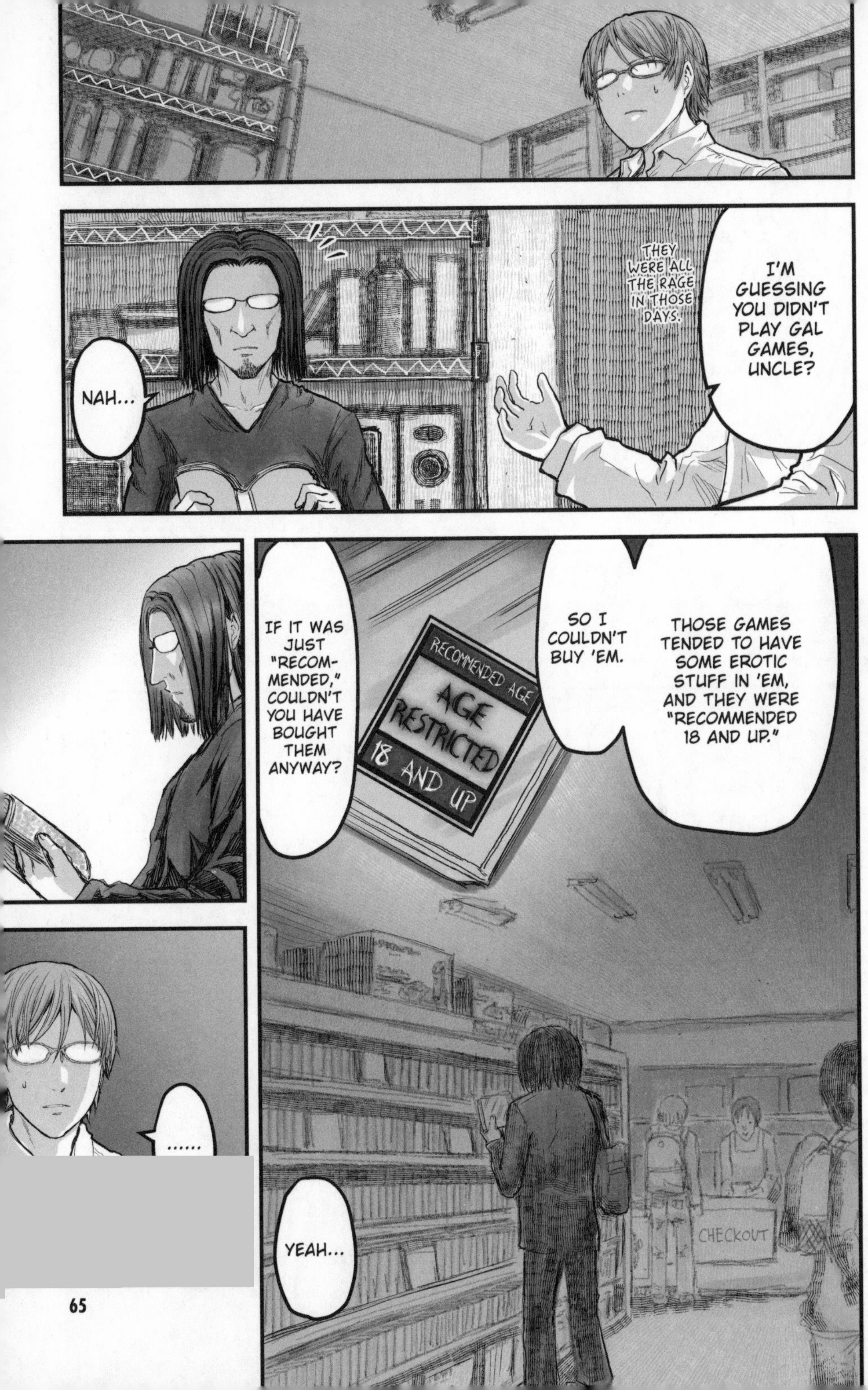

I'M GUESSING YOU DIDN'T PLAY GAL GAMES, UNCLE?
THEY WERE ALL THE RAGE IN THOSE DAYS.
NAH...
THOSE GAMES TENDED TO HAVE SOME EROTIC STUFF IN 'EM, AND THEY WERE "RECOMMENDED 18 AND UP."
SO I COULDN'T BUY 'EM.
RECOMMENDED AGE
AGE RESTRICTED
18 AND UP
IF IT WAS JUST "RECOMMENDED," COULDN'T YOU HAVE BOUGHT THEM ANYWAY?
YEAH...
CHECKOUT
......

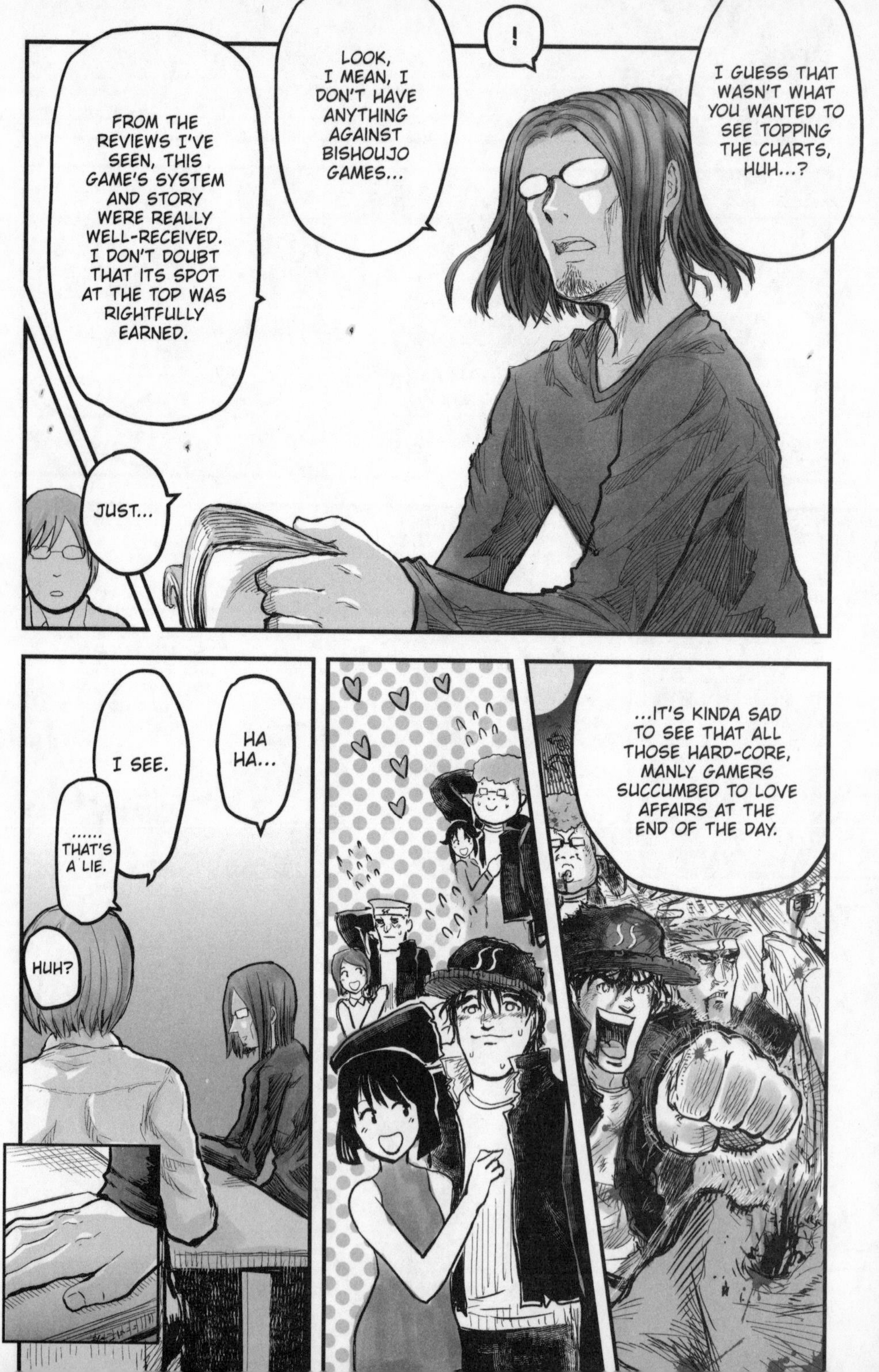
I GUESS THAT WASN'T WHAT YOU WANTED TO SEE TOPPING THE CHARTS, HUH...?
!
LOOK, I MEAN, I DON'T HAVE ANYTHING AGAINST BISHOUJO GAMES...
FROM THE REVIEWS I'VE SEEN, THIS GAME'S SYSTEM AND STORY WERE REALLY WELL-RECEIVED. I DON'T DOUBT THAT ITS SPOT AT THE TOP WAS RIGHTFULLY EARNED.
JUST...
...IT'S KINDA SAD TO SEE THAT ALL THOSE HARD-CORE, MANLY GAMERS SUCCUMBED TO LOVE AFFAIRS AT THE END OF THE DAY.
HA HA...
I SEE.
...... THAT'S A LIE.
HUH?

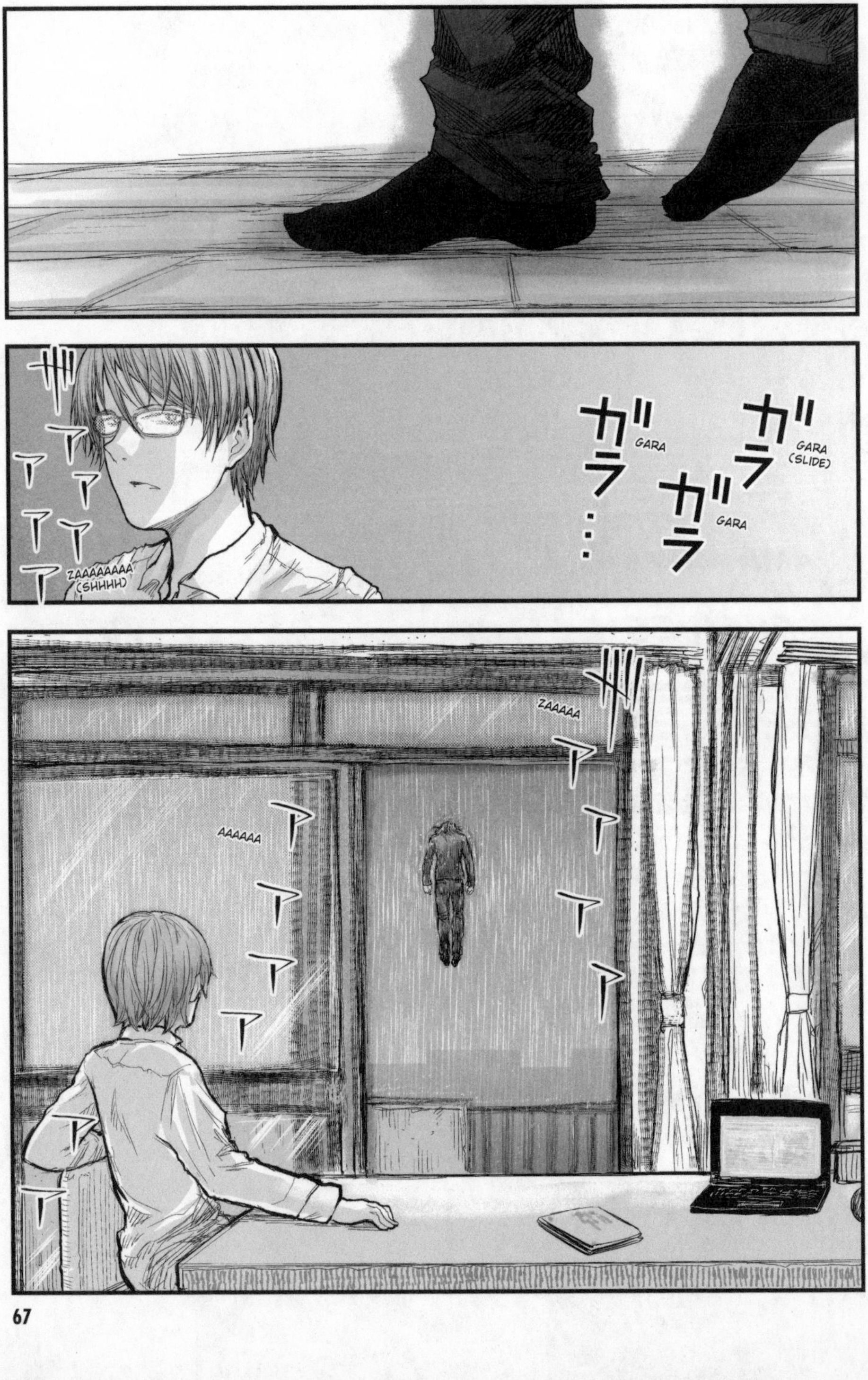
ガラ
GARA (SLIDE)
ガラ
GARA
ガラ…
GARA
ZAAAAAAAA (SHHHH)
ZAAAAA
AAAAAA

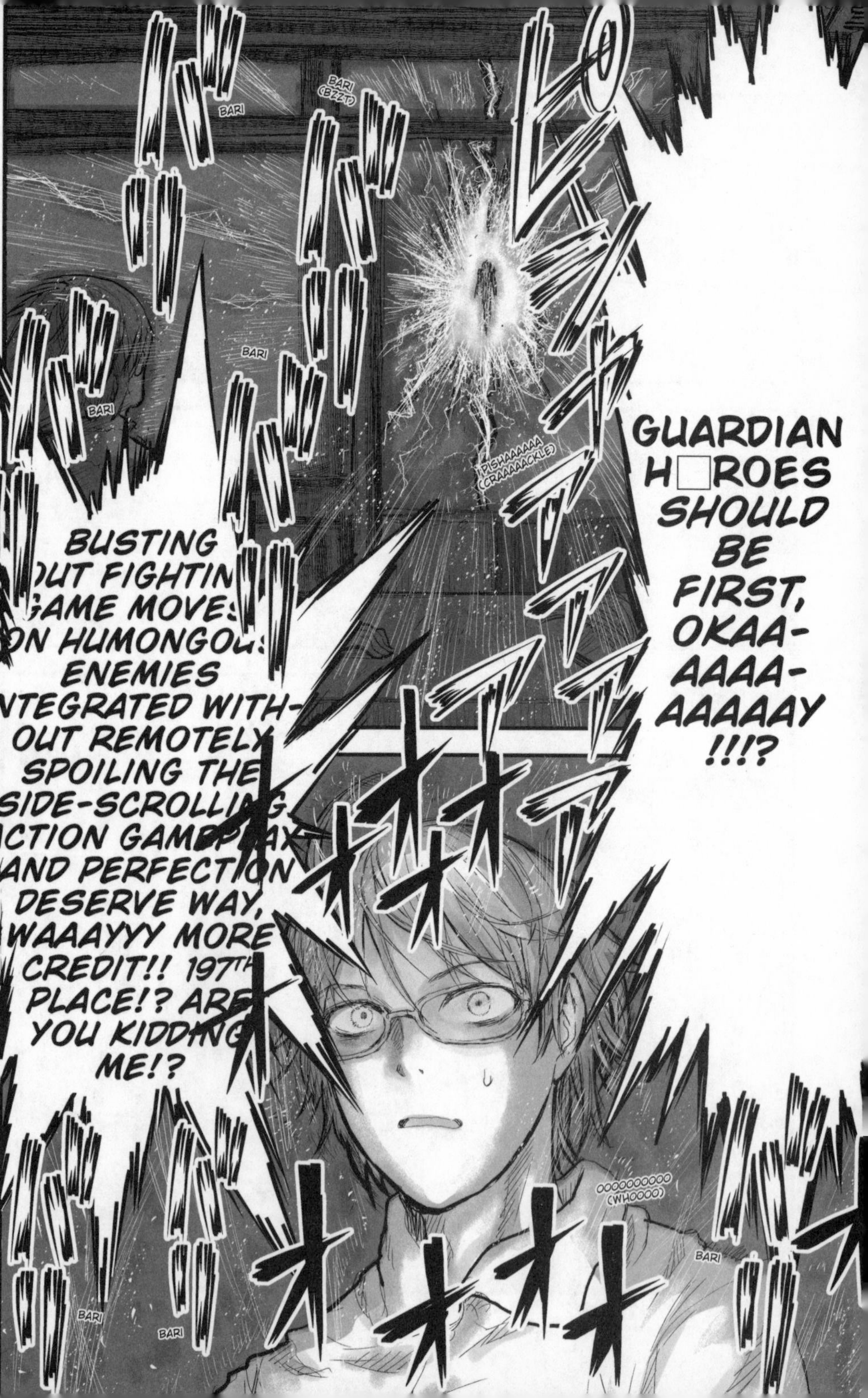
GUARDIAN H□ROES SHOULD BE FIRST, OKAA-AAAA-AAAAAY!!!?
PISHAAAAAAA (CRAAAAACKLE)
BARI (BZZT)
BARI
BARI
BARI
BUSTING OUT FIGHTING GAME MOVES ON HUMONGOUS ENEMIES INTEGRATED WITH-OUT REMOTELY SPOILING THE SIDE-SCROLLING ACTION GAMEPLAY AND PERFECTION DESERVE WAY, WAAAYYY MORE CREDIT!! 197TH PLACE!? ARE YOU KIDDING ME!?
OOOOOOOOOO (WHOOOO)
BARI
BARI
BARI

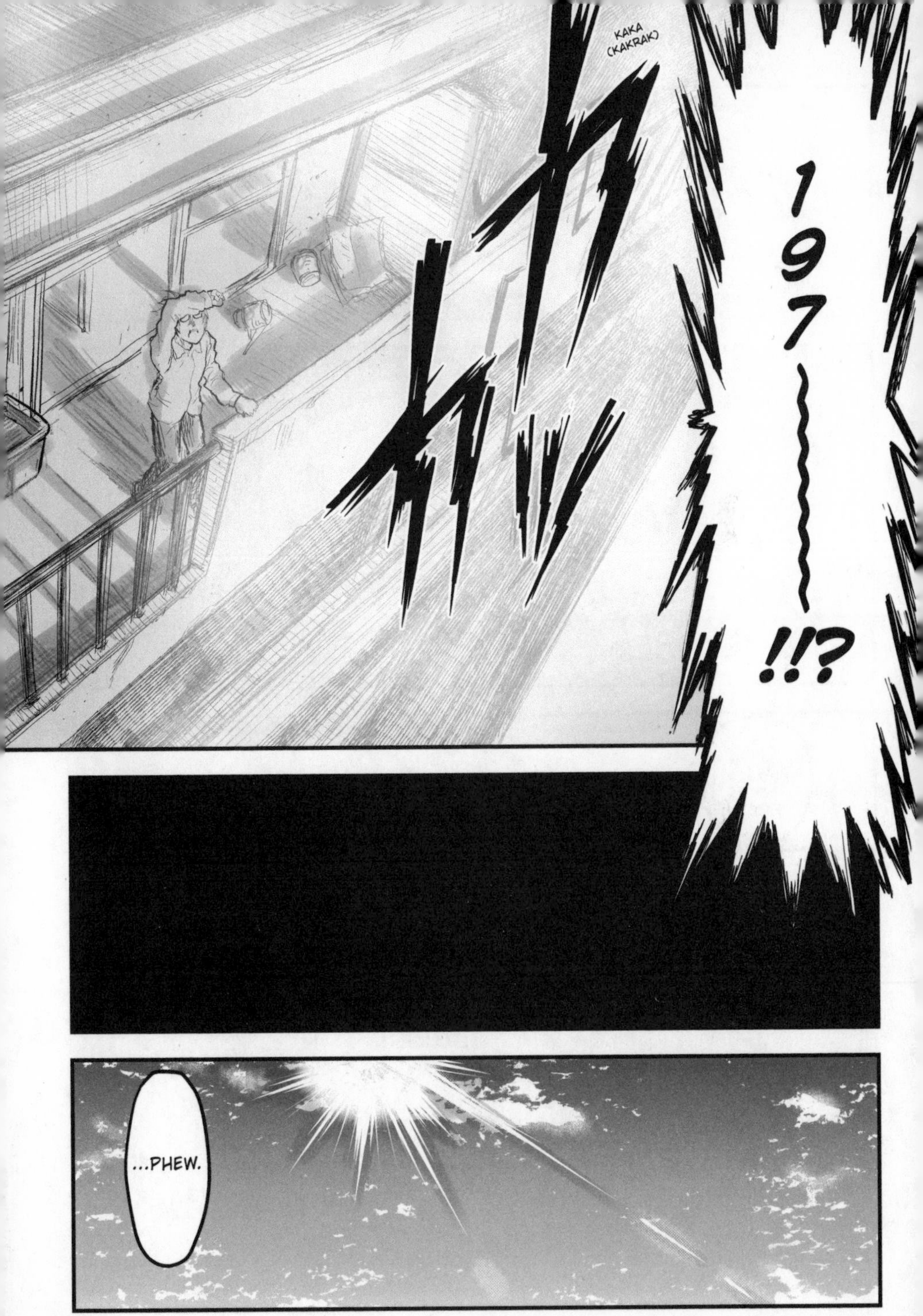
KAKA (KAKRAK)
197~!!?
...PHEW.

BUT HEY...
SECOND PLACE WENT TO AN ORIGINAL RPG FOR THE SATURN.
OH.
I DON'T PLAY RPGs.
YOU DON'T!?
......
THEY'RE ALWAYS FINE AT FIRST.
BUT THEN WHEN YOU GO BACK TO PLAY MORE THE NEXT DAY, YOU FORGET WHAT YOU WERE DOING AND WHERE YOU SHOULD BE GOING NEXT...
YOU NEED SALT TO DEFEAT SLUGS!
THE NEXT DAY
WHY AM I HOLDING SALT?
I SEE...

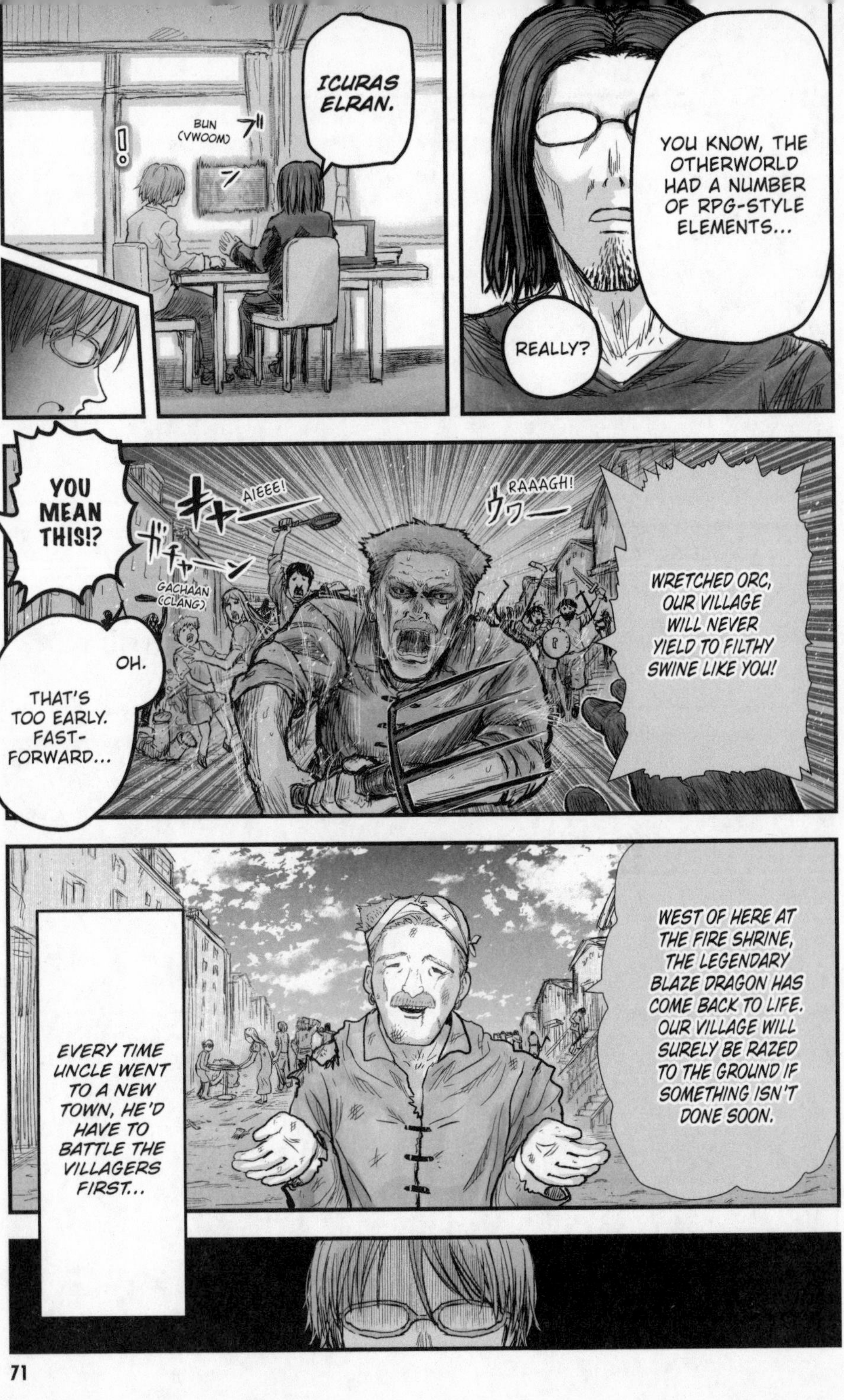
YOU KNOW, THE OTHERWORLD HAD A NUMBER OF RPG-STYLE ELEMENTS...
REALLY?
ICURAS ELRAN.
ブ
BUN (VWOOM)
!
WRETCHED ORC, OUR VILLAGE WILL NEVER YIELD TO FILTHY SWINE LIKE YOU!
ウワー
RAAAGH!
キャー
AIEEE!
ガチャーン
GACHAAN (CLANG)
YOU MEAN THIS!?
OH.
THAT'S TOO EARLY. FAST-FORWARD...
WEST OF HERE AT THE FIRE SHRINE, THE LEGENDARY BLAZE DRAGON HAS COME BACK TO LIFE. OUR VILLAGE WILL SURELY BE RAZED TO THE GROUND IF SOMETHING ISN'T DONE SOON.
EVERY TIME UNCLE WENT TO A NEW TOWN, HE'D HAVE TO BATTLE THE VILLAGERS FIRST...

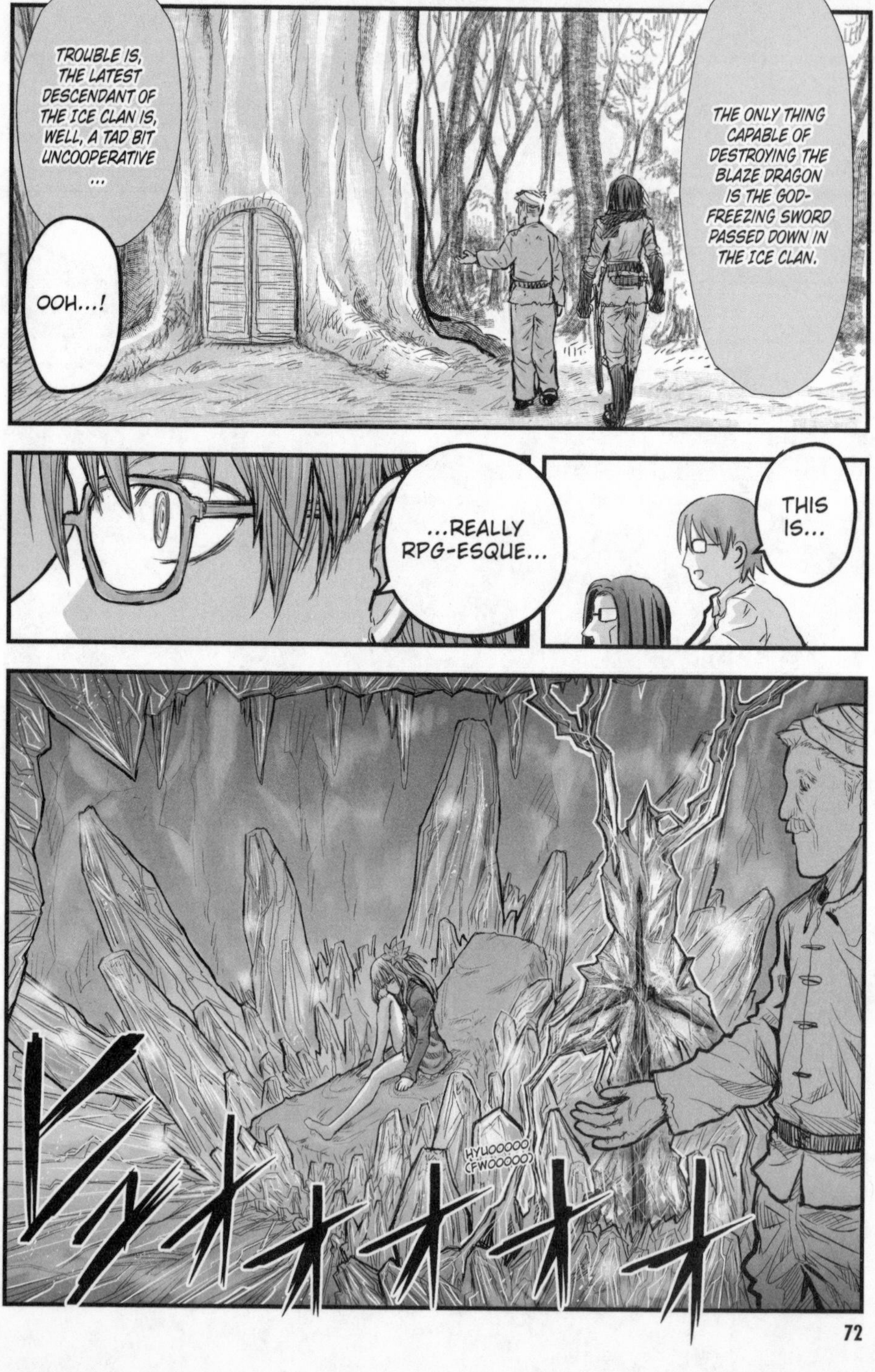
THE ONLY THING CAPABLE OF DESTROYING THE BLAZE DRAGON IS THE GOD-FREEZING SWORD PASSED DOWN IN THE ICE CLAN.
TROUBLE IS, THE LATEST DESCENDANT OF THE ICE CLAN IS, WELL, A TAD BIT UNCOOPERATIVE ...
OOH...!
THIS IS...
...REALLY RPG-ESQUE...
HYUOOOOOO (FWOOOOOO)

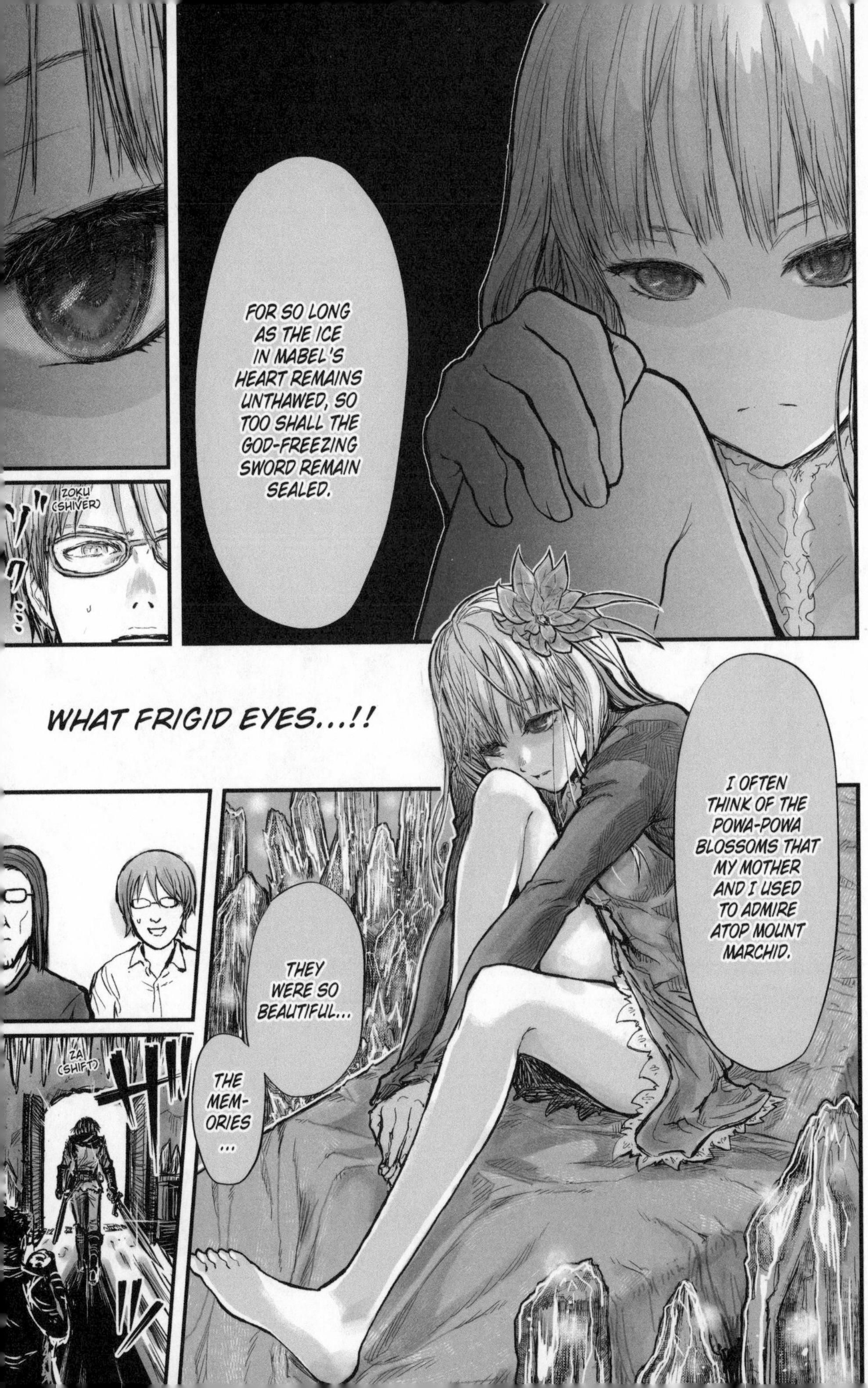
FOR SO LONG AS THE ICE IN MABEL'S HEART REMAINS UNTHAWED, SO TOO SHALL THE GOD-FREEZING SWORD REMAIN SEALED.
ZOKU (SHIVER)
WHAT FRIGID EYES...!!
I OFTEN THINK OF THE POWA-POWA BLOSSOMS THAT MY MOTHER AND I USED TO ADMIRE ATOP MOUNT MARCHID.
THEY WERE SO BEAUTIFUL...
THE MEM-ORIES...
ZA (SHIFT)

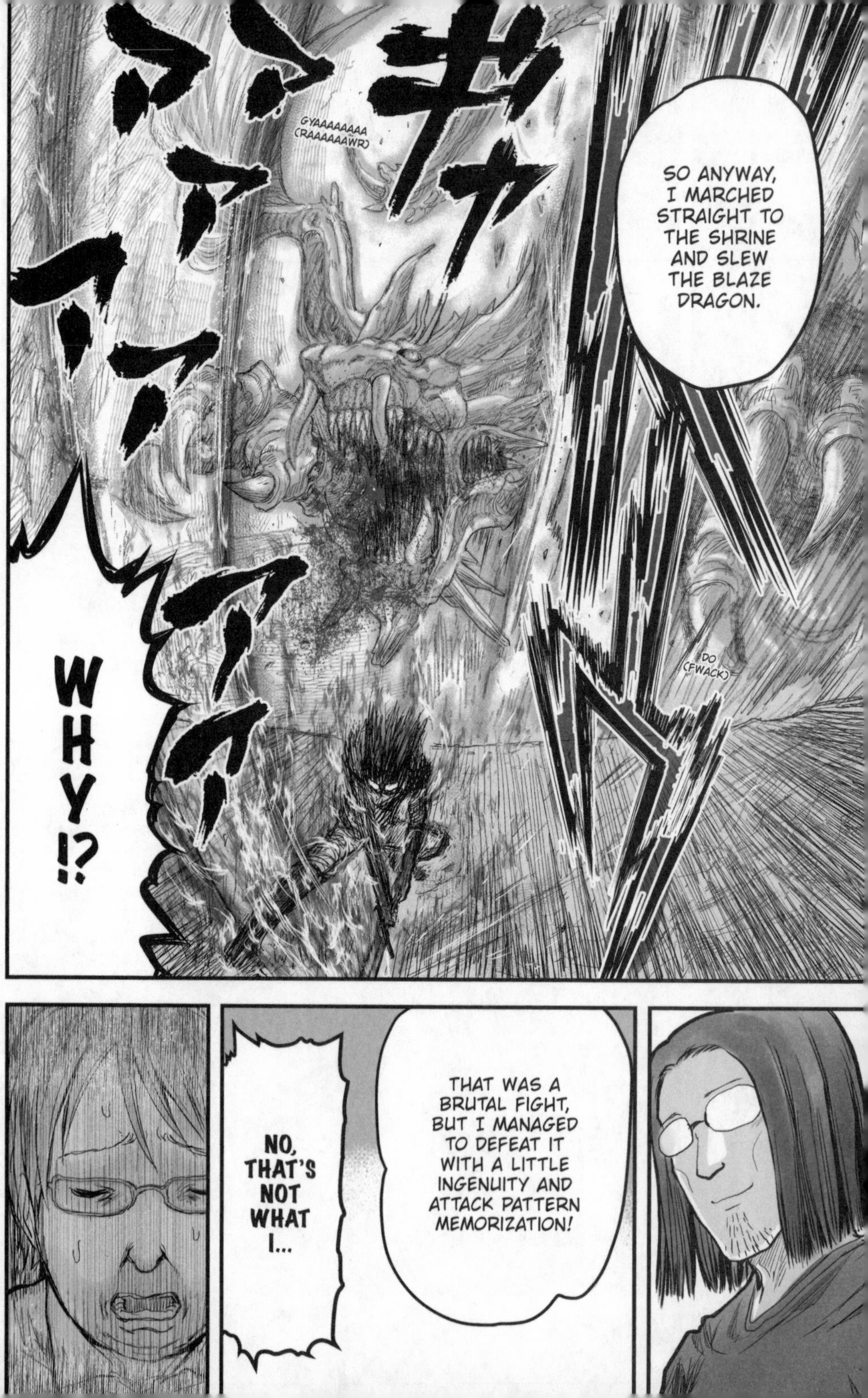
SO ANYWAY, I MARCHED STRAIGHT TO THE SHRINE AND SLEW THE BLAZE DRAGON.
GYAAAAAAAA (RAAAAAAWR)
DO (FWACK)
WHY!?
THAT WAS A BRUTAL FIGHT, BUT I MANAGED TO DEFEAT IT WITH A LITTLE INGENUITY AND ATTACK PATTERN MEMORIZATION!
NO, THAT'S NOT WHAT I...

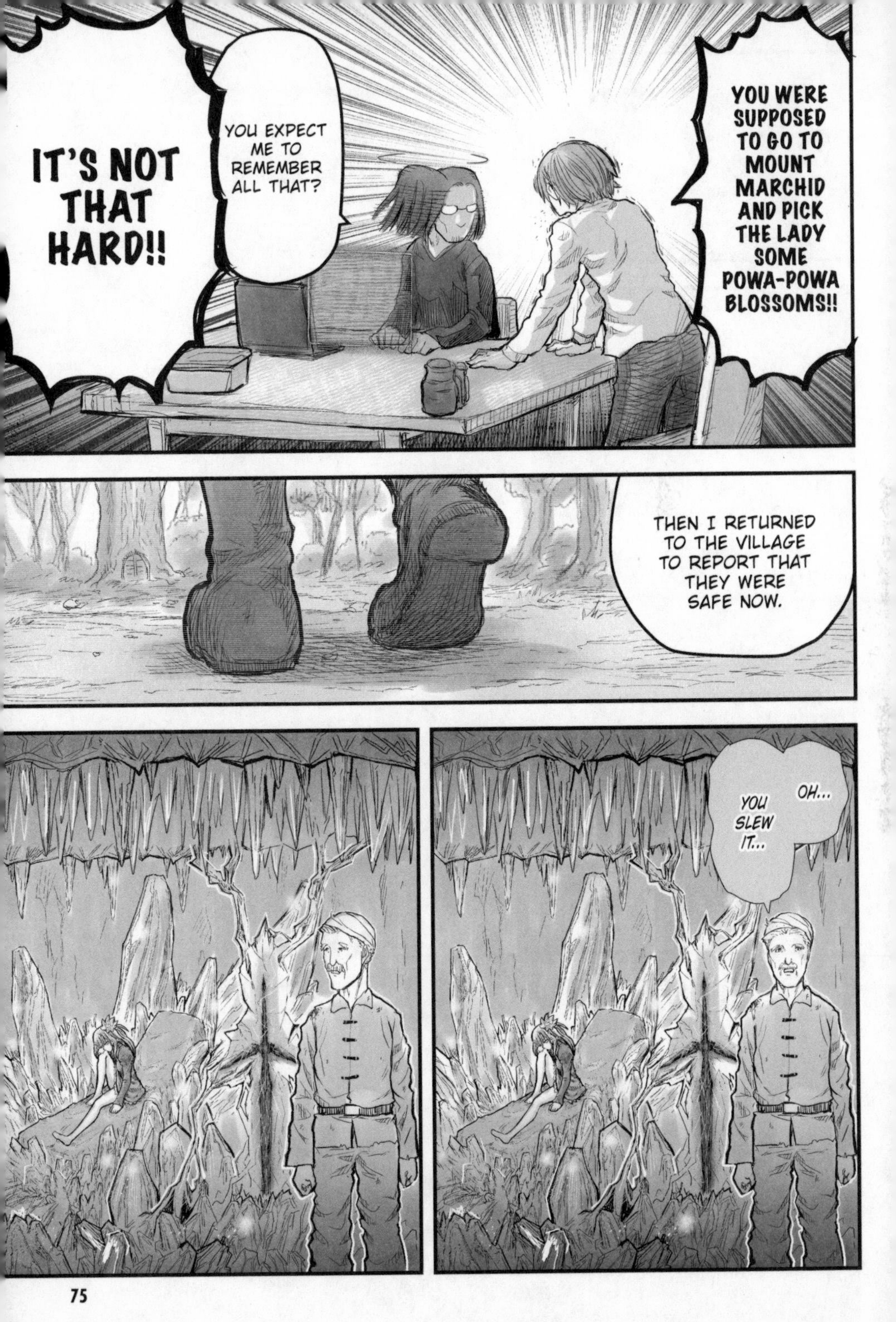
YOU WERE SUPPOSED TO GO TO MOUNT MARCHID AND PICK THE LADY SOME POWA-POWA BLOSSOMS!!
YOU EXPECT ME TO REMEMBER ALL THAT?
IT'S NOT THAT HARD!!
THEN I RETURNED TO THE VILLAGE TO REPORT THAT THEY WERE SAFE NOW.
OH... YOU SLEW IT...

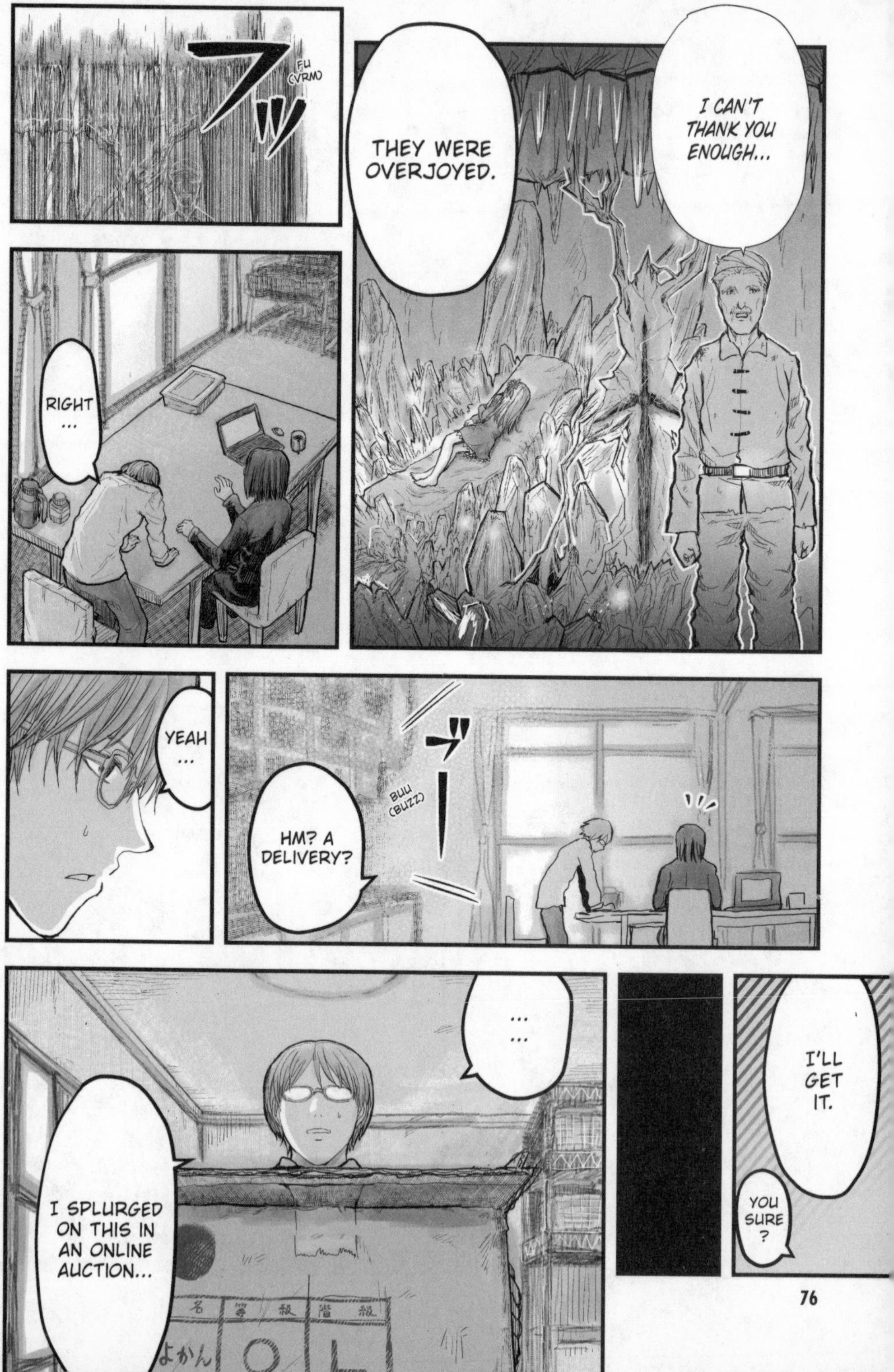
I CAN'T THANK YOU ENOUGH...
THEY WERE OVERJOYED.
FU (VRM)
RIGHT ...
BUU (BUZZ)
HM? A DELIVERY?
YEAH ...
I'LL GET IT.
YOU SURE?
... ...
I SPLURGED ON THIS IN AN ONLINE AUCTION...

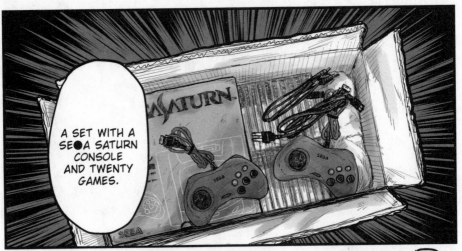

A SET WITH A SE●A SATURN CONSOLE AND TWENTY GAMES.

I'D PLANNED ON IT BEING A SURPRISE, BUT...

AH...

OH...

WHAT'S THAT?

TAKA-FUMI?

...AFTER ALL THAT TALK ABOUT CUTTING BACK ON UNNECESSARY SPENDING, I WONDER IF HE'LL GET MAD...

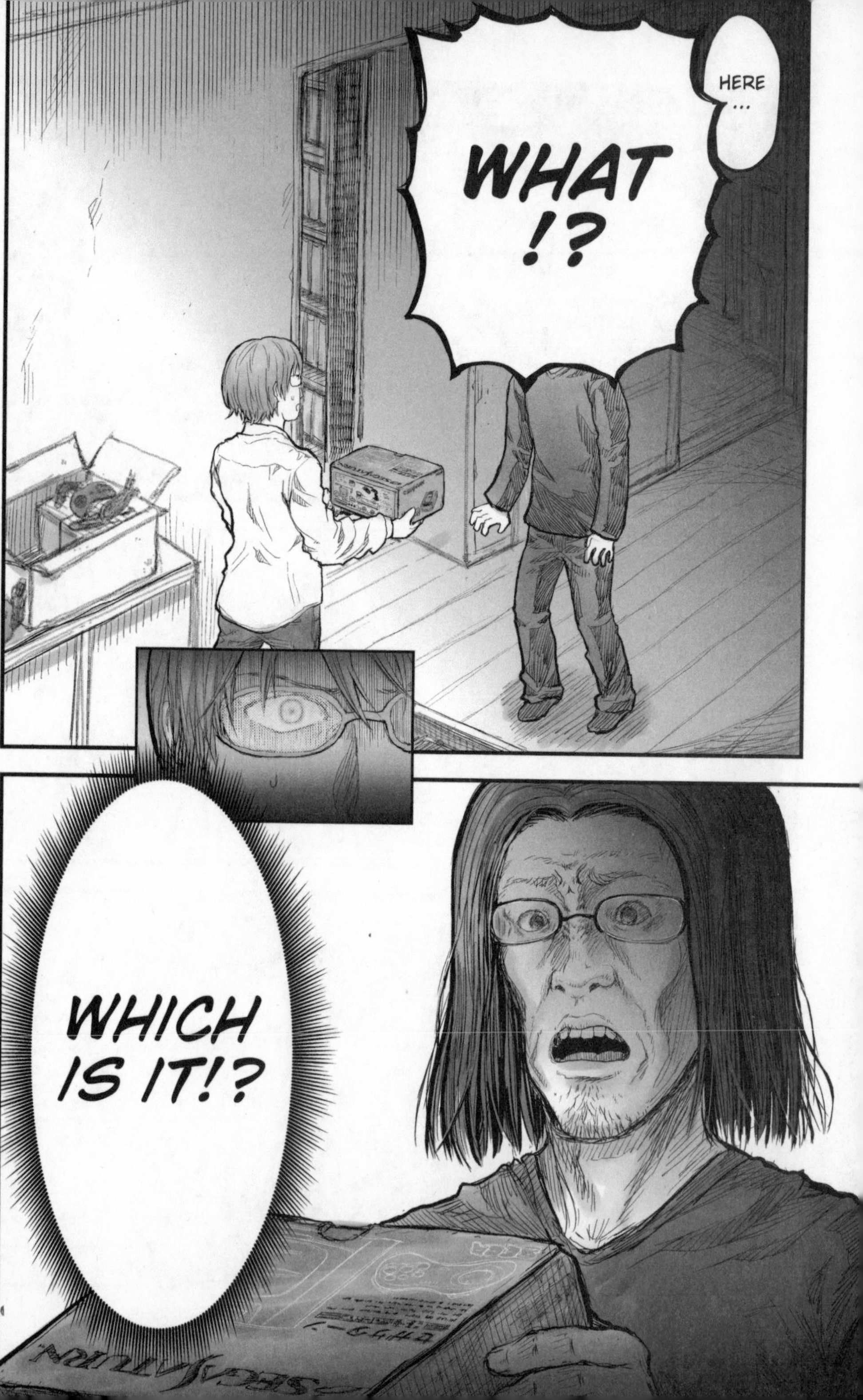
HERE ...
WHAT !?
WHICH IS IT!?

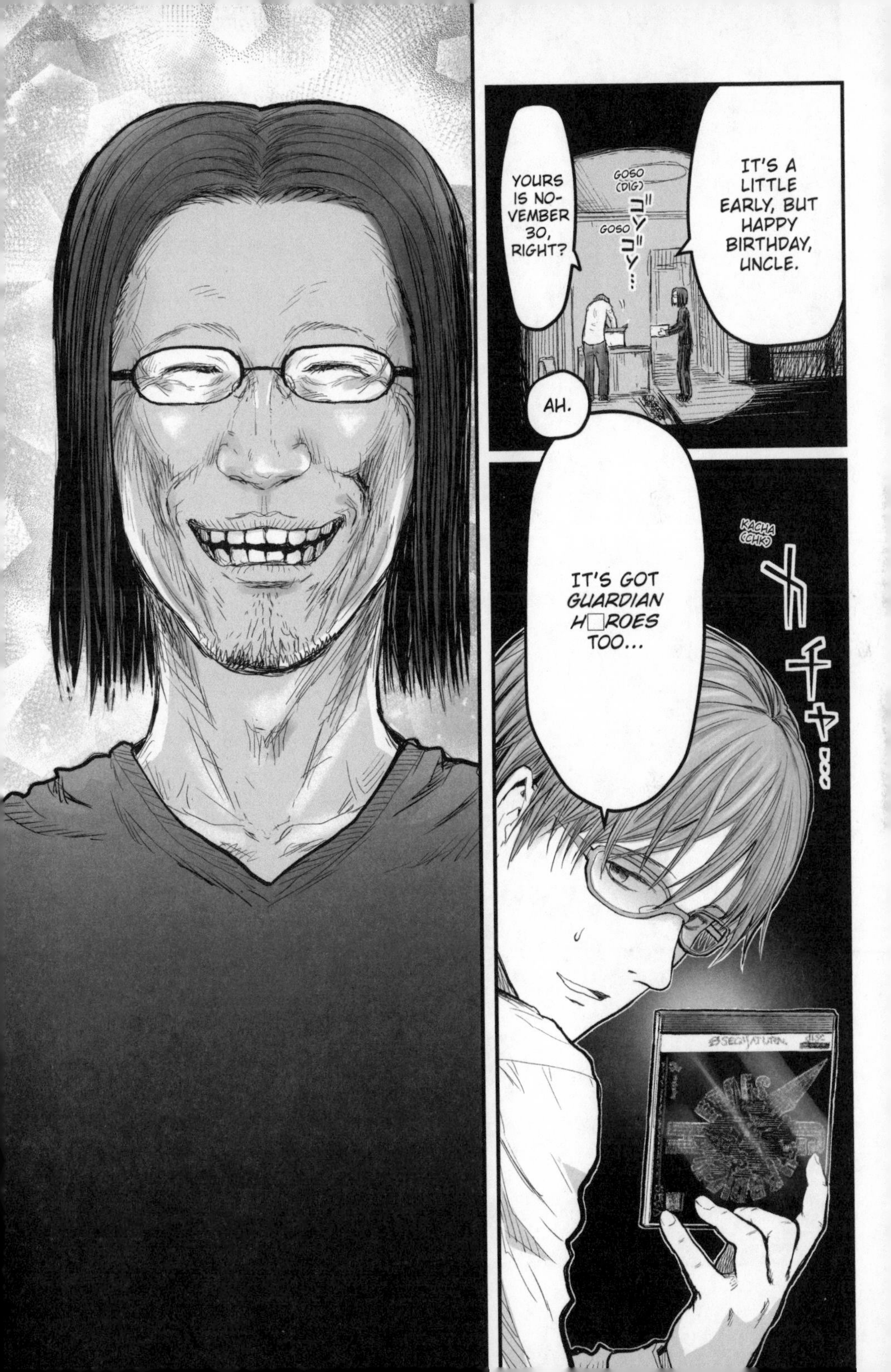
IT'S A LITTLE EARLY, BUT HAPPY BIRTHDAY, UNCLE.
GOSO (DIG)
ゴソ
GOSO
ゴソ…
YOURS IS NO-VEMBER 30, RIGHT?
AH.
IT'S GOT GUARDIAN H□ROES TOO…
KACHA (CHK)
カチャ

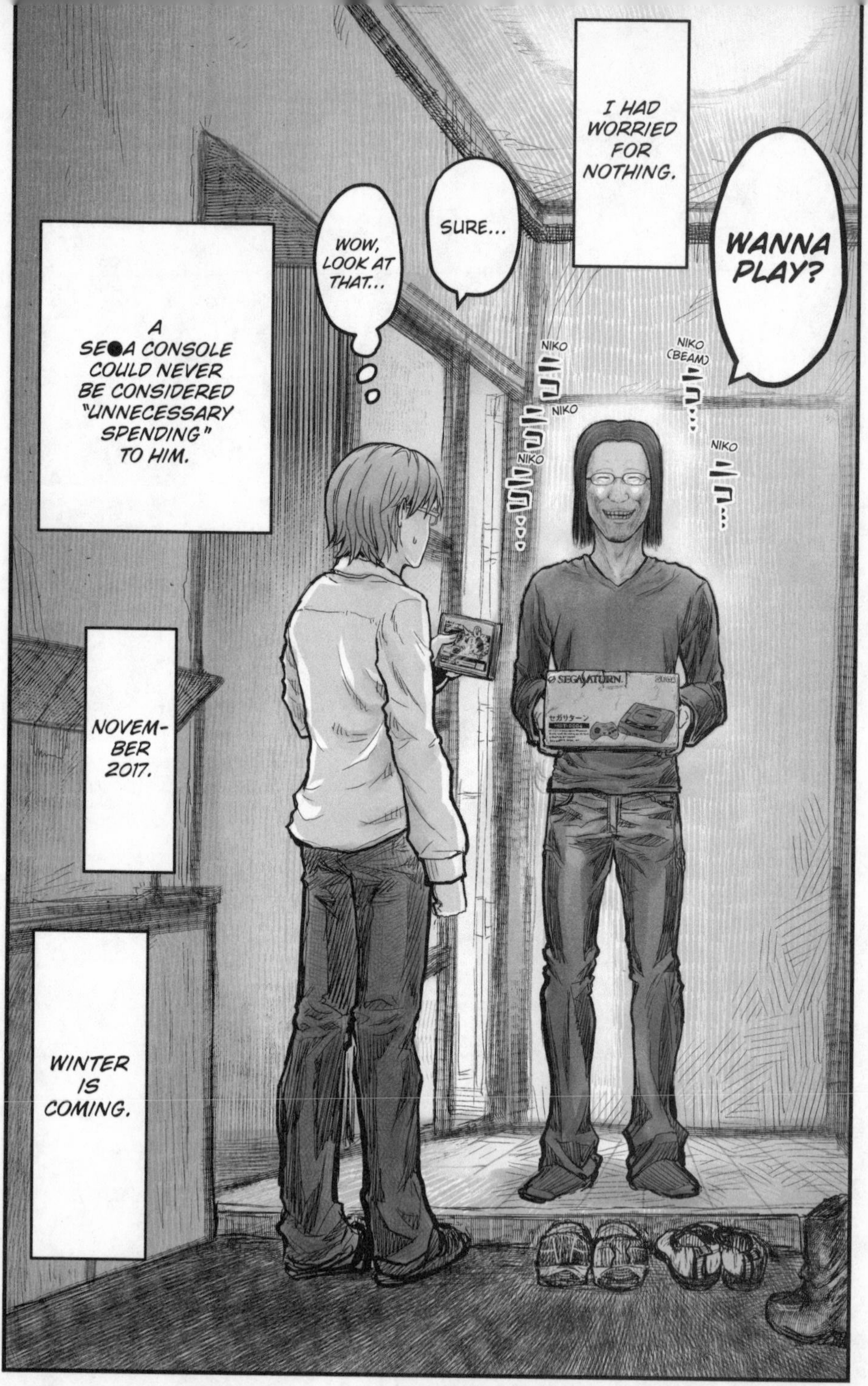
WANNA PLAY?
I HAD WORRIED FOR NOTHING.
SURE...
WOW, LOOK AT THAT...
NIKO (BEAM)
NIKO
NIKO
NIKO
NIKO
SEGA SATURN
セガサターン
A SE●A CONSOLE COULD NEVER BE CONSIDERED "UNNECESSARY SPENDING" TO HIM.
NOVEMBER 2017.
WINTER IS COMING.

1st Place in Reader Polls

EVE Burst Error

TIPS

UNCLE from ANOTHER WORLD

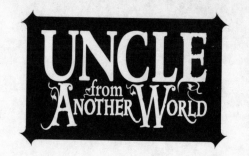

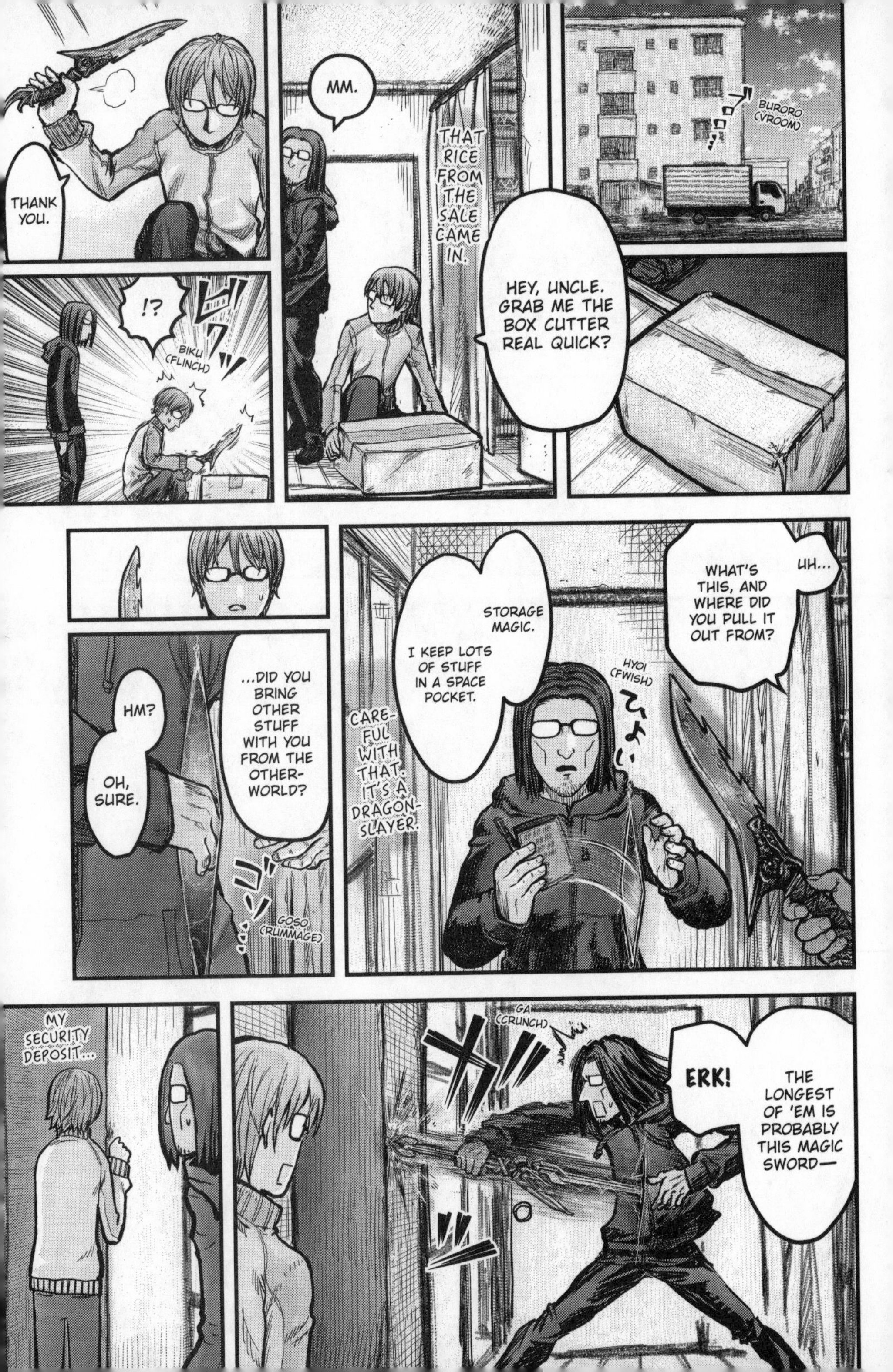
BURORO (VROOM)
THAT RICE FROM THE SALE CAME IN.
HEY, UNCLE. GRAB ME THE BOX CUTTER REAL QUICK?
MM.
THANK YOU.
!?
BIKU (FLINCH)
UH...
WHAT'S THIS, AND WHERE DID YOU PULL IT OUT FROM?
STORAGE MAGIC.
I KEEP LOTS OF STUFF IN A SPACE POCKET.
HYOI (FWISH)
CARE-FUL WITH THAT. IT'S A DRAGON-SLAYER.
...DID YOU BRING OTHER STUFF WITH YOU FROM THE OTHER-WORLD?
HM?
OH, SURE.
GOSO (RUMMAGE)
THE LONGEST OF 'EM IS PROBABLY THIS MAGIC SWORD—
ERK!
GA (CRUNCH)
MY SECURITY DEPOSIT...

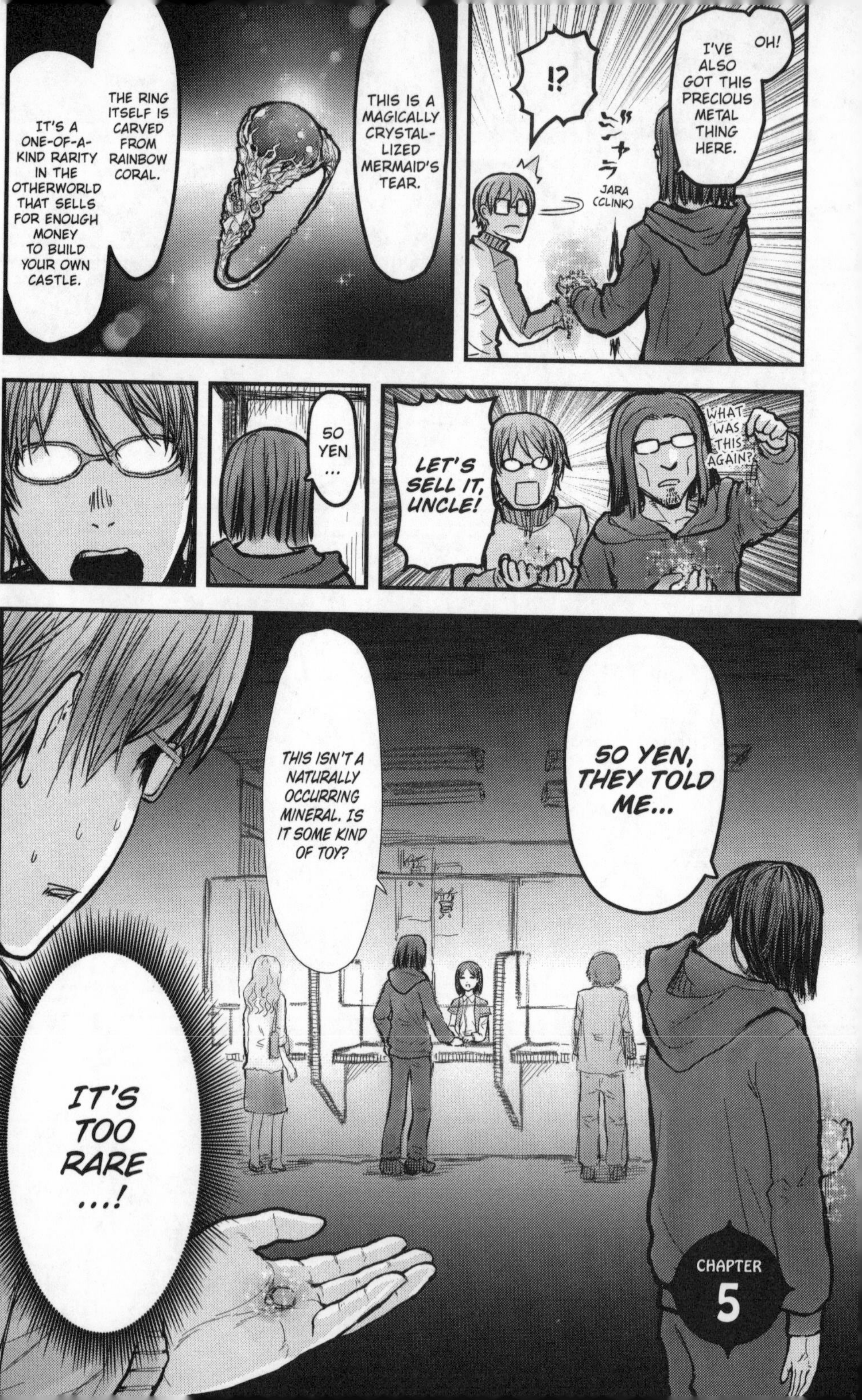
OH!
I'VE ALSO GOT THIS PRECIOUS METAL THING HERE.
!?
JARA (CLINK)
THIS IS A MAGICALLY CRYSTALLIZED MERMAID'S TEAR.
THE RING ITSELF IS CARVED FROM RAINBOW CORAL.
IT'S A ONE-OF-A-KIND RARITY IN THE OTHERWORLD THAT SELLS FOR ENOUGH MONEY TO BUILD YOUR OWN CASTLE.
WHAT WAS THIS AGAIN?
LET'S SELL IT, UNCLE!
SO YEN...
SO YEN, THEY TOLD ME...
THIS ISN'T A NATURALLY OCCURRING MINERAL. IS IT SOME KIND OF TOY?
IT'S TOO RARE...!
CHAPTER 5

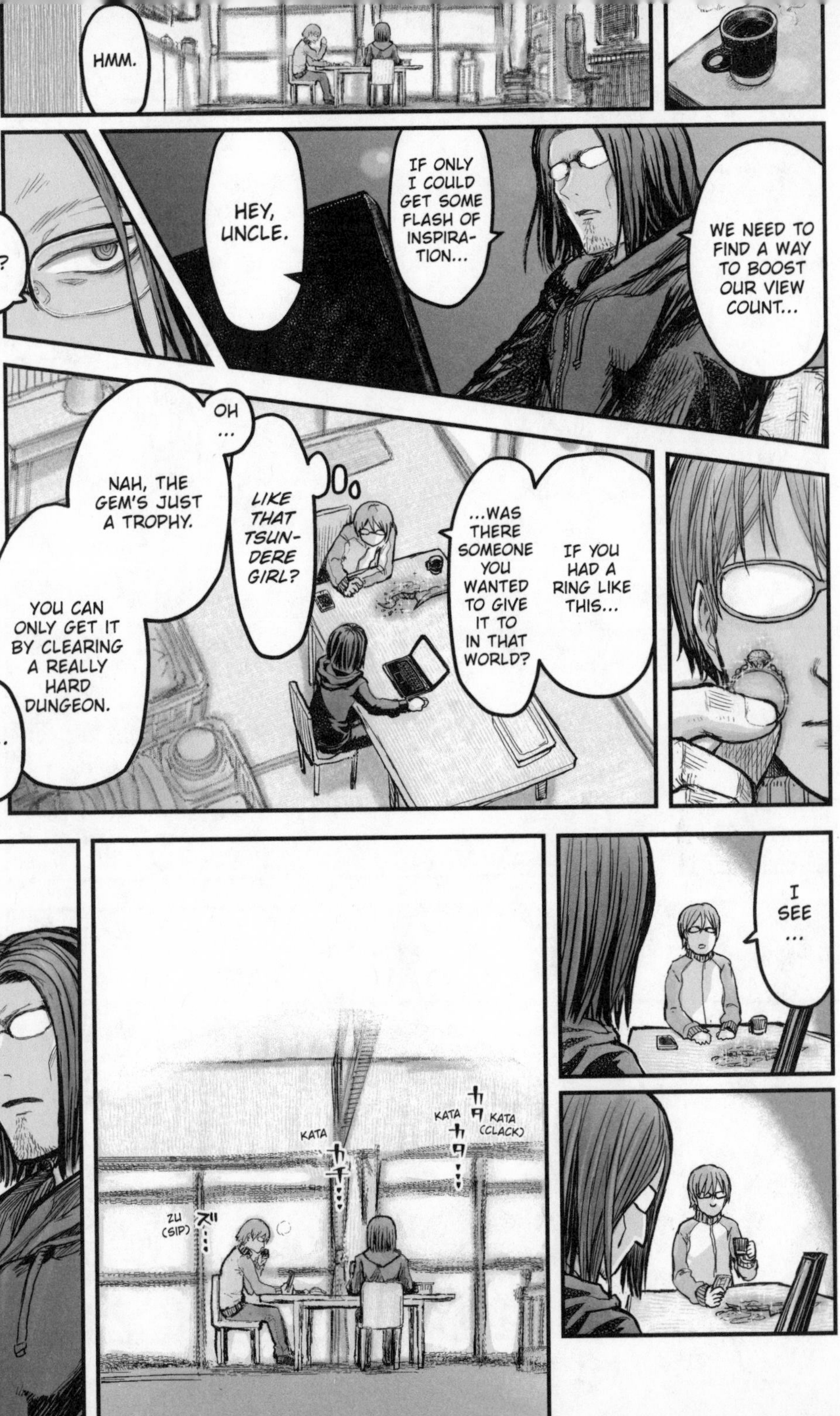
HMM.
WE NEED TO FIND A WAY TO BOOST OUR VIEW COUNT...
IF ONLY I COULD GET SOME FLASH OF INSPIRA-TION...
HEY, UNCLE.
HM?
IF YOU HAD A RING LIKE THIS...
...WAS THERE SOMEONE YOU WANTED TO GIVE IT TO IN THAT WORLD?
LIKE THAT TSUN-DERE GIRL?
OH ...
NAH, THE GEM'S JUST A TROPHY.
YOU CAN ONLY GET IT BY CLEARING A REALLY HARD DUNGEON.
AH...
I SEE ...
KATA KATA (CLACK)
KATA
ZU (SIP)

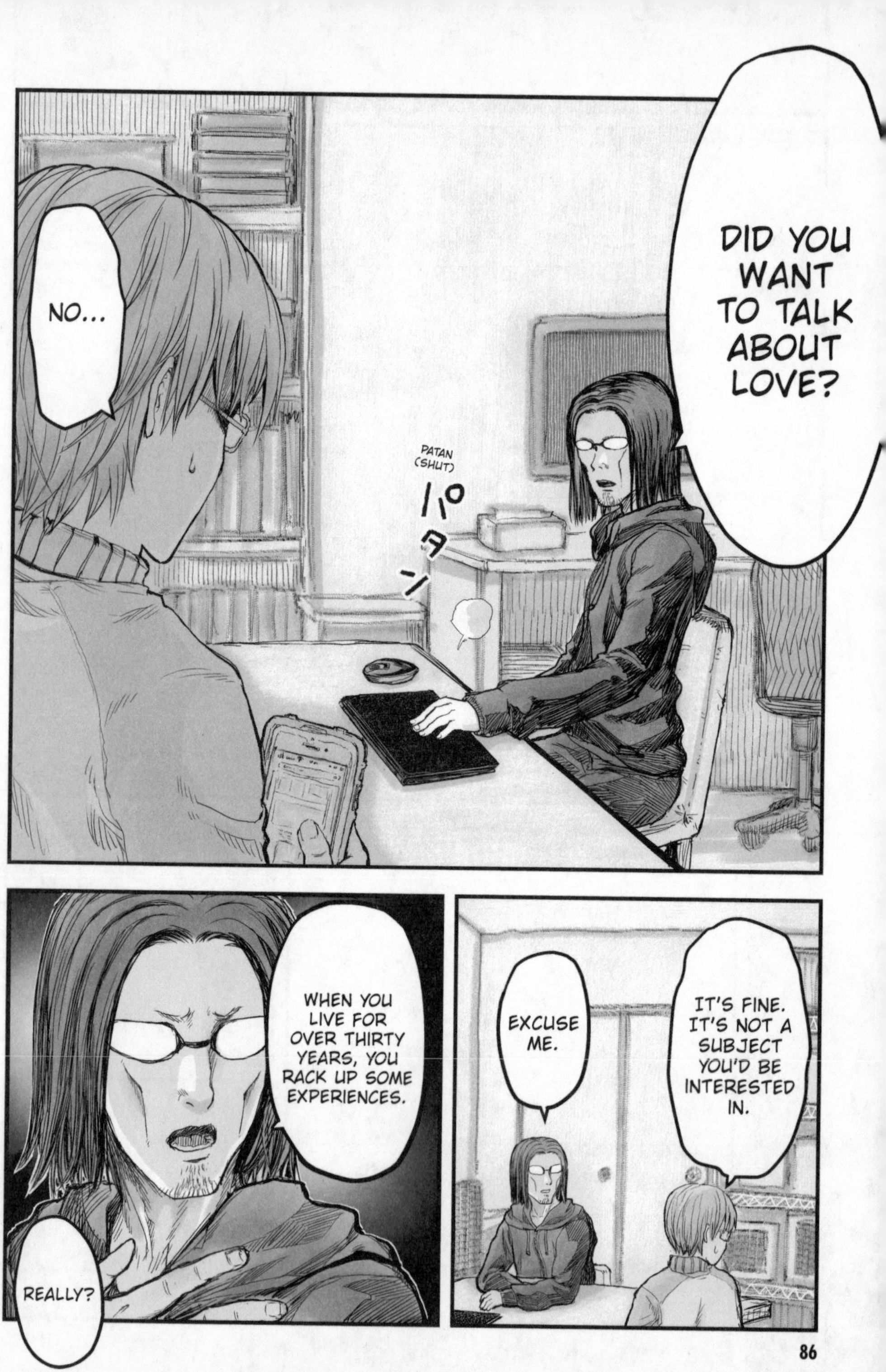
DID YOU WANT TO TALK ABOUT LOVE?
PATAN (SHUT)
パタン
NO...
IT'S FINE. IT'S NOT A SUBJECT YOU'D BE INTERESTED IN.
EXCUSE ME.
WHEN YOU LIVE FOR OVER THIRTY YEARS, YOU RACK UP SOME EXPERIENCES.
REALLY?

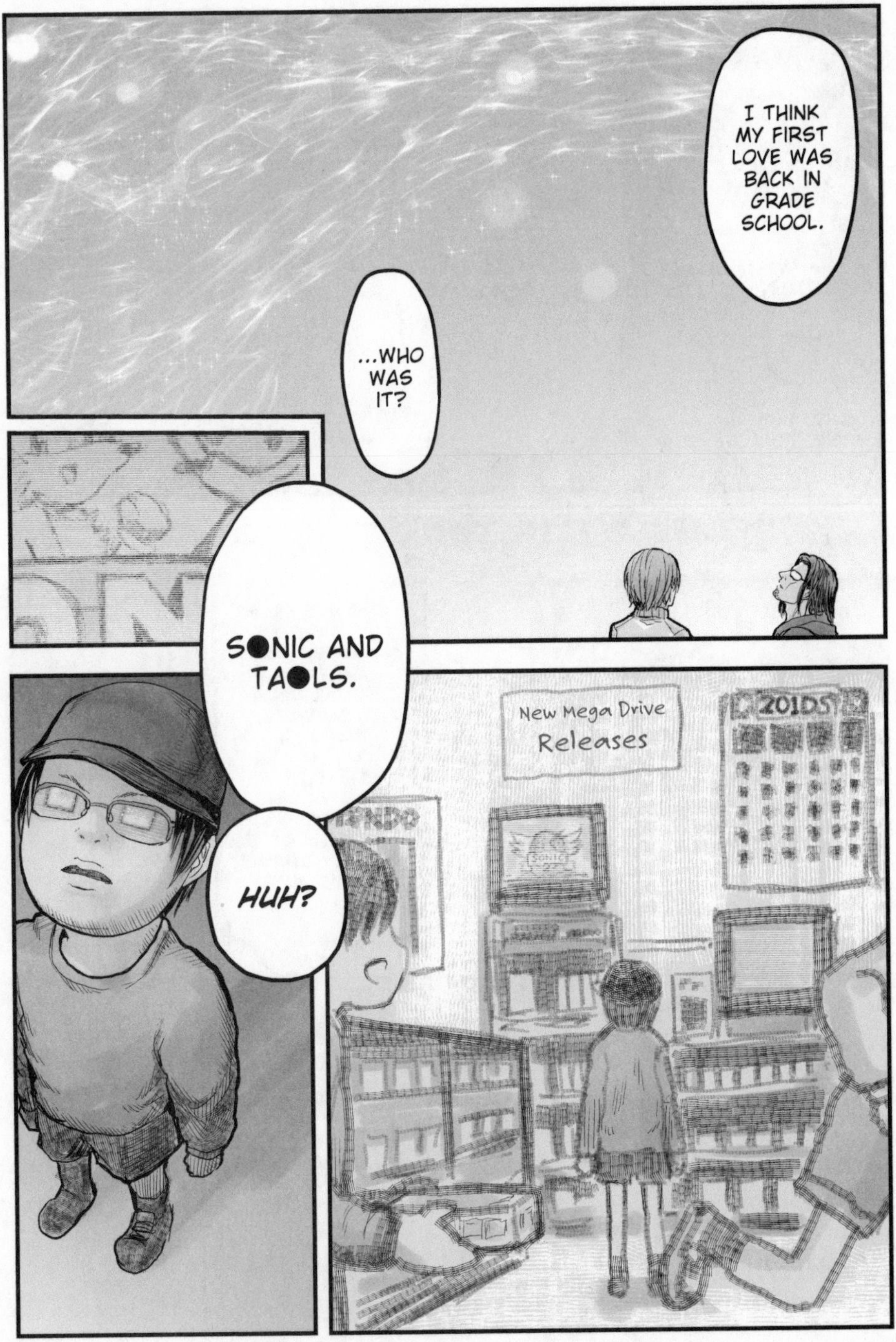
I THINK MY FIRST LOVE WAS BACK IN GRADE SCHOOL.
...WHO WAS IT?
S●NIC AND TA●LS.
New Mega Drive Releases
HUH?

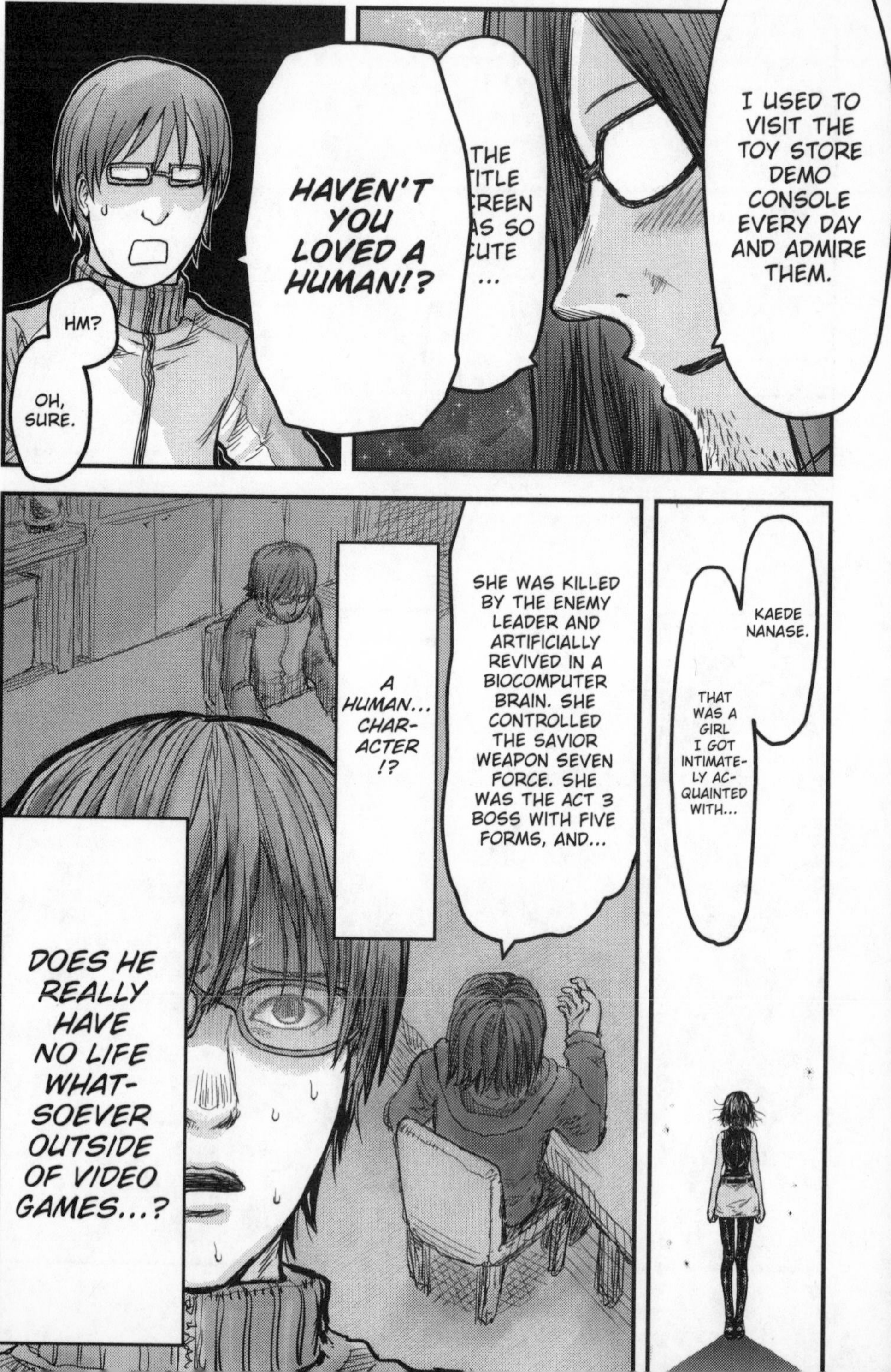
I USED TO VISIT THE TOY STORE DEMO CONSOLE EVERY DAY AND ADMIRE THEM.
THE ITLE CREEN AS SO CUTE ...
HAVEN'T YOU LOVED A HUMAN!?
HM?
OH, SURE.
KAEDE NANASE.
THAT WAS A GIRL I GOT INTIMATELY ACQUAINTED WITH...
SHE WAS KILLED BY THE ENEMY LEADER AND ARTIFICIALLY REVIVED IN A BIOCOMPUTER BRAIN. SHE CONTROLLED THE SAVIOR WEAPON SEVEN FORCE. SHE WAS THE ACT 3 BOSS WITH FIVE FORMS, AND...
A HUMAN... CHARACTER!?
DOES HE REALLY HAVE NO LIFE WHATSOEVER OUTSIDE OF VIDEO GAMES...?

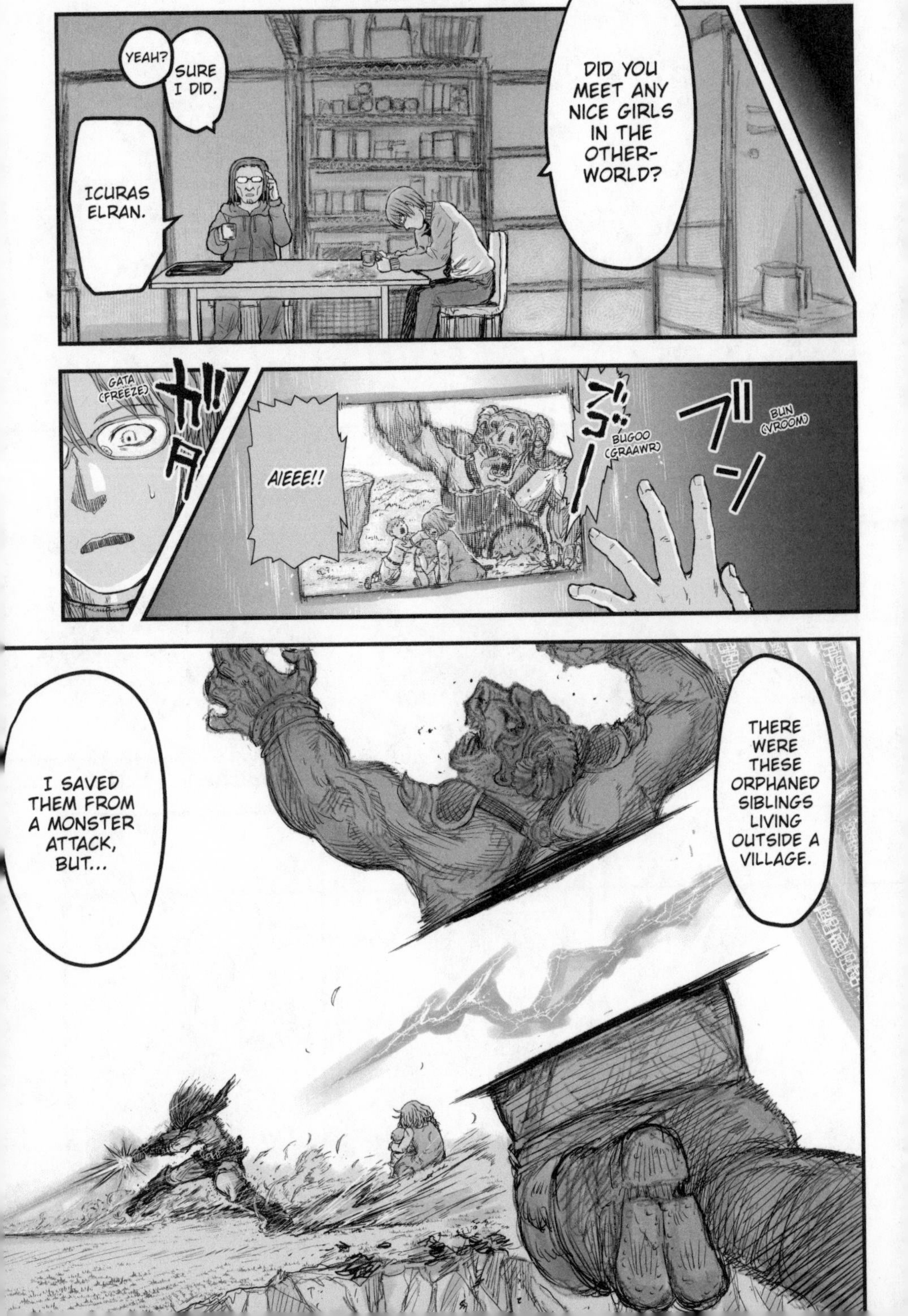
DID YOU MEET ANY NICE GIRLS IN THE OTHER-WORLD?
SURE I DID.
YEAH?
ICURAS ELRAN.
BUN (VROOM)
BUGOO (GRAAWR)
AIEEE!!
GATA (FREEZE)
THERE WERE THESE ORPHANED SIBLINGS LIVING OUTSIDE A VILLAGE.
I SAVED THEM FROM A MONSTER ATTACK, BUT...

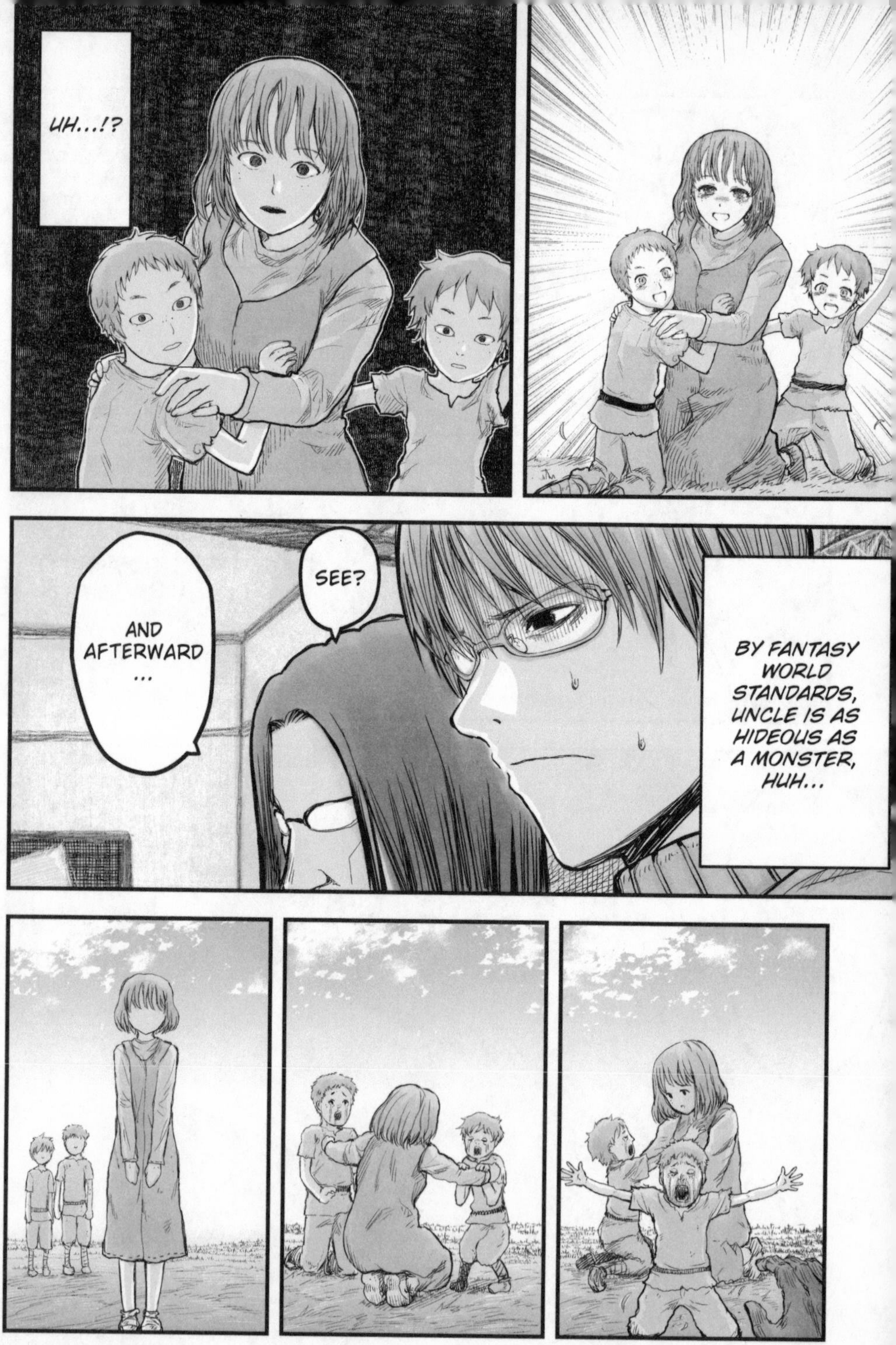
UH...!?
BY FANTASY WORLD STANDARDS, UNCLE IS AS HIDEOUS AS A MONSTER, HUH...
SEE?
AND AFTERWARD ...

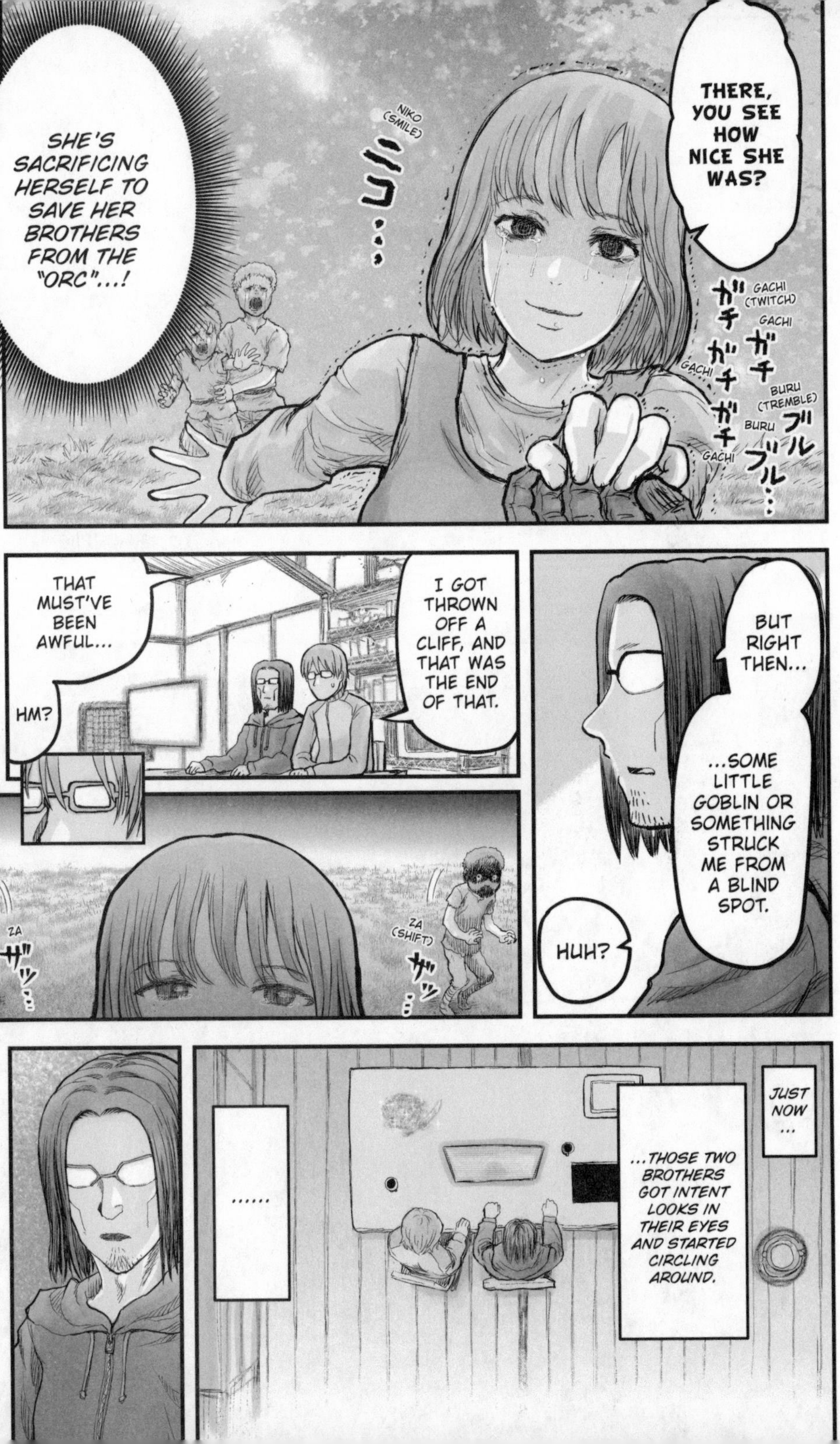
THERE, YOU SEE HOW NICE SHE WAS?
GACHI (TWITCH) GACHI GACHI GACHI
BURU (TREMBLE) BURU
NIKO (SMILE)
SHE'S SACRIFICING HERSELF TO SAVE HER BROTHERS FROM THE "ORC"...!
BUT RIGHT THEN...
...SOME LITTLE GOBLIN OR SOMETHING STRUCK ME FROM A BLIND SPOT.
HUH?
I GOT THROWN OFF A CLIFF, AND THAT WAS THE END OF THAT.
THAT MUST'VE BEEN AWFUL...
HM?
ZA (SHIFT)
ZA
JUST NOW...
...THOSE TWO BROTHERS GOT INTENT LOOKS IN THEIR EYES AND STARTED CIRCLING AROUND.
......

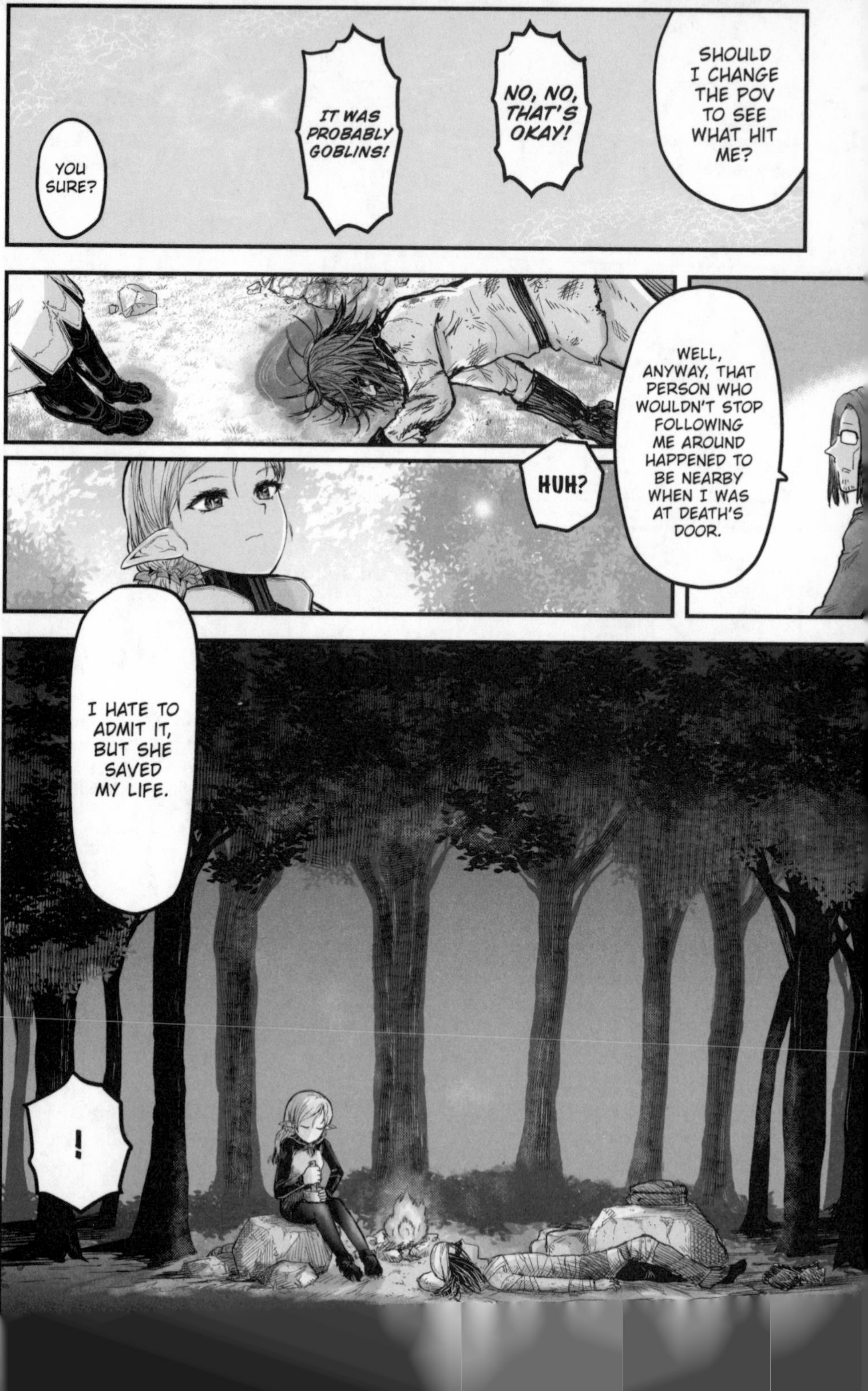
SHOULD I CHANGE THE POV TO SEE WHAT HIT ME?
NO, NO, THAT'S OKAY!
IT WAS PROBABLY GOBLINS!
YOU SURE?
WELL, ANYWAY, THAT PERSON WHO WOULDN'T STOP FOLLOWING ME AROUND HAPPENED TO BE NEARBY WHEN I WAS AT DEATH'S DOOR.
HUH?
I HATE TO ADMIT IT, BUT SHE SAVED MY LIFE.
!

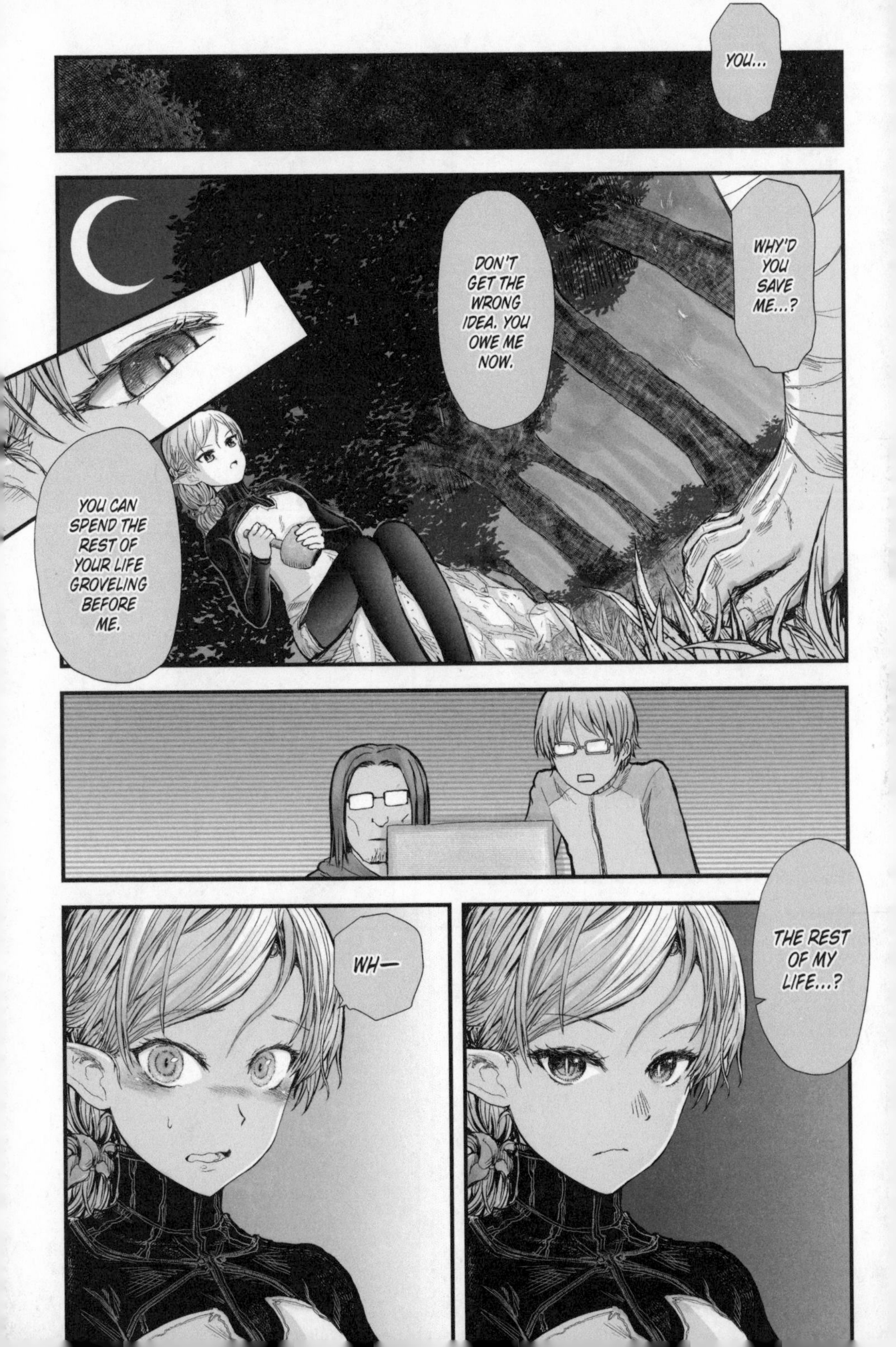
YOU...
WHY'D YOU SAVE ME...?
DON'T GET THE WRONG IDEA. YOU OWE ME NOW.
YOU CAN SPEND THE REST OF YOUR LIFE GROVELING BEFORE ME.
THE REST OF MY LIFE...?
WH—

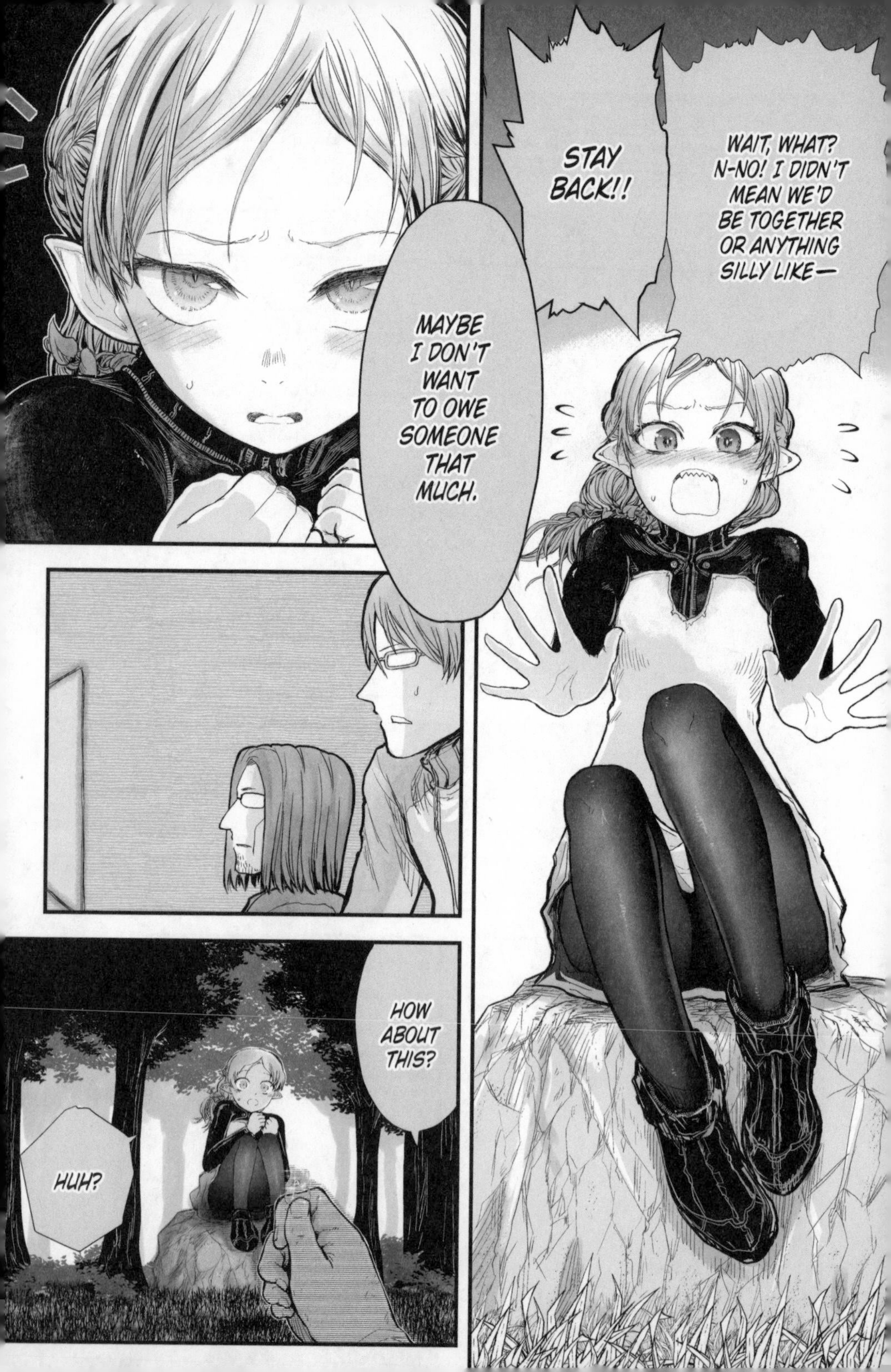
WAIT, WHAT? N-NO! I DIDN'T MEAN WE'D BE TOGETHER OR ANYTHING SILLY LIKE—
STAY BACK!!
MAYBE I DON'T WANT TO OWE SOMEONE THAT MUCH.
HOW ABOUT THIS?
HUH?

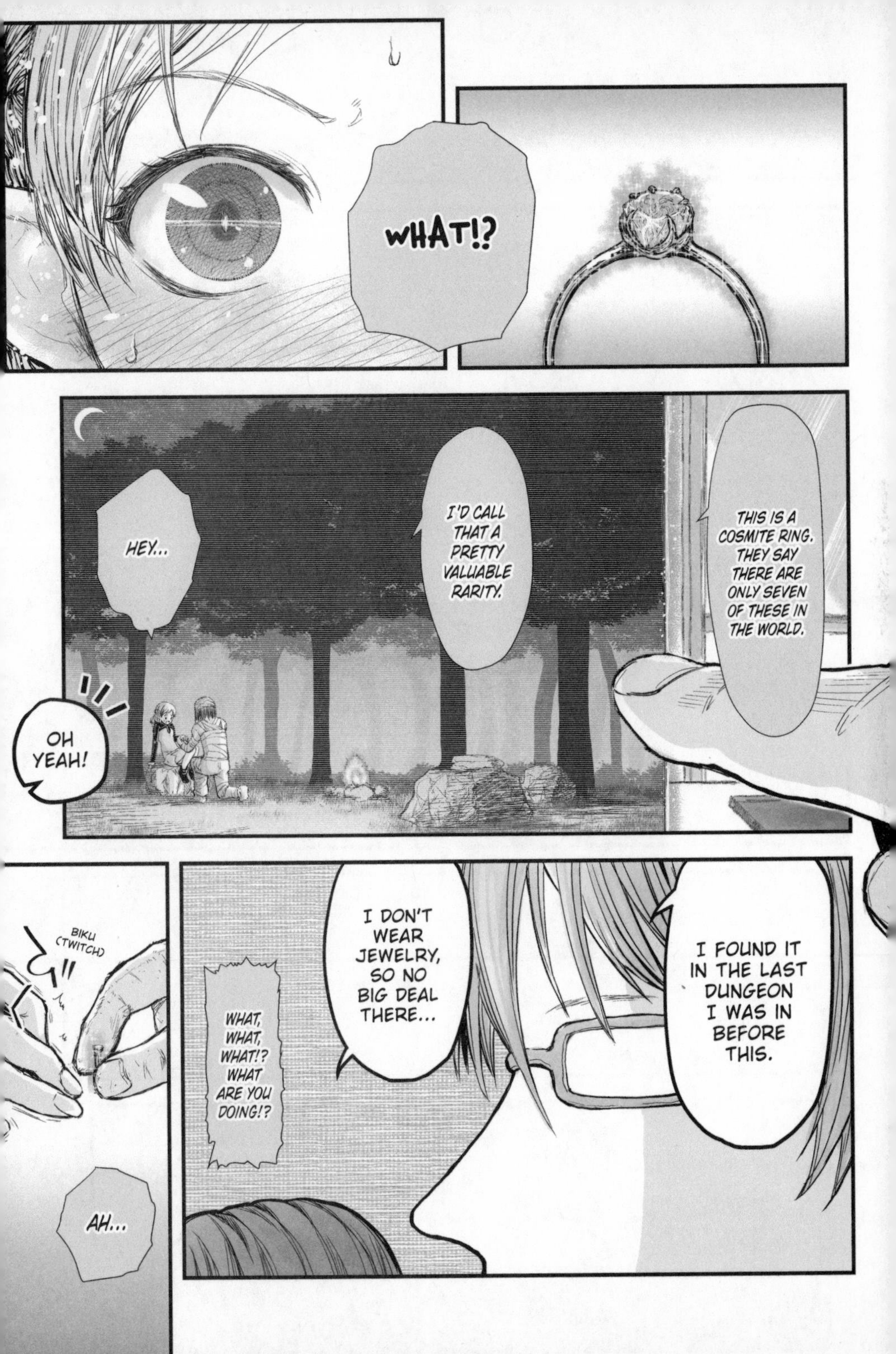
WHAT!?
THIS IS A COSMITE RING. THEY SAY THERE ARE ONLY SEVEN OF THESE IN THE WORLD.
I'D CALL THAT A PRETTY VALUABLE RARITY.
HEY...
OH YEAH!
I FOUND IT IN THE LAST DUNGEON I WAS IN BEFORE THIS.
I DON'T WEAR JEWELRY, SO NO BIG DEAL THERE...
WHAT, WHAT, WHAT!? WHAT ARE YOU DOING!?
BIKU (TWITCH)
AH...

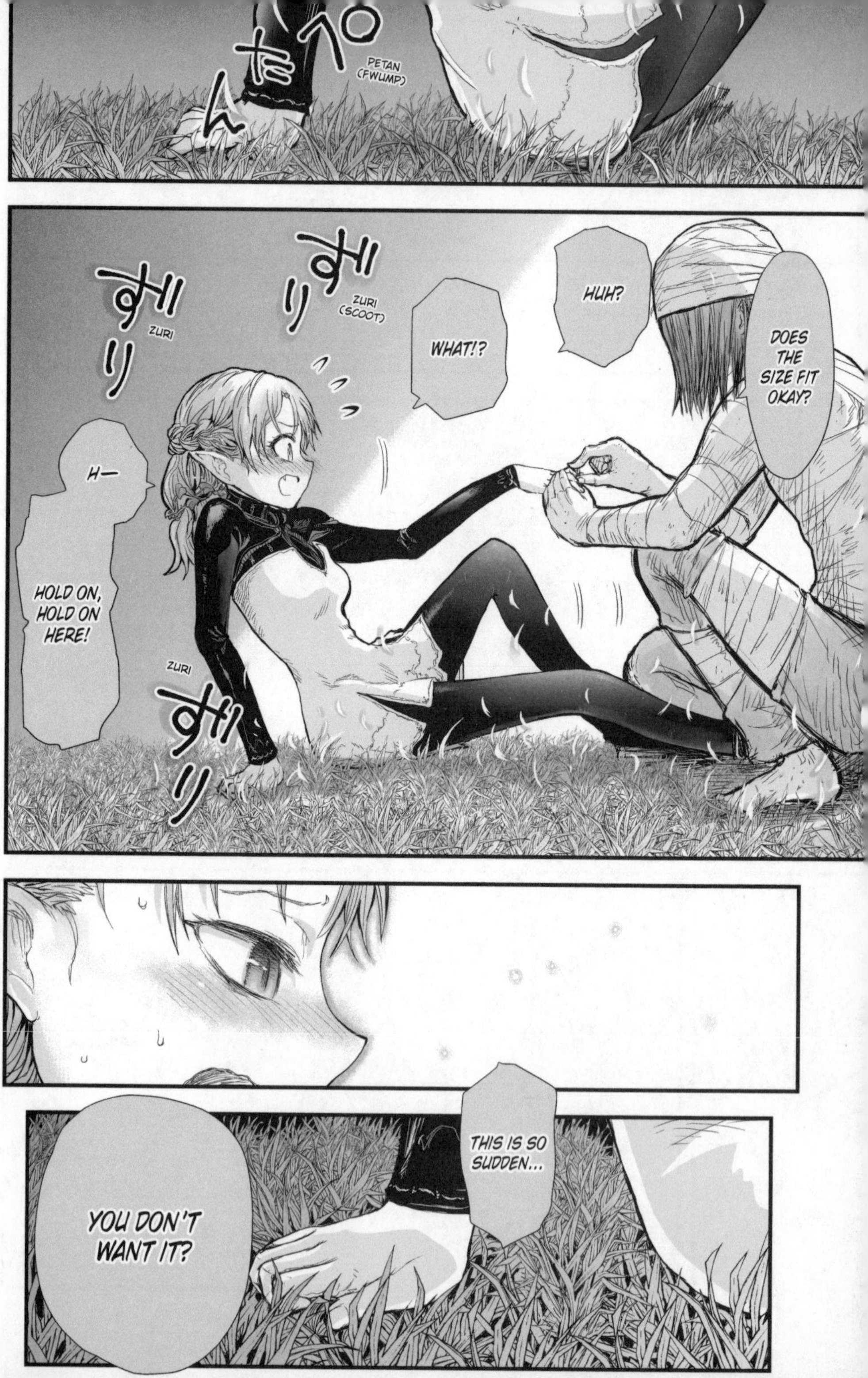
ぺたん
PETAN (FWUMP)
DOES THE SIZE FIT OKAY?
HUH?
WHAT!?
ずり
ZURI (SCOOT)
ずり
ZURI
H—
HOLD ON, HOLD ON HERE!
ZURI
ずり
THIS IS SO SUDDEN...
YOU DON'T WANT IT?

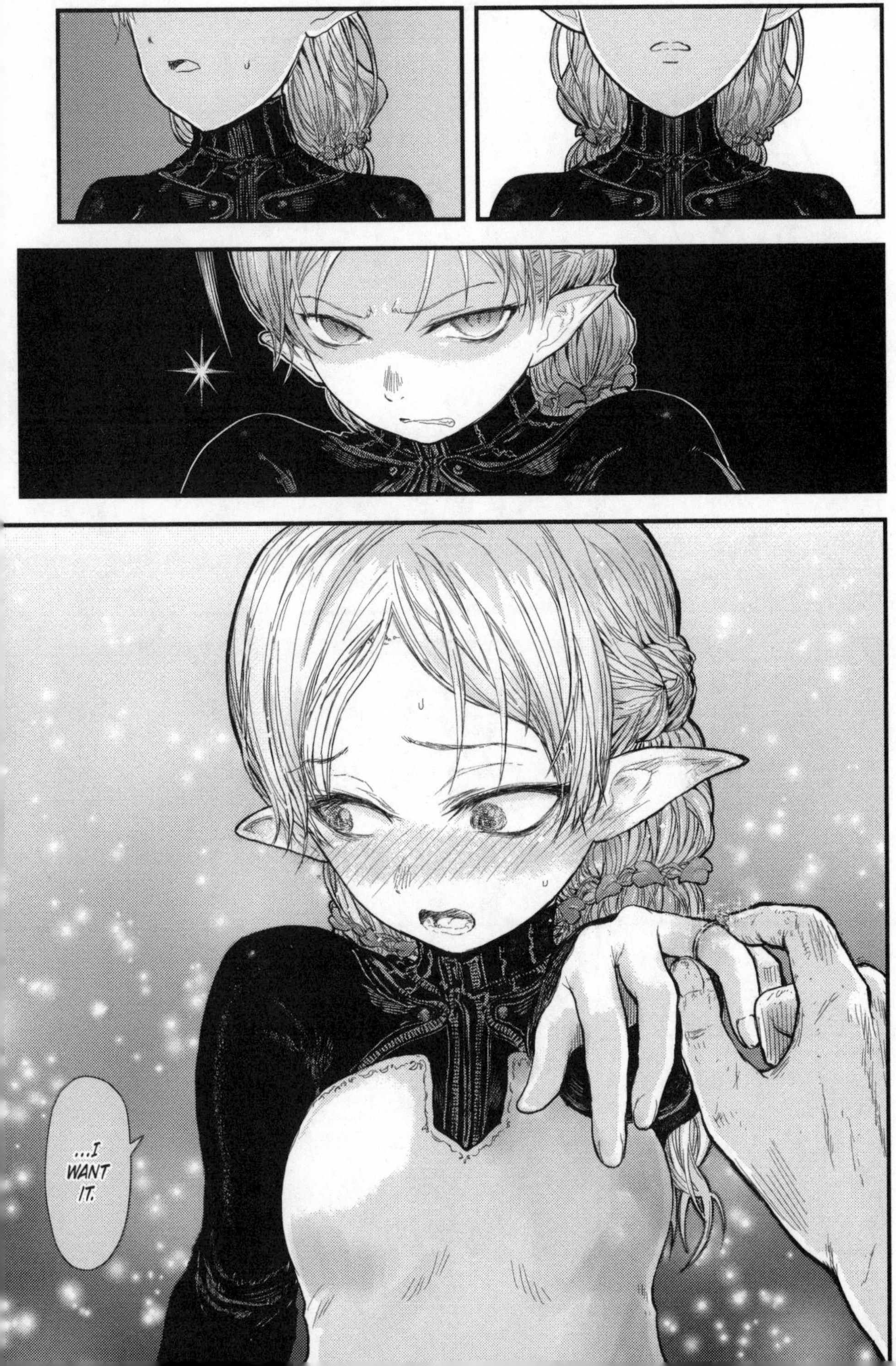
...I WANT IT.

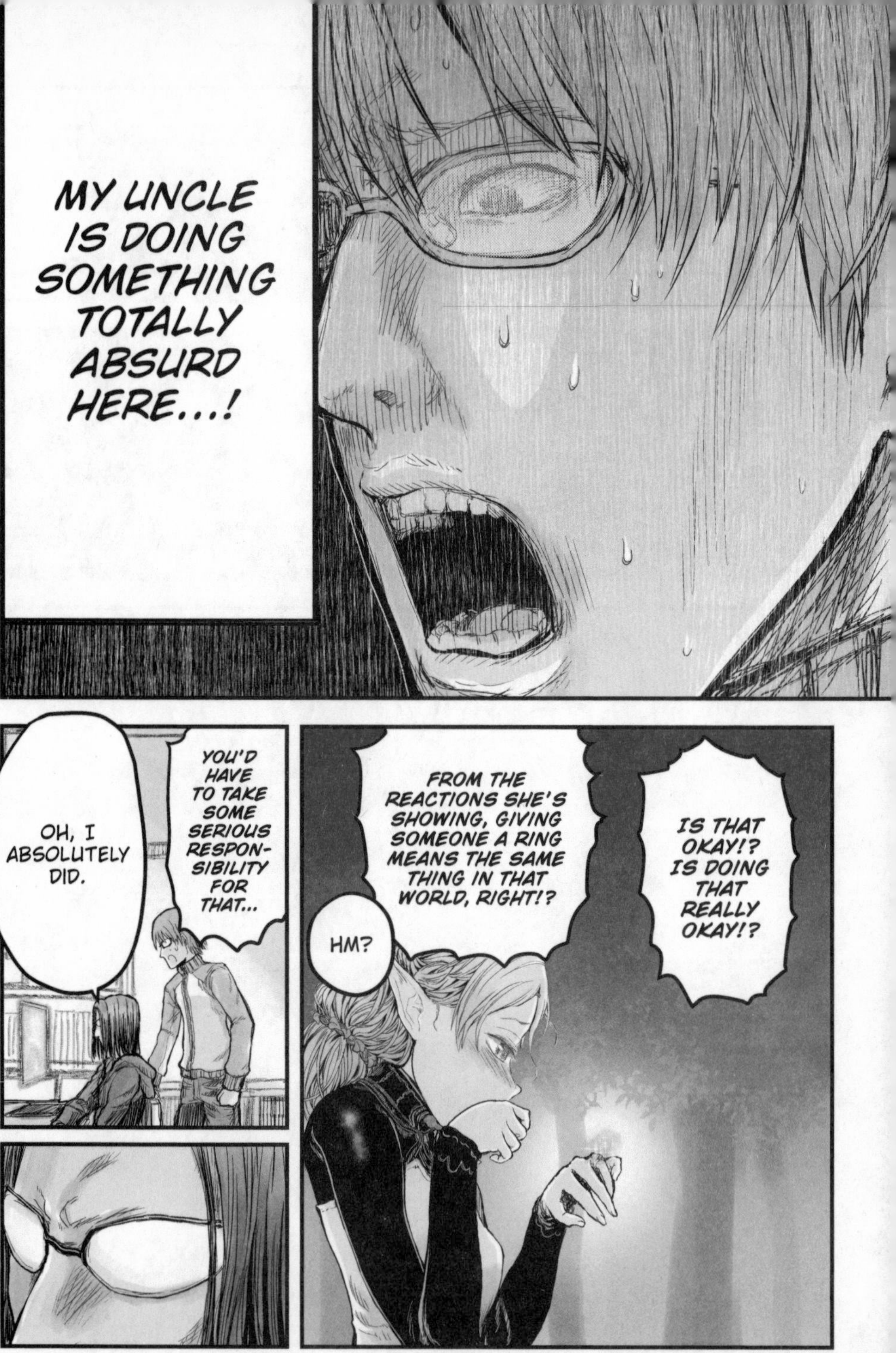
MY UNCLE IS DOING SOMETHING TOTALLY ABSURD HERE...!
FROM THE REACTIONS SHE'S SHOWING, GIVING SOMEONE A RING MEANS THE SAME THING IN THAT WORLD, RIGHT!?
IS THAT OKAY!? IS DOING THAT REALLY OKAY!?
HM?
YOU'D HAVE TO TAKE SOME SERIOUS RESPON-SIBILITY FOR THAT...
OH, I ABSOLUTELY DID.

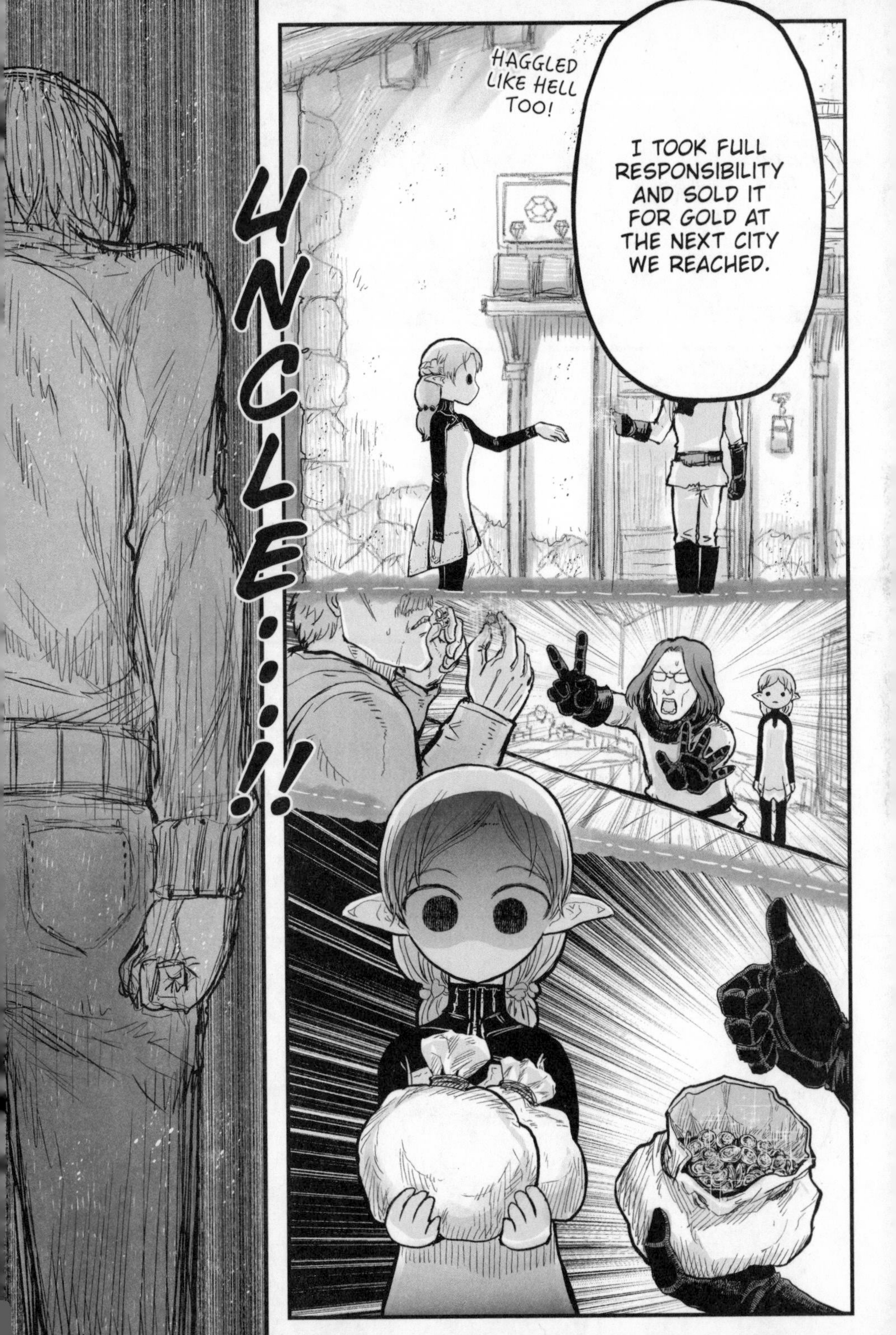
I TOOK FULL RESPONSIBILITY AND SOLD IT FOR GOLD AT THE NEXT CITY WE REACHED.
HAGGLED LIKE HELL TOO!
UNCLE...!!

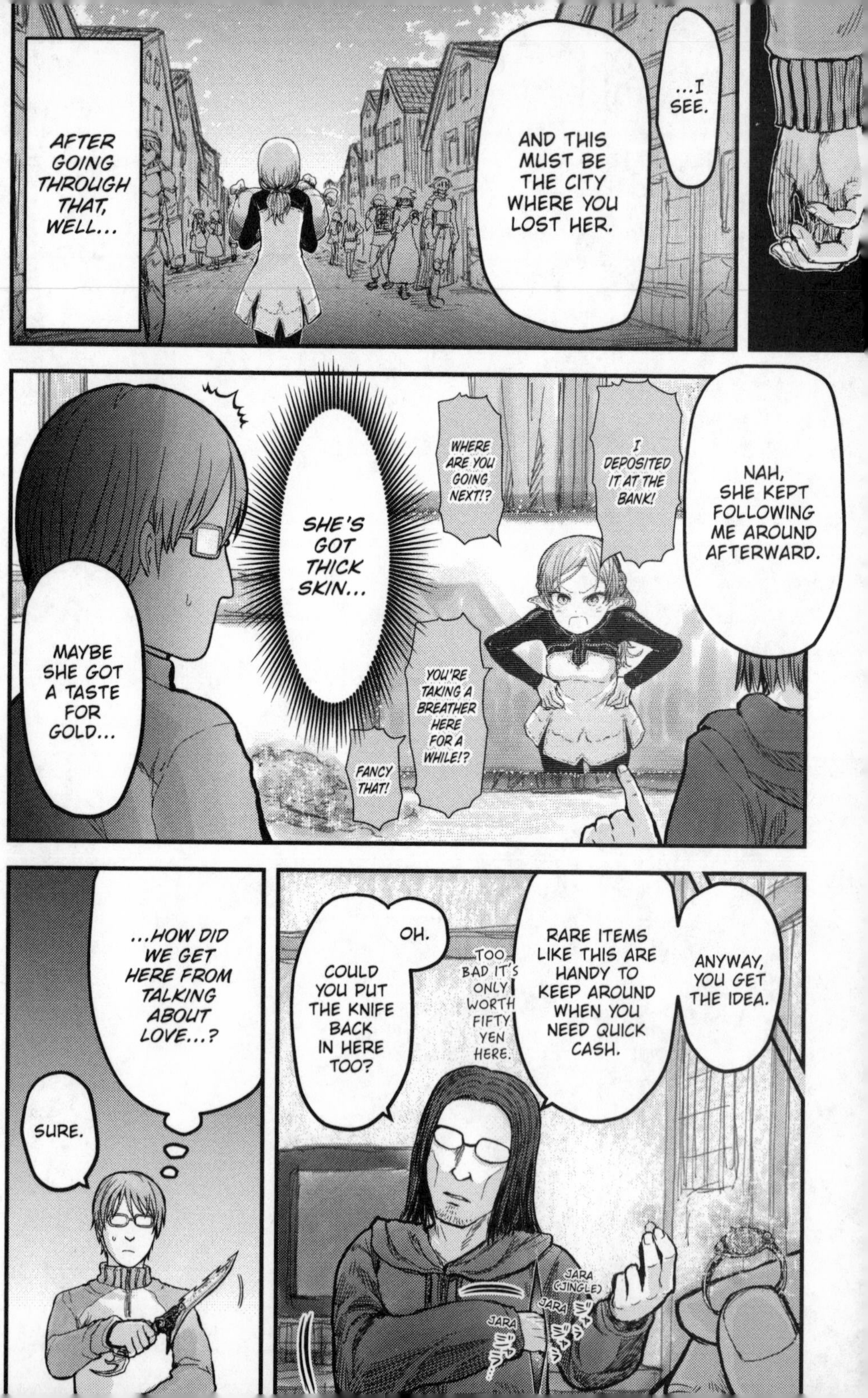
...I SEE.
AND THIS MUST BE THE CITY WHERE YOU LOST HER.
AFTER GOING THROUGH THAT, WELL...
NAH, SHE KEPT FOLLOWING ME AROUND AFTERWARD.
I DEPOSITED IT AT THE BANK!
WHERE ARE YOU GOING NEXT!?
YOU'RE TAKING A BREATHER HERE FOR A WHILE!?
FANCY THAT!
SHE'S GOT THICK SKIN...
MAYBE SHE GOT A TASTE FOR GOLD...
ANYWAY, YOU GET THE IDEA.
RARE ITEMS LIKE THIS ARE HANDY TO KEEP AROUND WHEN YOU NEED QUICK CASH.
TOO BAD IT'S ONLY WORTH FIFTY YEN HERE.
OH.
COULD YOU PUT THE KNIFE BACK IN HERE TOO?
JARA (JINGLE)
JARA
JARA
...HOW DID WE GET HERE FROM TALKING ABOUT LOVE...?
SURE.

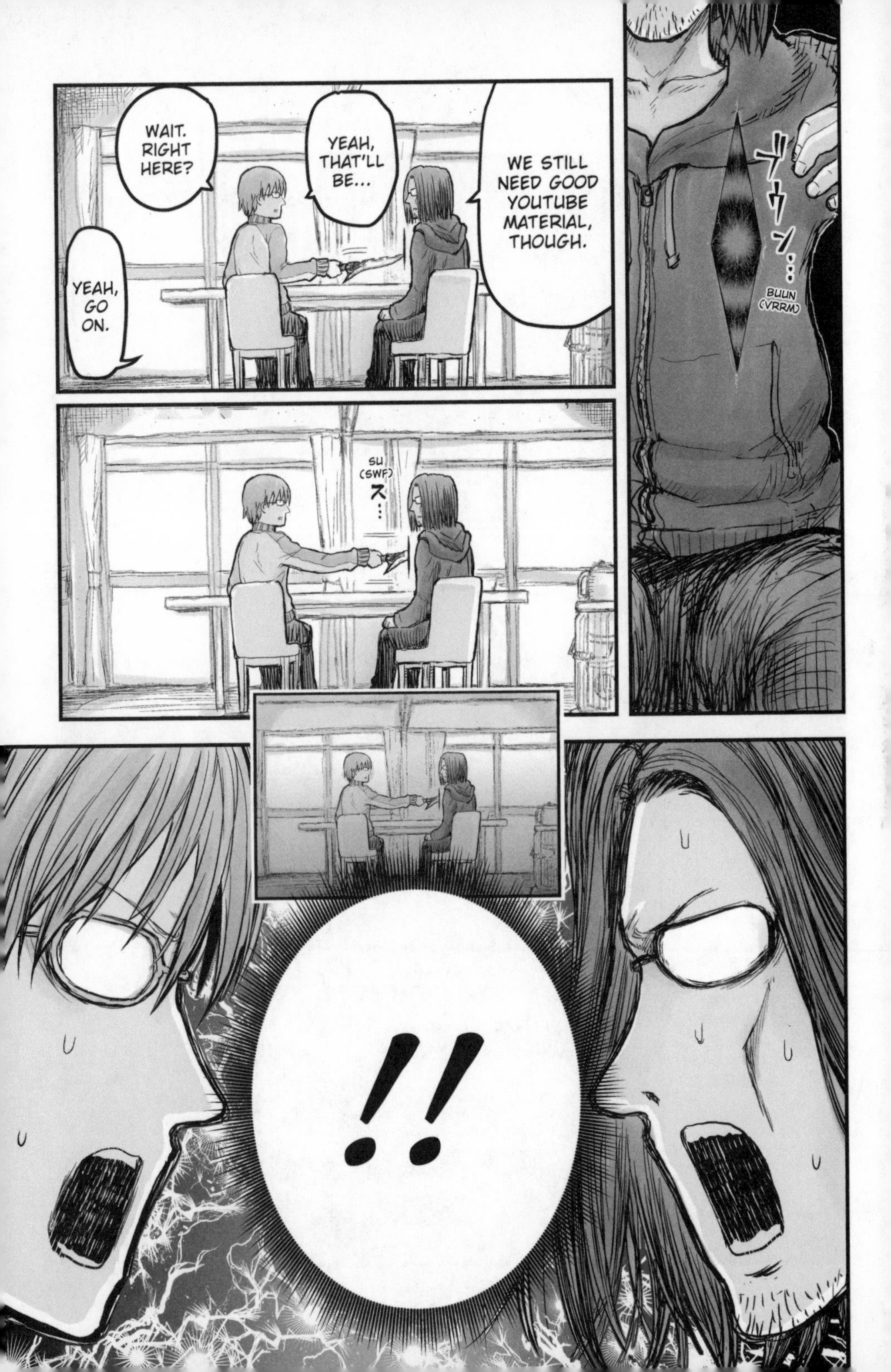

ブゥン…
BUUN (VRRM)
WE STILL NEED GOOD YOUTUBE MATERIAL, THOUGH.
YEAH, THAT'LL BE...
WAIT. RIGHT HERE?
YEAH, GO ON.
SU (SWF)
ス…
!!

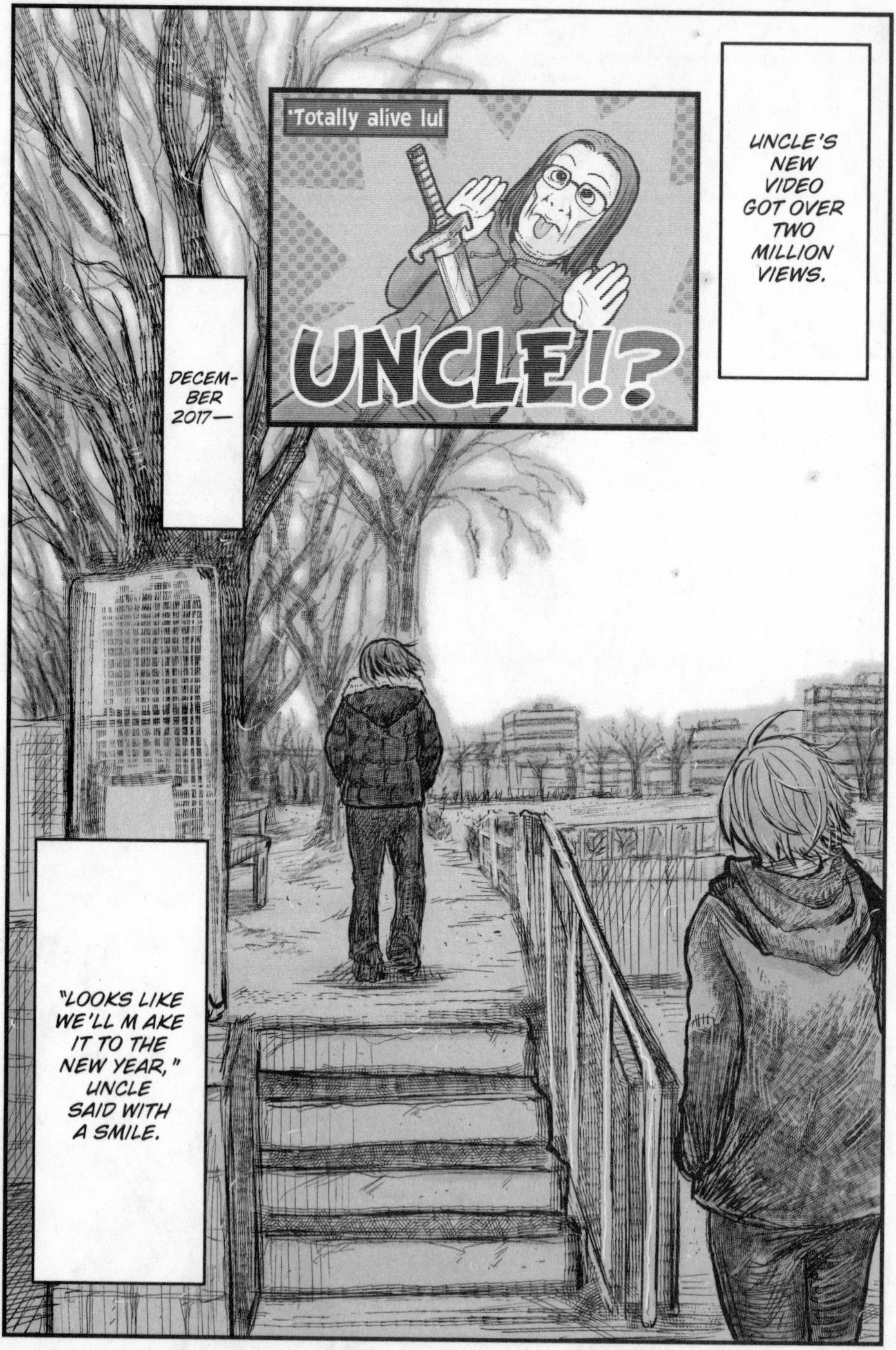
UNCLE'S NEW VIDEO GOT OVER TWO MILLION VIEWS.
'Totally alive lul
UNCLE!?
DECEMBER 2017—
"LOOKS LIKE WE'LL MAKE IT TO THE NEW YEAR," UNCLE SAID WITH A SMILE.

YouTuber

A new field of work that has gained an increasing presence in the public consciousness since the late 2010s, in which one's primary source of income is ad revenue from YouTube video views.

TIPS

UNCLE from ANOTHER WORLD

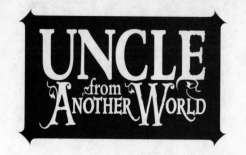

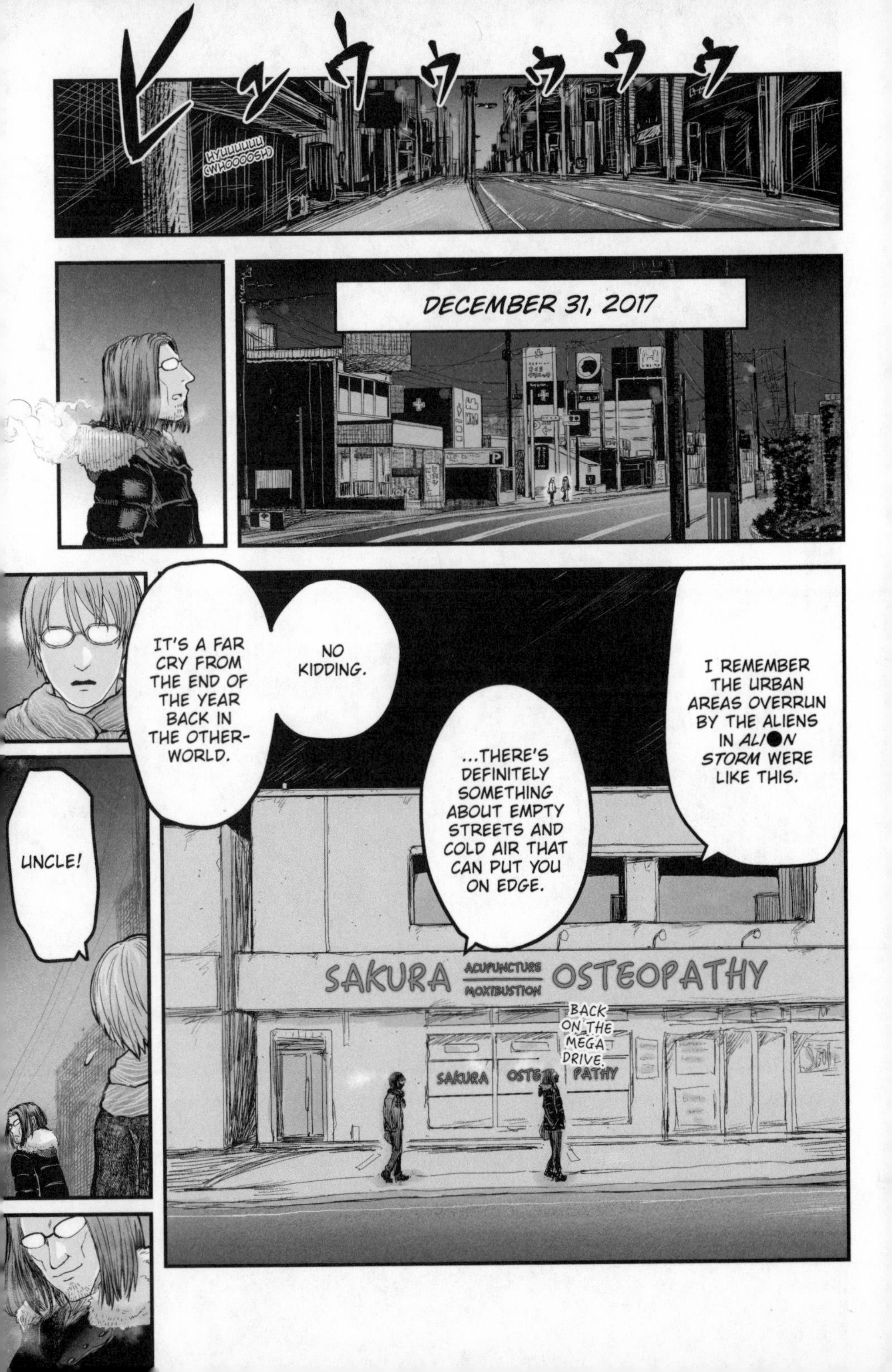
ヒュウウウウウ
HYUUUUUU (WHOOOOSH)
DECEMBER 31, 2017
I REMEMBER THE URBAN AREAS OVERRUN BY THE ALIENS IN ALI●N STORM WERE LIKE THIS.
...THERE'S DEFINITELY SOMETHING ABOUT EMPTY STREETS AND COLD AIR THAT CAN PUT YOU ON EDGE.
NO KIDDING.
IT'S A FAR CRY FROM THE END OF THE YEAR BACK IN THE OTHER-WORLD.
SAKURA ACUPUNCTURE MOXIBUSTION OSTEOPATHY
BACK ON THE MEGA DRIVE.
SAKURA OSTE PATHY
UNCLE!

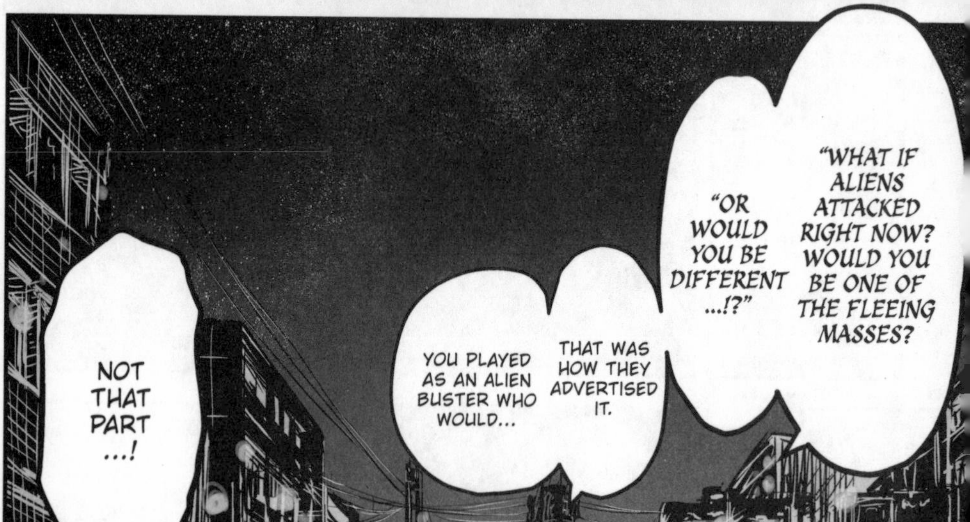
"WHAT IF ALIENS ATTACKED RIGHT NOW? WOULD YOU BE ONE OF THE FLEEING MASSES?
"OR WOULD YOU BE DIFFERENT ...!?"
THAT WAS HOW THEY ADVERTISED IT.
YOU PLAYED AS AN ALIEN BUSTER WHO WOULD...
NOT THAT PART ...!

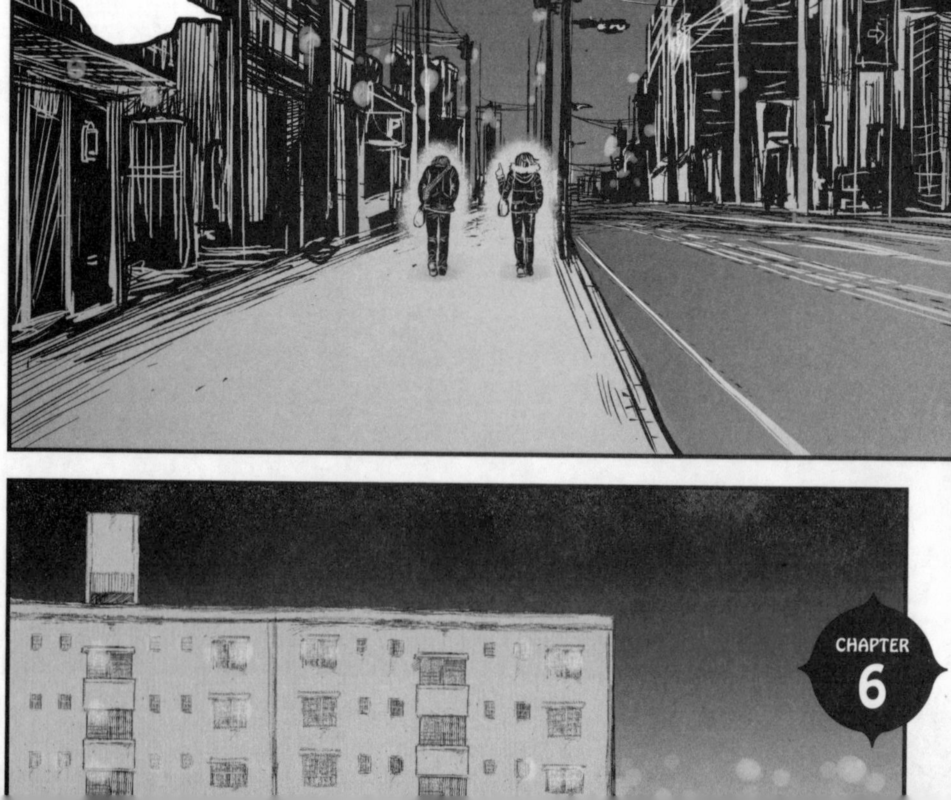
CHAPTER 6

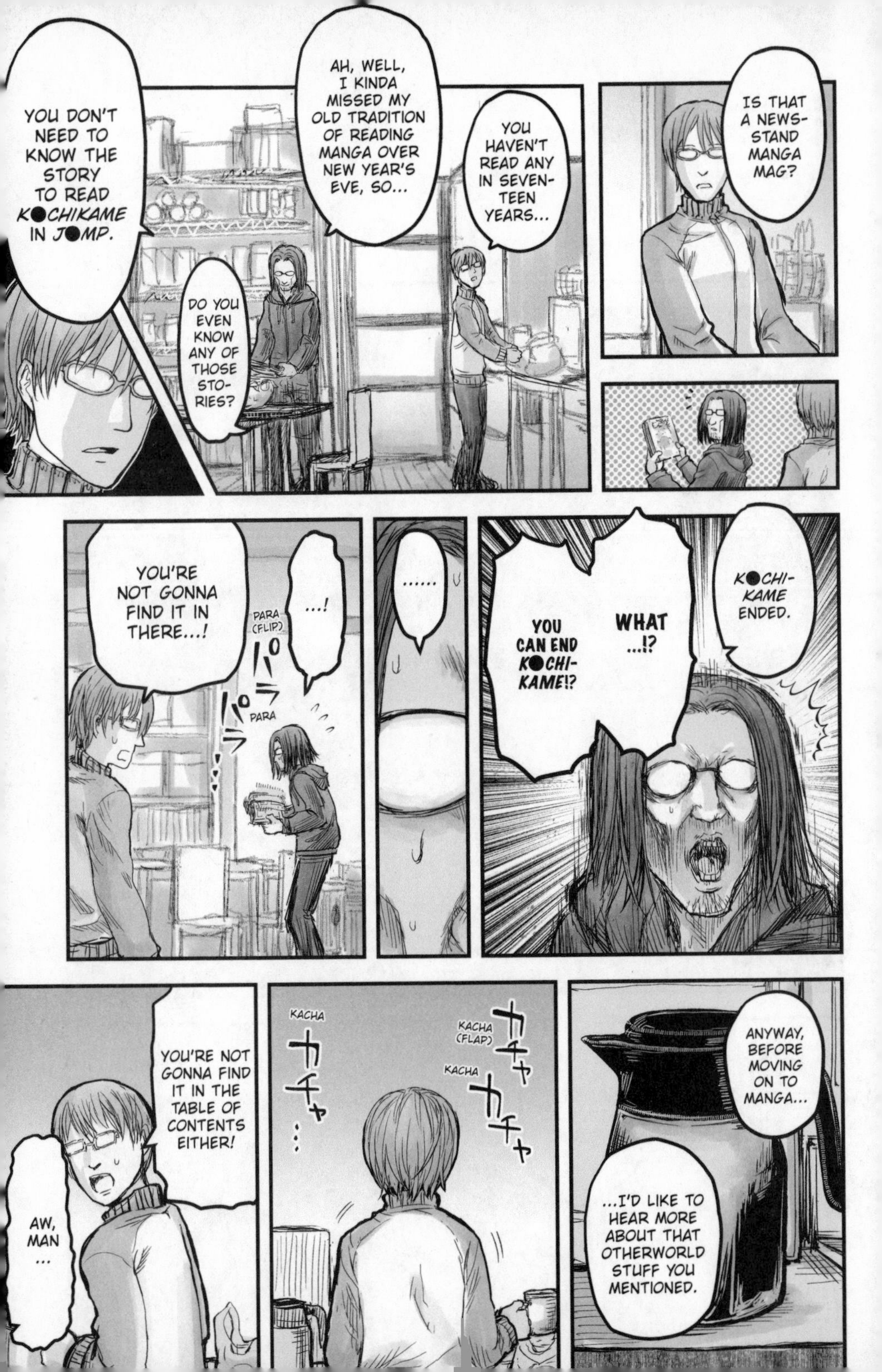
IS THAT A NEWS-STAND MANGA MAG?
YOU HAVEN'T READ ANY IN SEVEN-TEEN YEARS...
AH, WELL, I KINDA MISSED MY OLD TRADITION OF READING MANGA OVER NEW YEAR'S EVE, SO...
DO YOU EVEN KNOW ANY OF THOSE STO-RIES?
YOU DON'T NEED TO KNOW THE STORY TO READ K●CHIKAME IN J●MP.
K●CHI-KAME ENDED.
WHAT ...!?
YOU CAN END K●CHI-KAME!?
......
...!
PARA (FLIP)
PARA
YOU'RE NOT GONNA FIND IT IN THERE...!
ANYWAY, BEFORE MOVING ON TO MANGA...
...I'D LIKE TO HEAR MORE ABOUT THAT OTHERWORLD STUFF YOU MENTIONED.
KACHA (FLAP)
KACHA
KACHA
YOU'RE NOT GONNA FIND IT IN THE TABLE OF CONTENTS EITHER!
AW, MAN ...

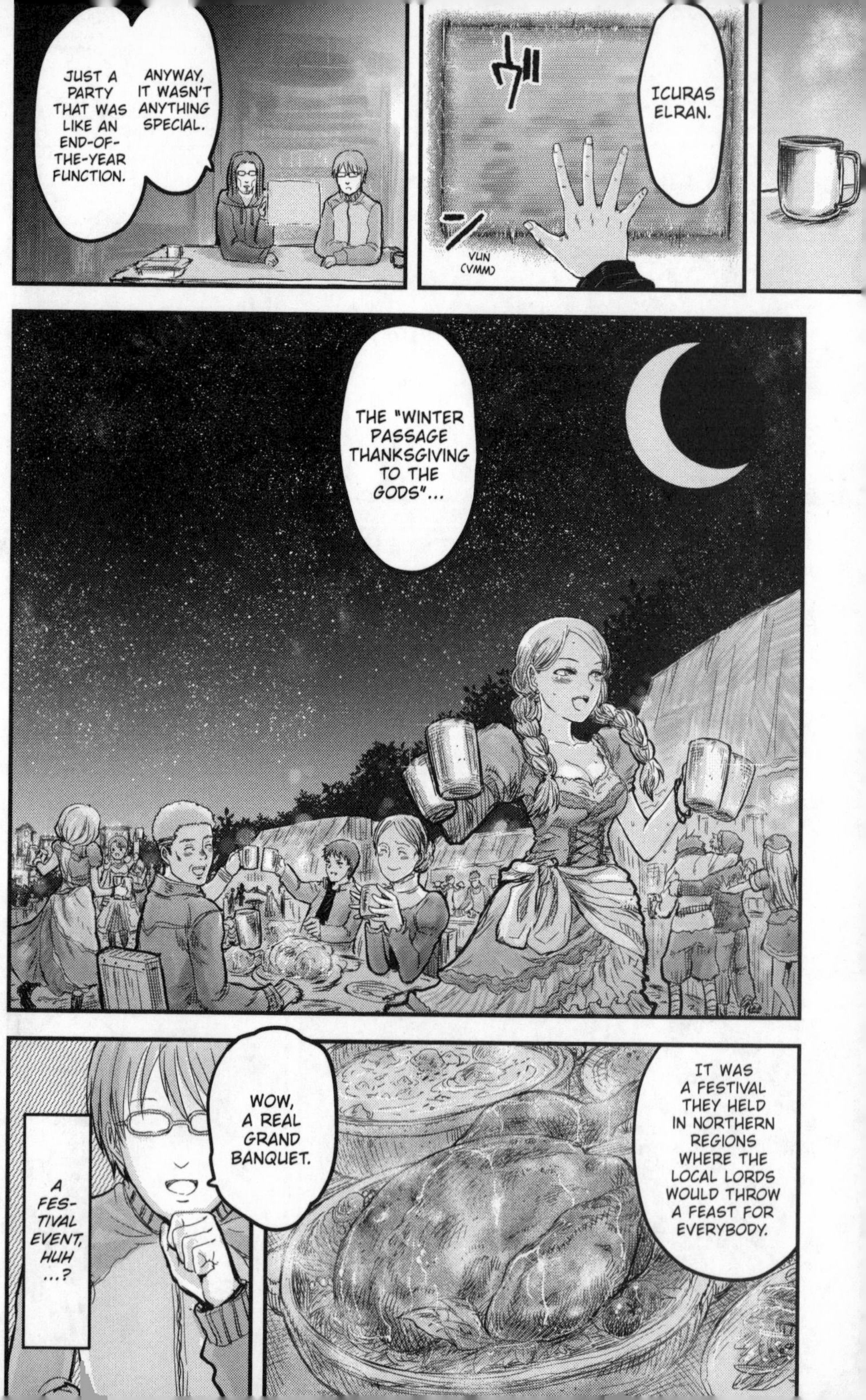
ICURAS ELRAN.
VUN (VMM)
ANYWAY, IT WASN'T ANYTHING SPECIAL.
JUST A PARTY THAT WAS LIKE AN END-OF-THE-YEAR FUNCTION.
THE "WINTER PASSAGE THANKSGIVING TO THE GODS"...
IT WAS A FESTIVAL THEY HELD IN NORTHERN REGIONS WHERE THE LOCAL LORDS WOULD THROW A FEAST FOR EVERYBODY.
WOW, A REAL GRAND BANQUET.
A FES-TIVAL EVENT, HUH ...?

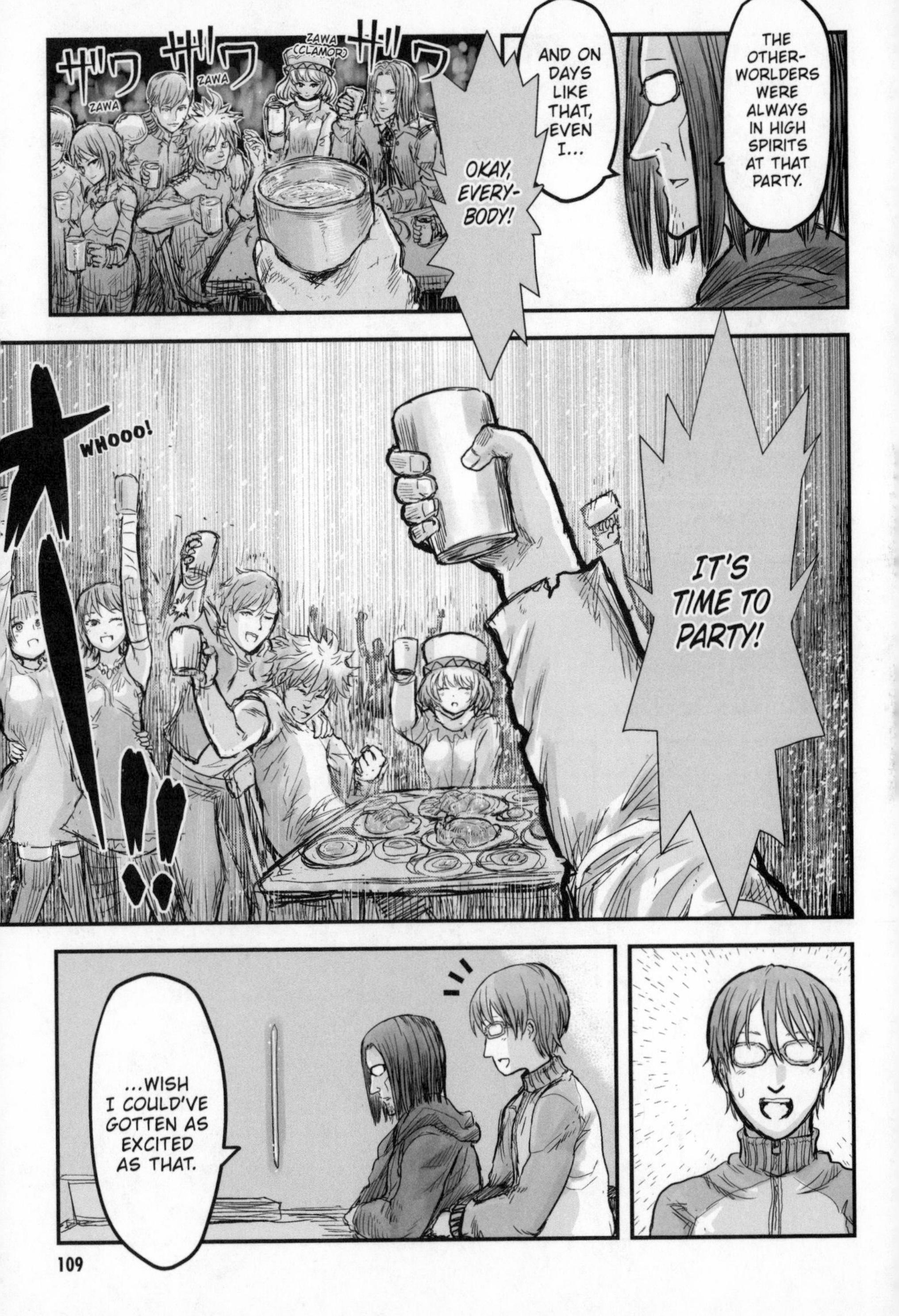
THE OTHER-WORLDERS WERE ALWAYS IN HIGH SPIRITS AT THAT PARTY.
AND ON DAYS LIKE THAT, EVEN I...
ザワ ザワ ザワ
ZAWA (CLAMOR)
ZAWA
ZAWA
OKAY, EVERYBODY!
IT'S TIME TO PARTY!
オ!!
WHOOO!
...WISH I COULD'VE GOTTEN AS EXCITED AS THAT.

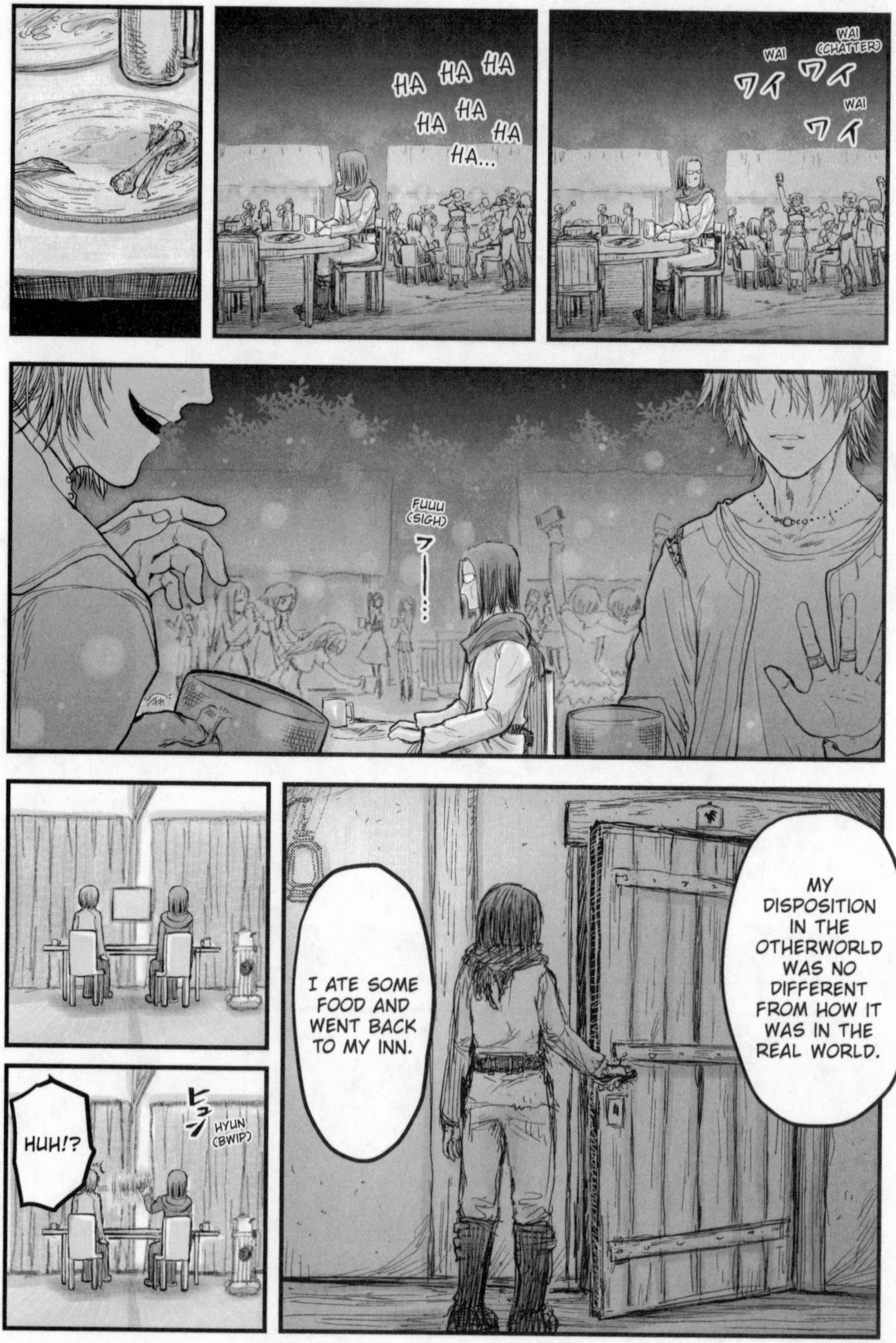
WAI
WAI (CHATTER)
ワイワイ
WAI
ワイ
HA HA HA HA HA HA HA...
FUUU (SIGH)
フー…
MY DISPOSITION IN THE OTHERWORLD WAS NO DIFFERENT FROM HOW IT WAS IN THE REAL WORLD.
I ATE SOME FOOD AND WENT BACK TO MY INN.
HYUN (BWIP)
ヒュン
HUH!?

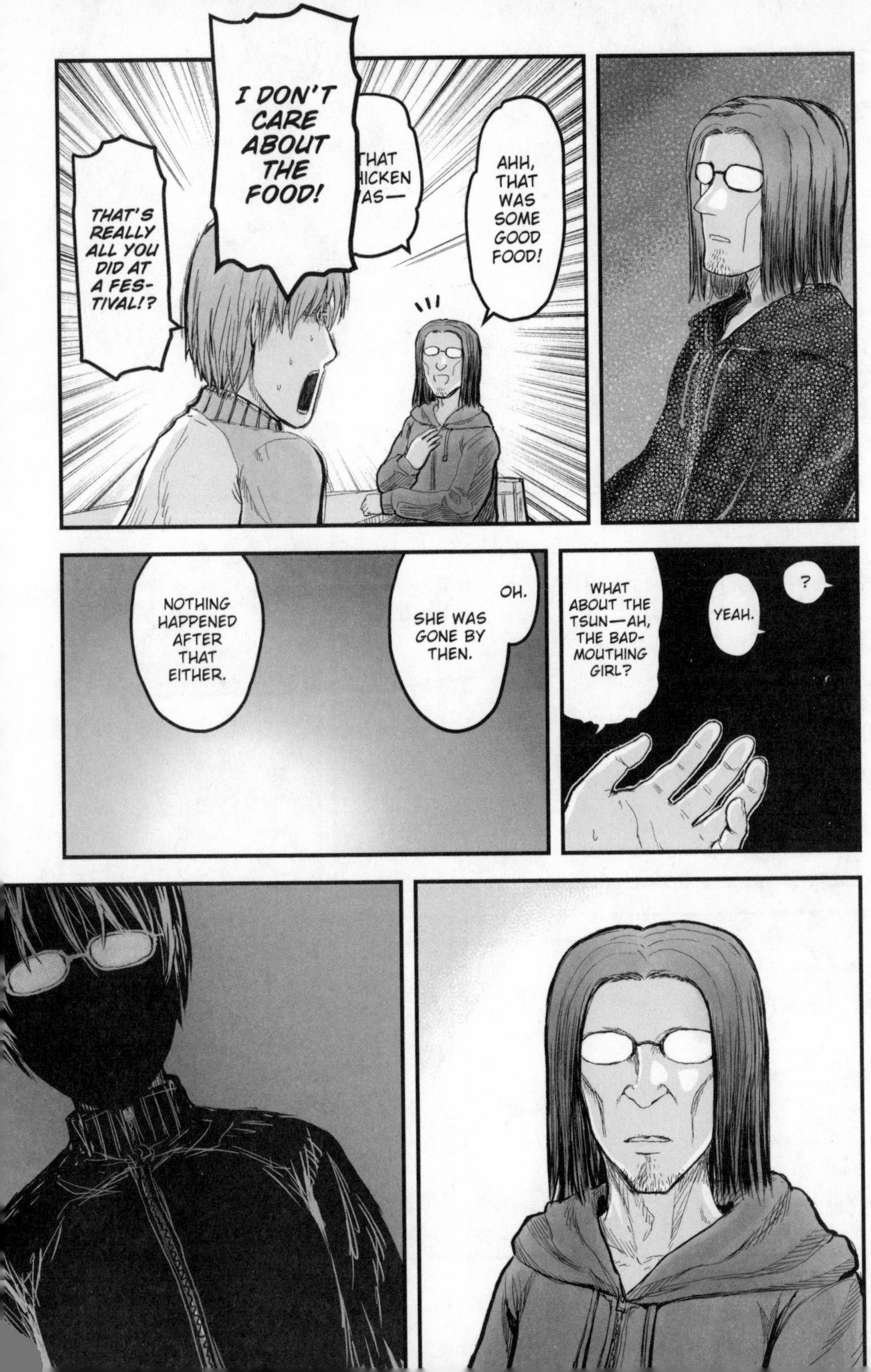
AHH, THAT WAS SOME GOOD FOOD!
THAT HICKEN AS—
I DON'T CARE ABOUT THE FOOD!
THAT'S REALLY ALL YOU DID AT A FES-TIVAL!?
?
YEAH.
WHAT ABOUT THE TSUN—AH, THE BAD-MOUTHING GIRL?
OH.
SHE WAS GONE BY THEN.
NOTHING HAPPENED AFTER THAT EITHER.

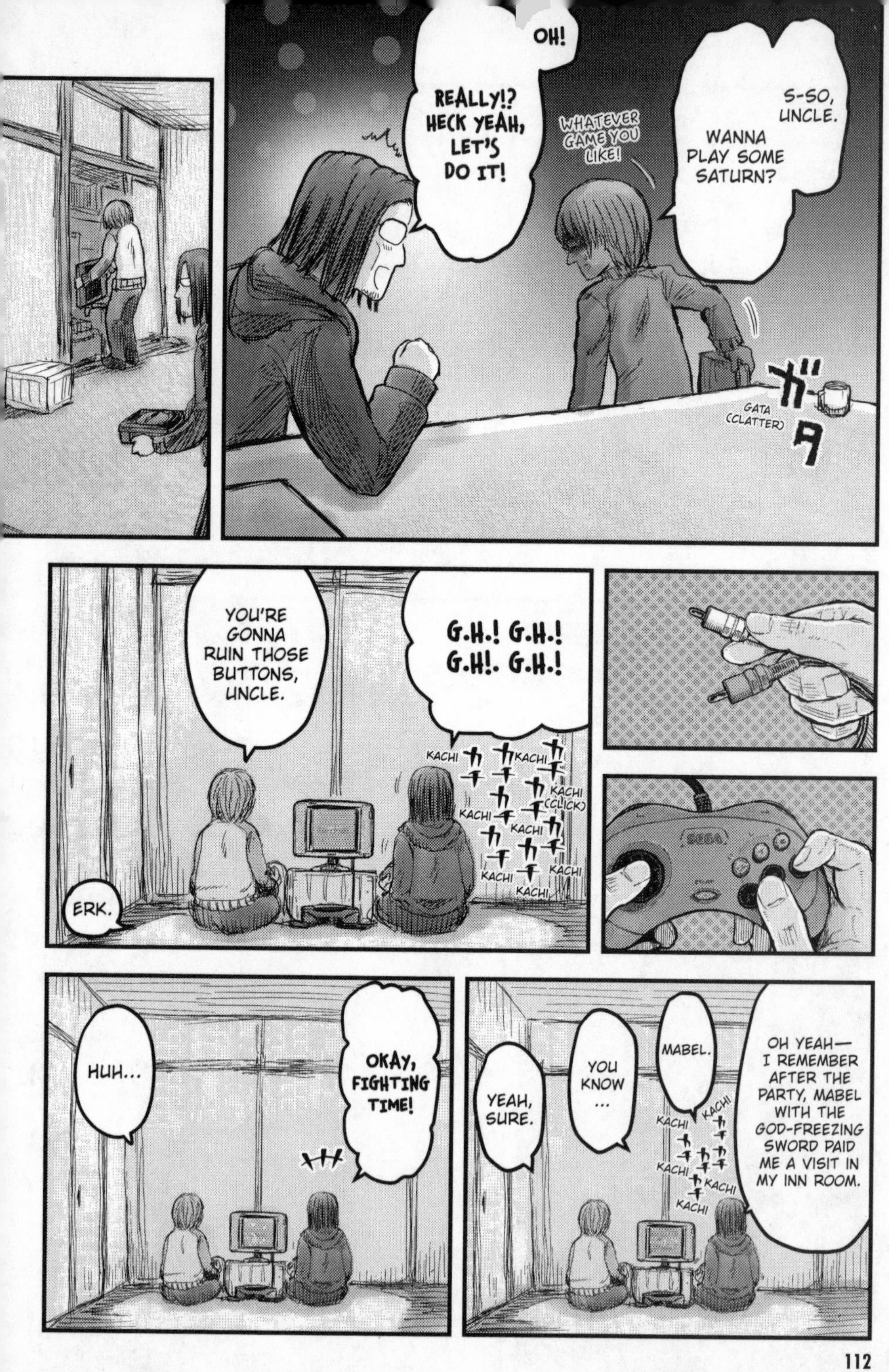
S-SO, UNCLE. WANNA PLAY SOME SATURN?
WHATEVER GAME YOU LIKE!
OH!
REALLY!? HECK YEAH, LET'S DO IT!
GATA (CLATTER)
SEGA
G.H.! G.H.! G.H!. G.H.!
KACHI KACHI KACHI (CLICK) KACHI KACHI KACHI KACHI KACHI
YOU'RE GONNA RUIN THOSE BUTTONS, UNCLE.
ERK.
OH YEAH— I REMEMBER AFTER THE PARTY, MABEL WITH THE GOD-FREEZING SWORD PAID ME A VISIT IN MY INN ROOM.
KACHI KACHI KACHI KACHI KACHI
MABEL.
YOU KNOW ...
YEAH, SURE.
OKAY, FIGHTING TIME!
HUH...

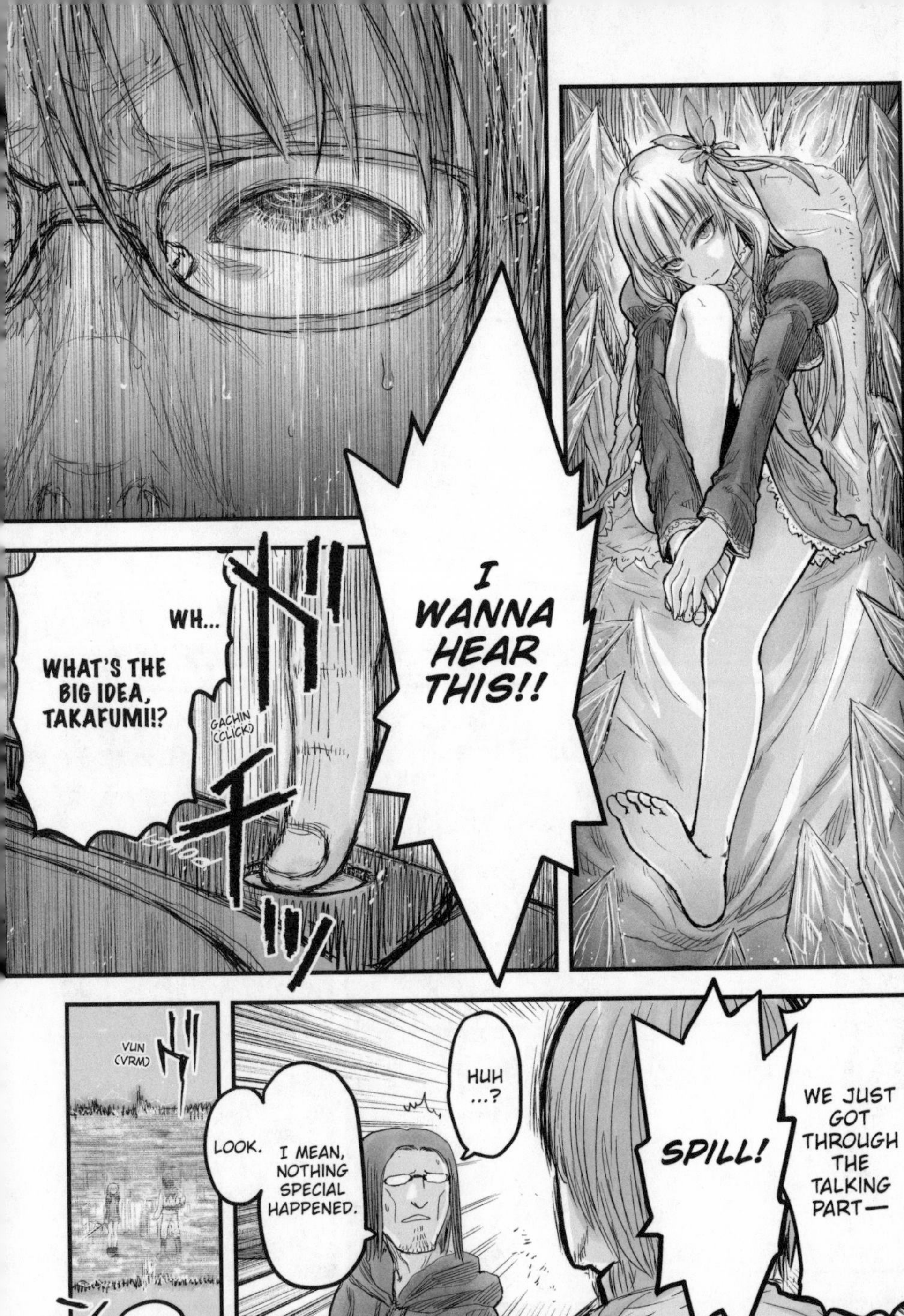

I WANNA HEAR THIS!!
WH...
WHAT'S THE BIG IDEA, TAKAFUMI!?
GACHIN (CLICK)
WE JUST GOT THROUGH THE TALKING PART—
SPILL!
HUH ...?
I MEAN, NOTHING SPECIAL HAPPENED.
LOOK.
VUN (VRM)
!

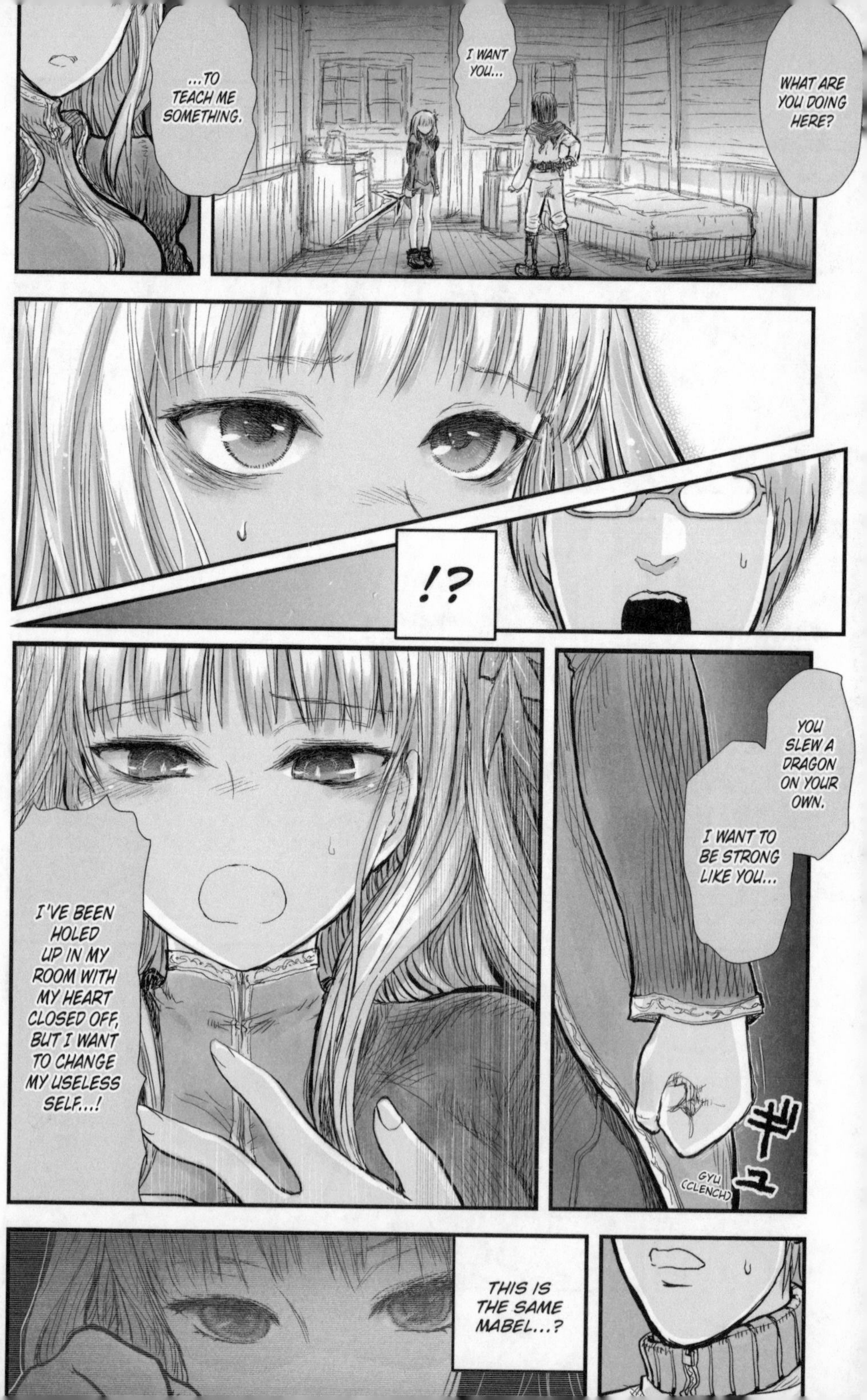
WHAT ARE YOU DOING HERE?
I WANT YOU...
...TO TEACH ME SOMETHING.
!?
YOU SLEW A DRAGON ON YOUR OWN.
I WANT TO BE STRONG LIKE YOU...
ギュ
GYU (CLENCH)
I'VE BEEN HOLED UP IN MY ROOM WITH MY HEART CLOSED OFF, BUT I WANT TO CHANGE MY USELESS SELF...!
THIS IS THE SAME MABEL...?

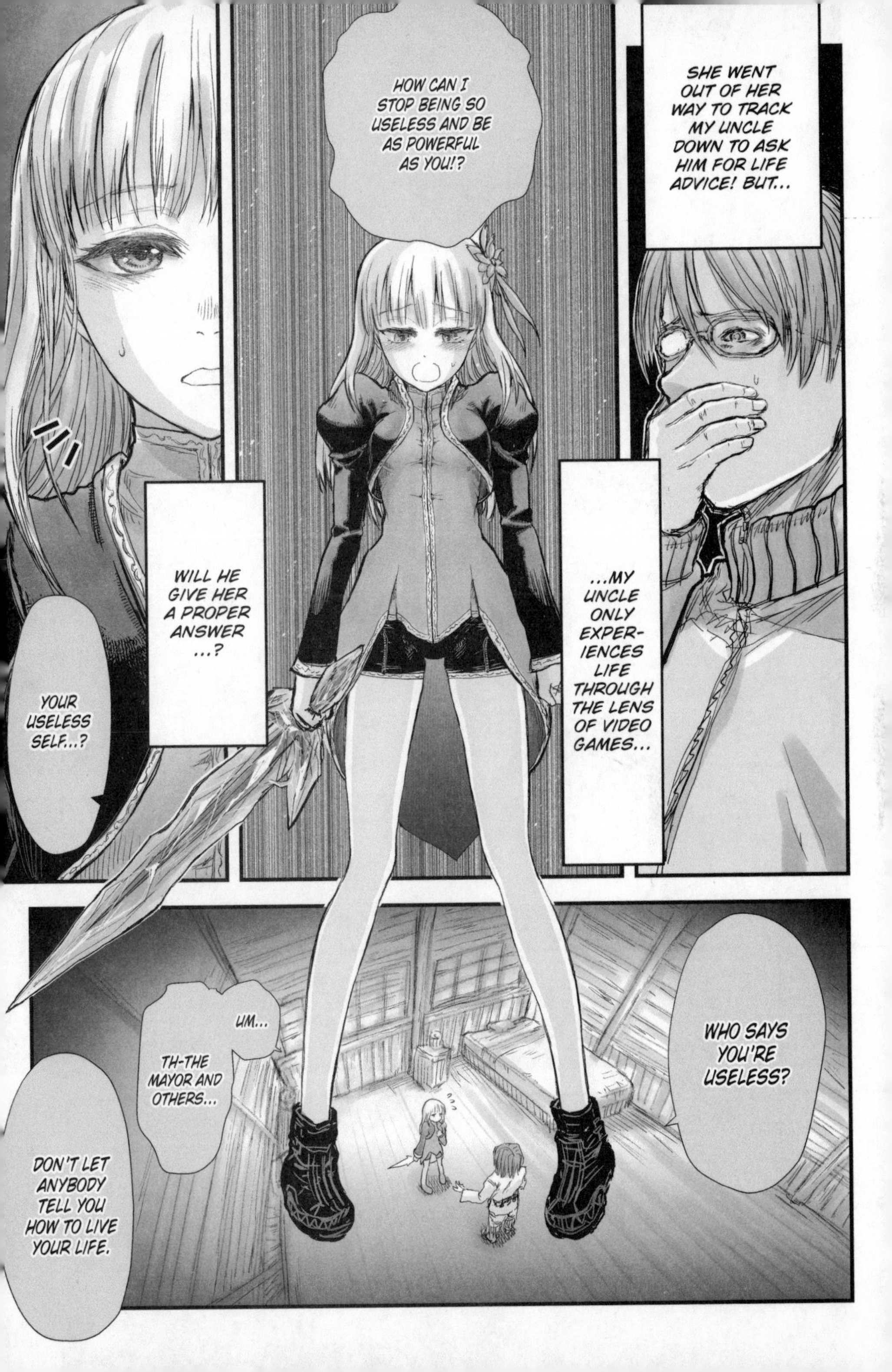
SHE WENT OUT OF HER WAY TO TRACK MY UNCLE DOWN TO ASK HIM FOR LIFE ADVICE! BUT...
...MY UNCLE ONLY EXPERIENCES LIFE THROUGH THE LENS OF VIDEO GAMES...
HOW CAN I STOP BEING SO USELESS AND BE AS POWERFUL AS YOU!?
WILL HE GIVE HER A PROPER ANSWER ...?
YOUR USELESS SELF...?
WHO SAYS YOU'RE USELESS?
UM...
TH-THE MAYOR AND OTHERS...
DON'T LET ANYBODY TELL YOU HOW TO LIVE YOUR LIFE.

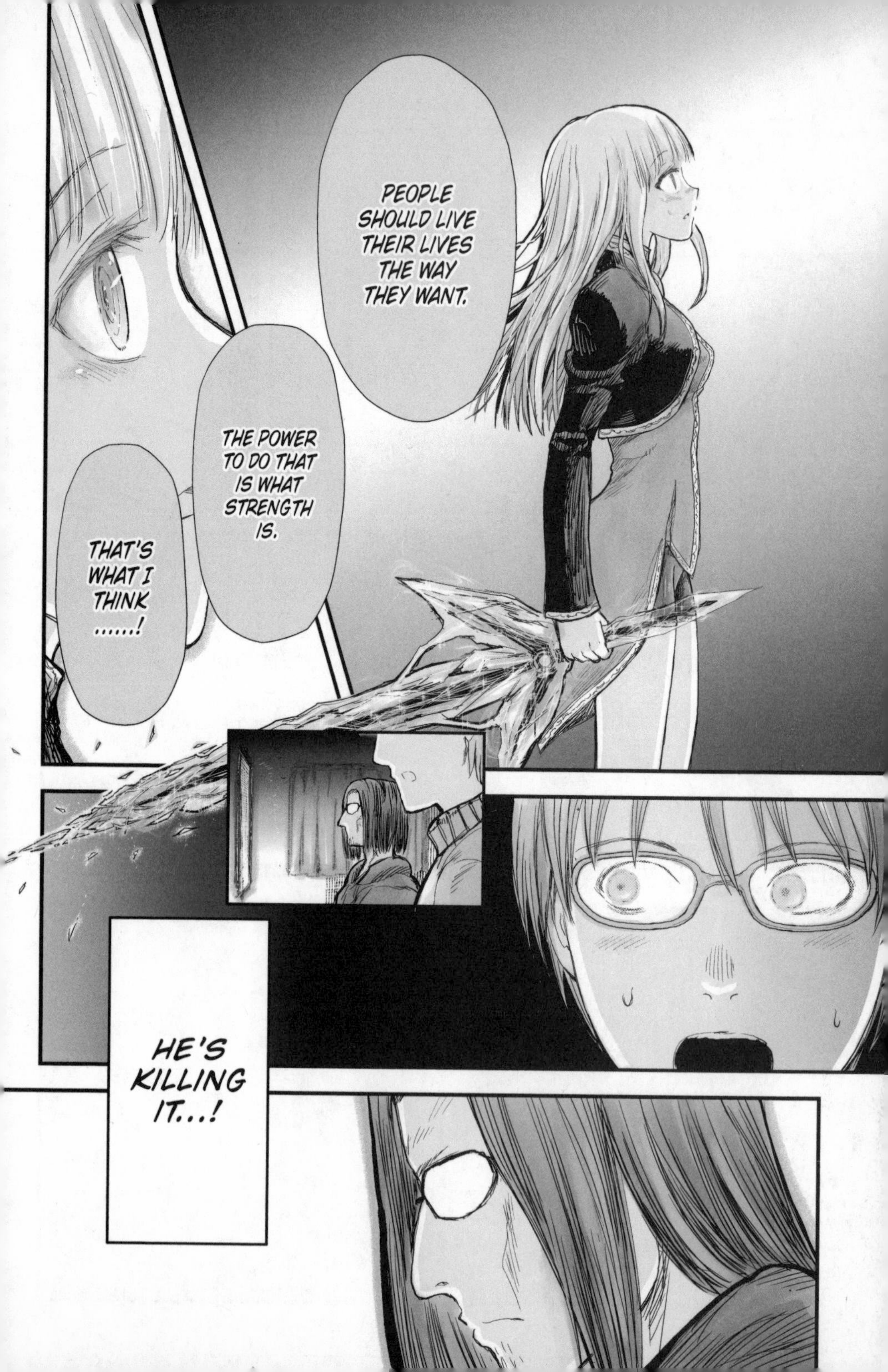
PEOPLE SHOULD LIVE THEIR LIVES THE WAY THEY WANT.
THE POWER TO DO THAT IS WHAT STRENGTH IS.
THAT'S WHAT I THINK ......!
HE'S KILLING IT...!

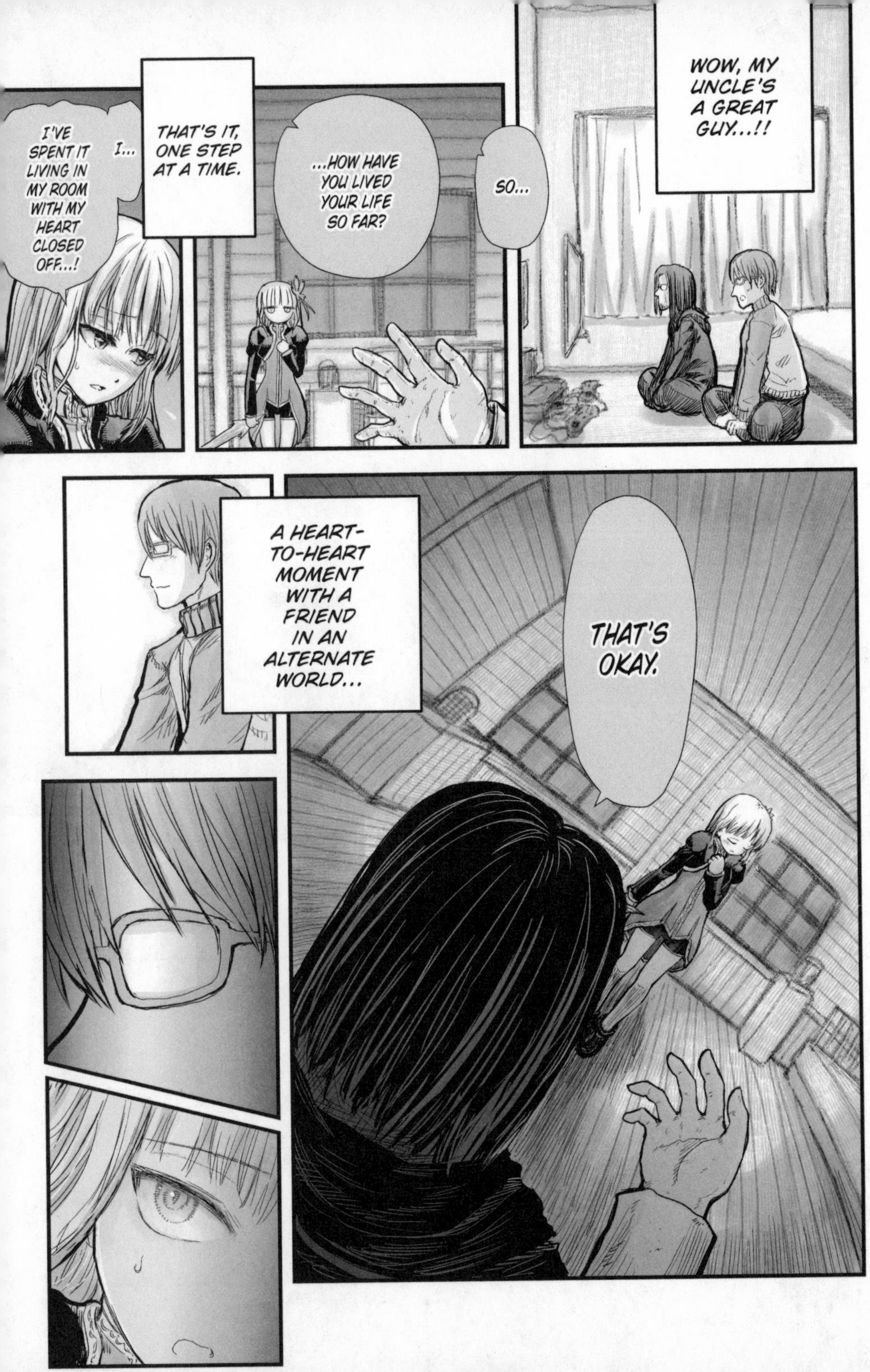
WOW, MY UNCLE'S A GREAT GUY...!!
SO...
...HOW HAVE YOU LIVED YOUR LIFE SO FAR?
THAT'S IT, ONE STEP AT A TIME.
I...
I'VE SPENT IT LIVING IN MY ROOM WITH MY HEART CLOSED OFF...!
THAT'S OKAY.
A HEART-TO-HEART MOMENT WITH A FRIEND IN AN ALTERNATE WORLD...

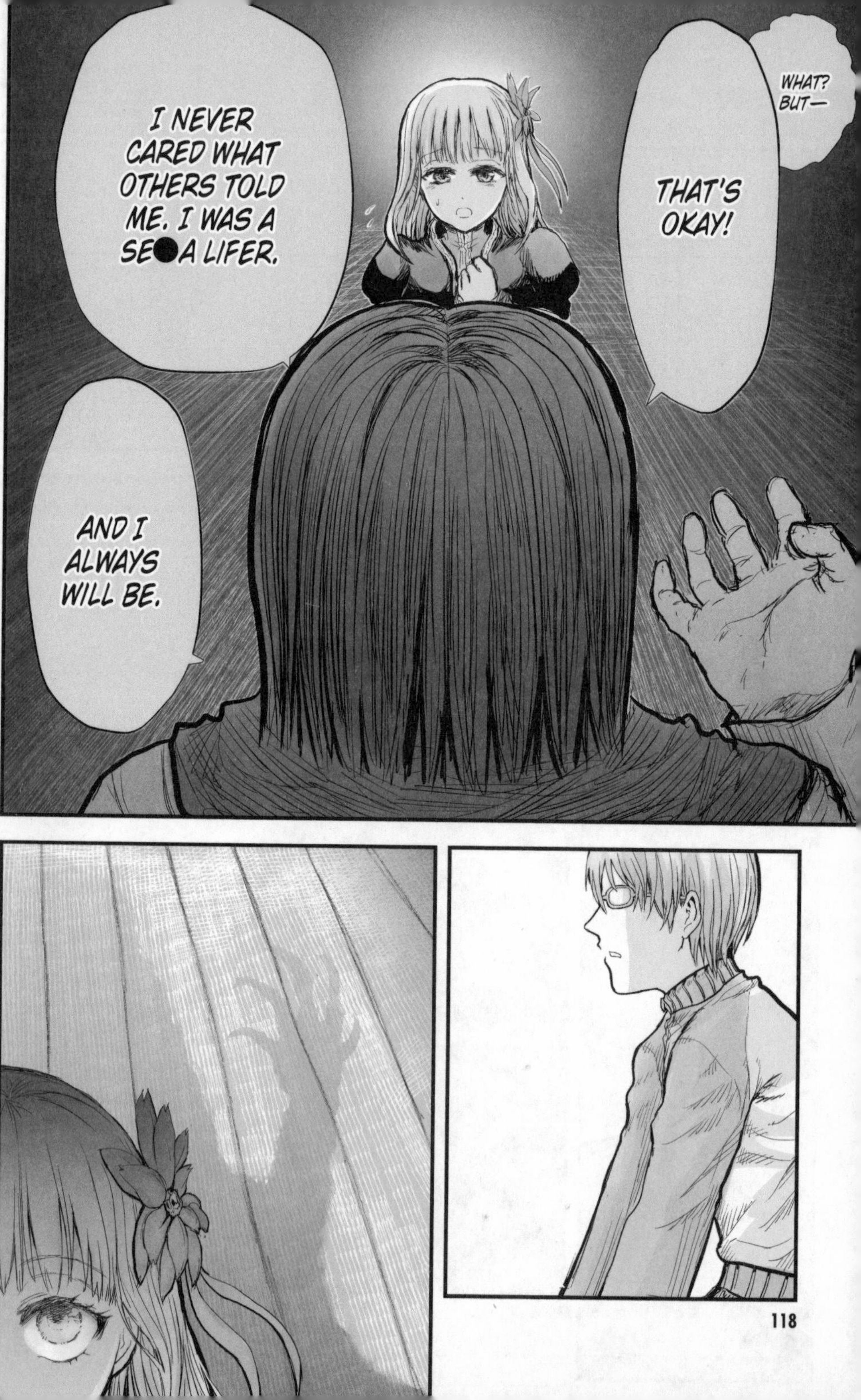
WHAT? BUT—
THAT'S OKAY!
I NEVER CARED WHAT OTHERS TOLD ME. I WAS A SE[redacted]A LIFER.
AND I ALWAYS WILL BE.

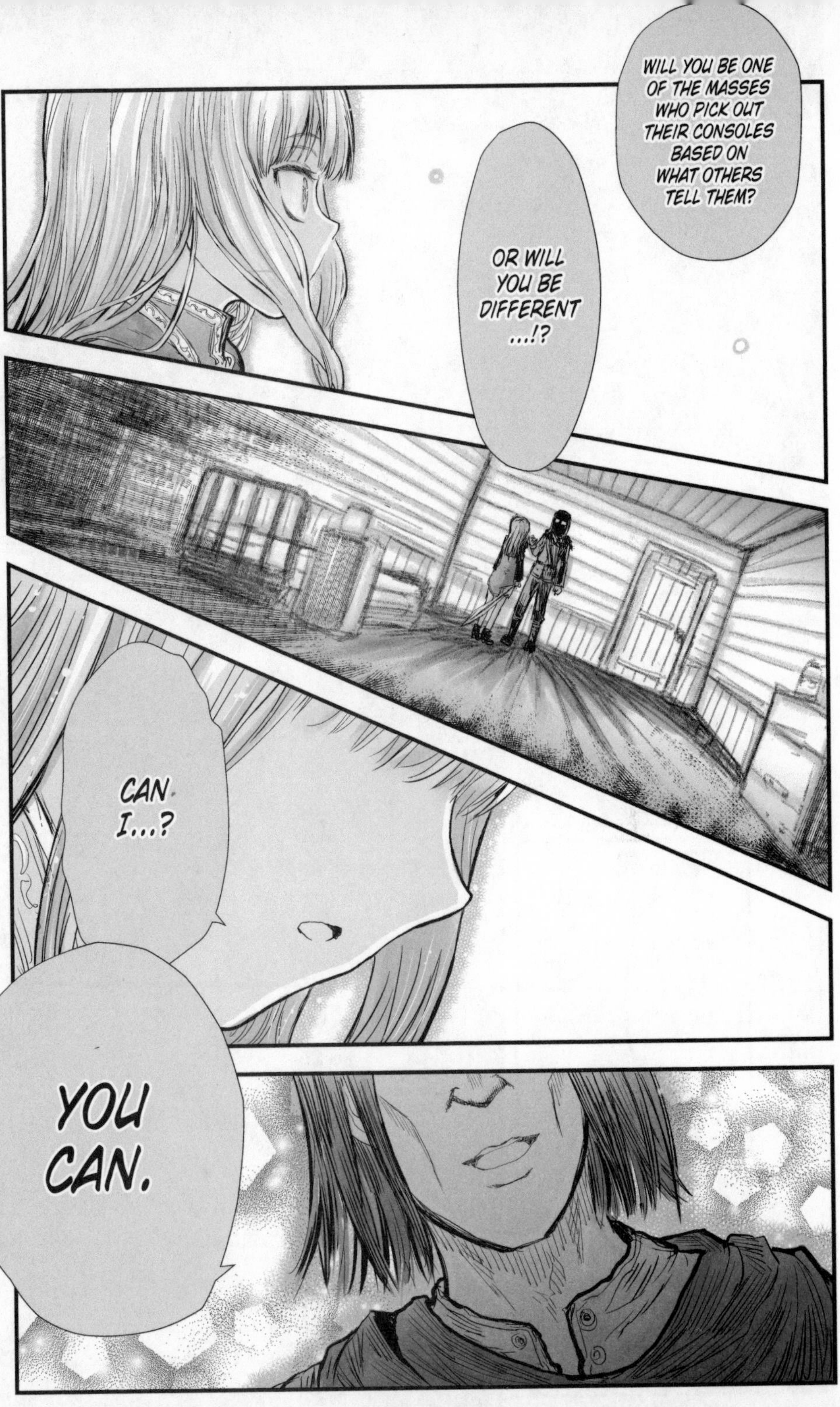
WILL YOU BE ONE OF THE MASSES WHO PICK OUT THEIR CONSOLES BASED ON WHAT OTHERS TELL THEM?
OR WILL YOU BE DIFFERENT ...!?
CAN I...?
YOU CAN.

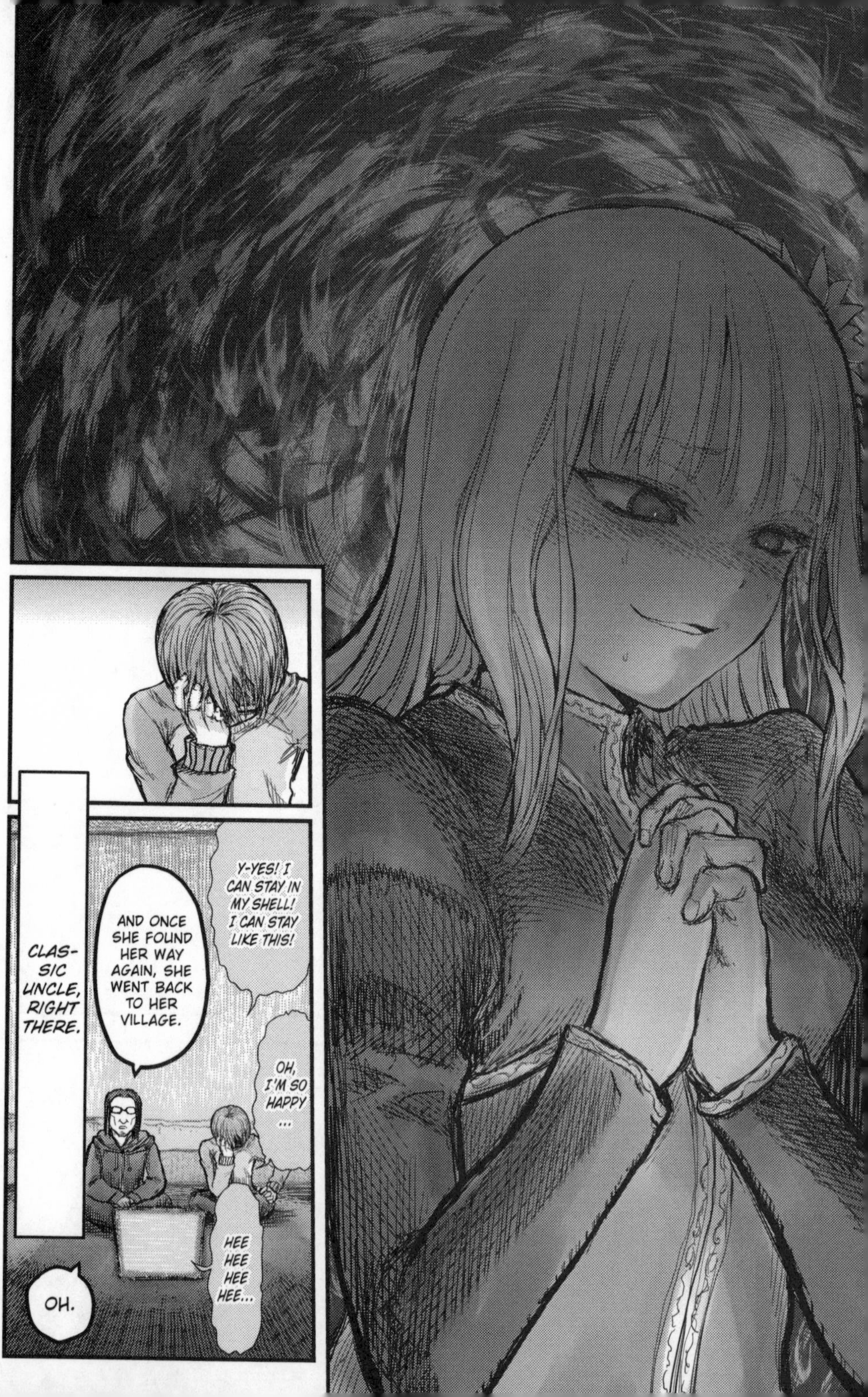

Y-YES! I CAN STAY IN MY SHELL! I CAN STAY LIKE THIS!
OH, I'M SO HAPPY ...
HEE HEE HEE HEE...
AND ONCE SHE FOUND HER WAY AGAIN, SHE WENT BACK TO HER VILLAGE.
CLAS-SIC UNCLE, RIGHT THERE.
OH.

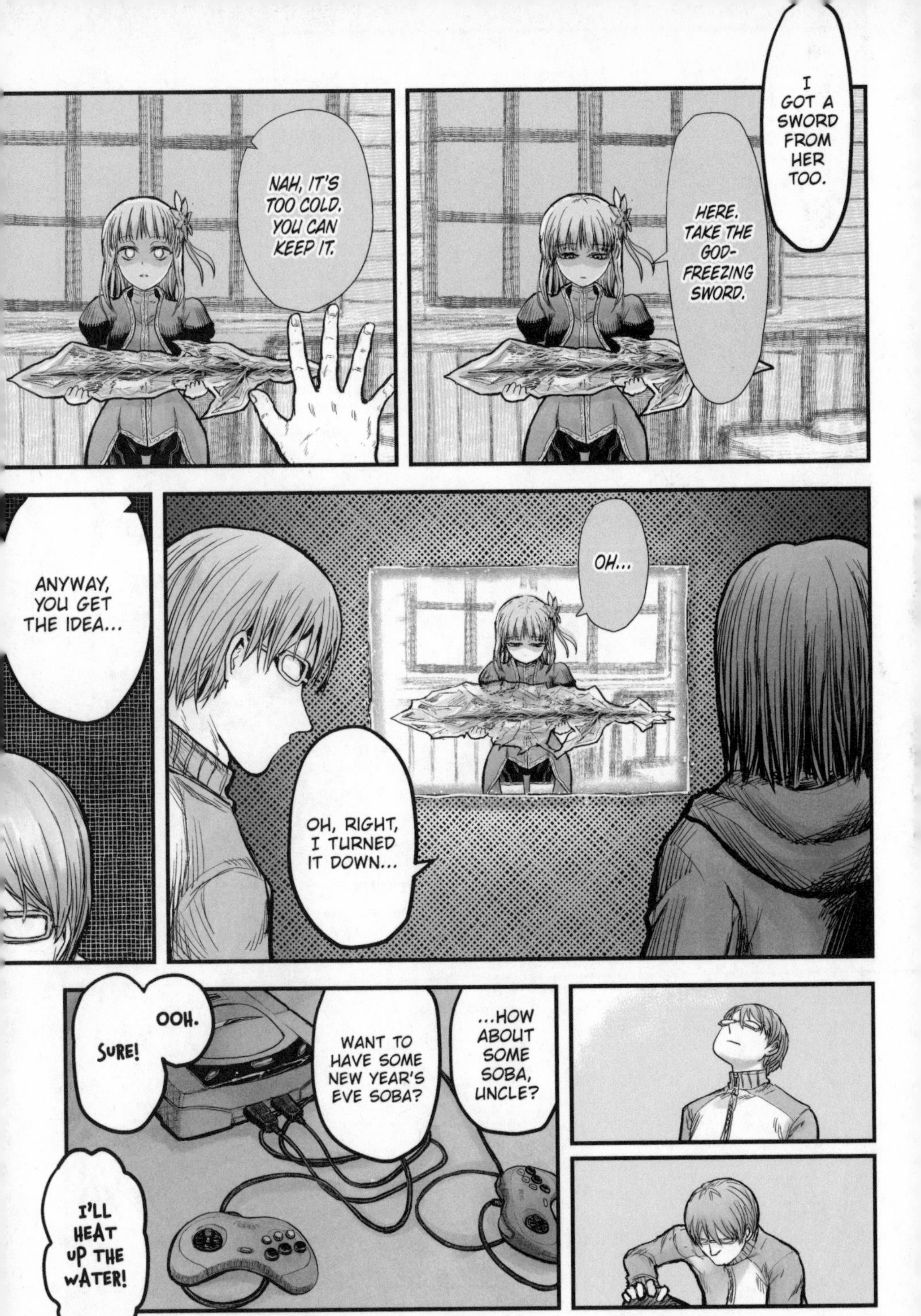
I GOT A SWORD FROM HER TOO.
HERE. TAKE THE GOD-FREEZING SWORD.
NAH, IT'S TOO COLD. YOU CAN KEEP IT.
OH...
OH, RIGHT, I TURNED IT DOWN...
ANYWAY, YOU GET THE IDEA...
...HOW ABOUT SOME SOBA, UNCLE?
WANT TO HAVE SOME NEW YEAR'S EVE SOBA?
OOH.
SURE!
I'LL HEAT UP THE WATER!

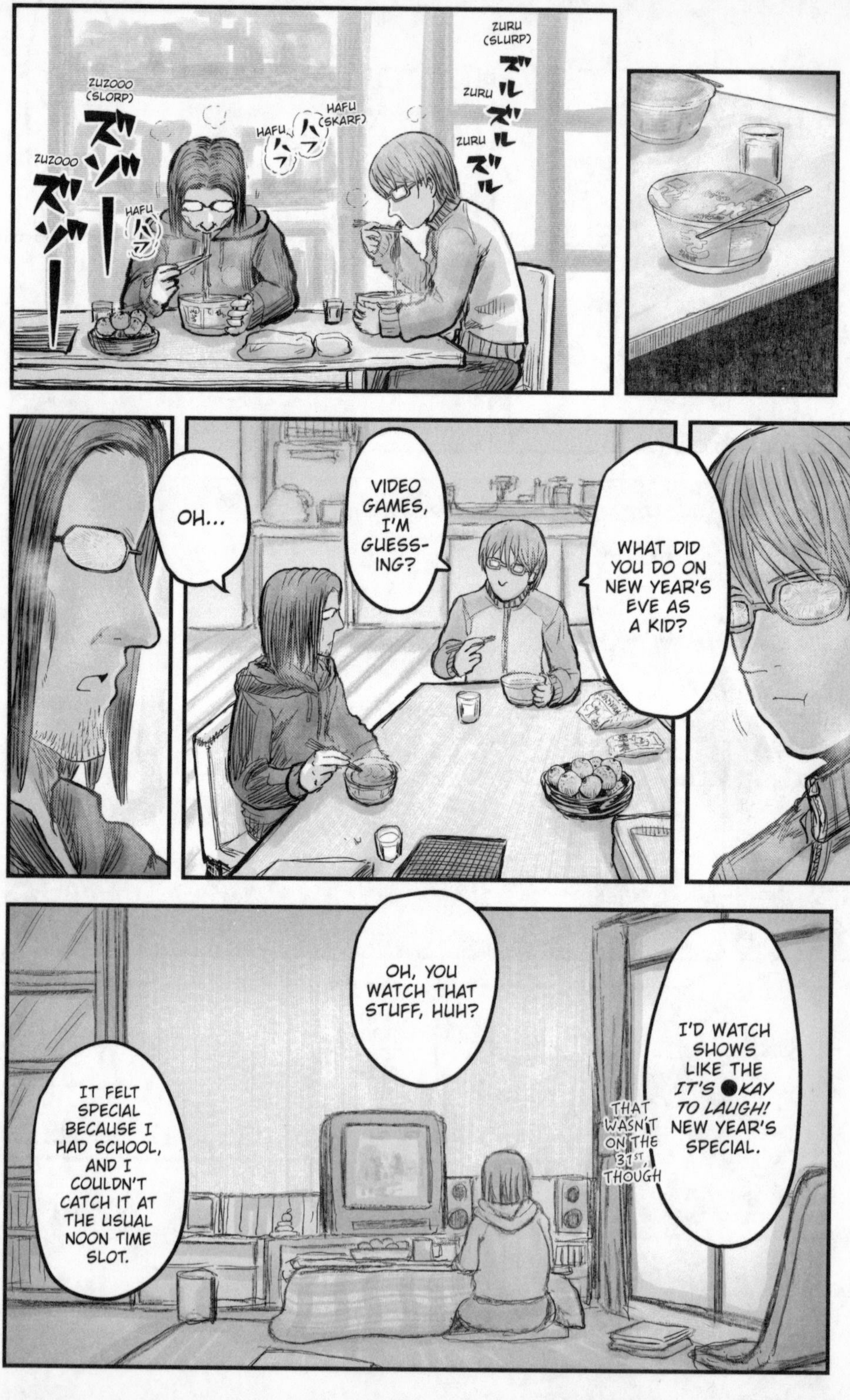
ZURU (SLURP) ズル
ZURU ズル
ZURU ズル
HAFU (SKARF) ハフ
HAFU ハフ
ZUZOOO (SLORP) ズゾー
ZUZOOO ズゾー
HAFU ハフ
WHAT DID YOU DO ON NEW YEAR'S EVE AS A KID?
VIDEO GAMES, I'M GUESSING?
OH...
I'D WATCH SHOWS LIKE THE *IT'S ●KAY TO LAUGH!* NEW YEAR'S SPECIAL.
THAT WASN'T ON THE 31ST, THOUGH
OH, YOU WATCH THAT STUFF, HUH?
IT FELT SPECIAL BECAUSE I HAD SCHOOL, AND I COULDN'T CATCH IT AT THE USUAL NOON TIME SLOT.

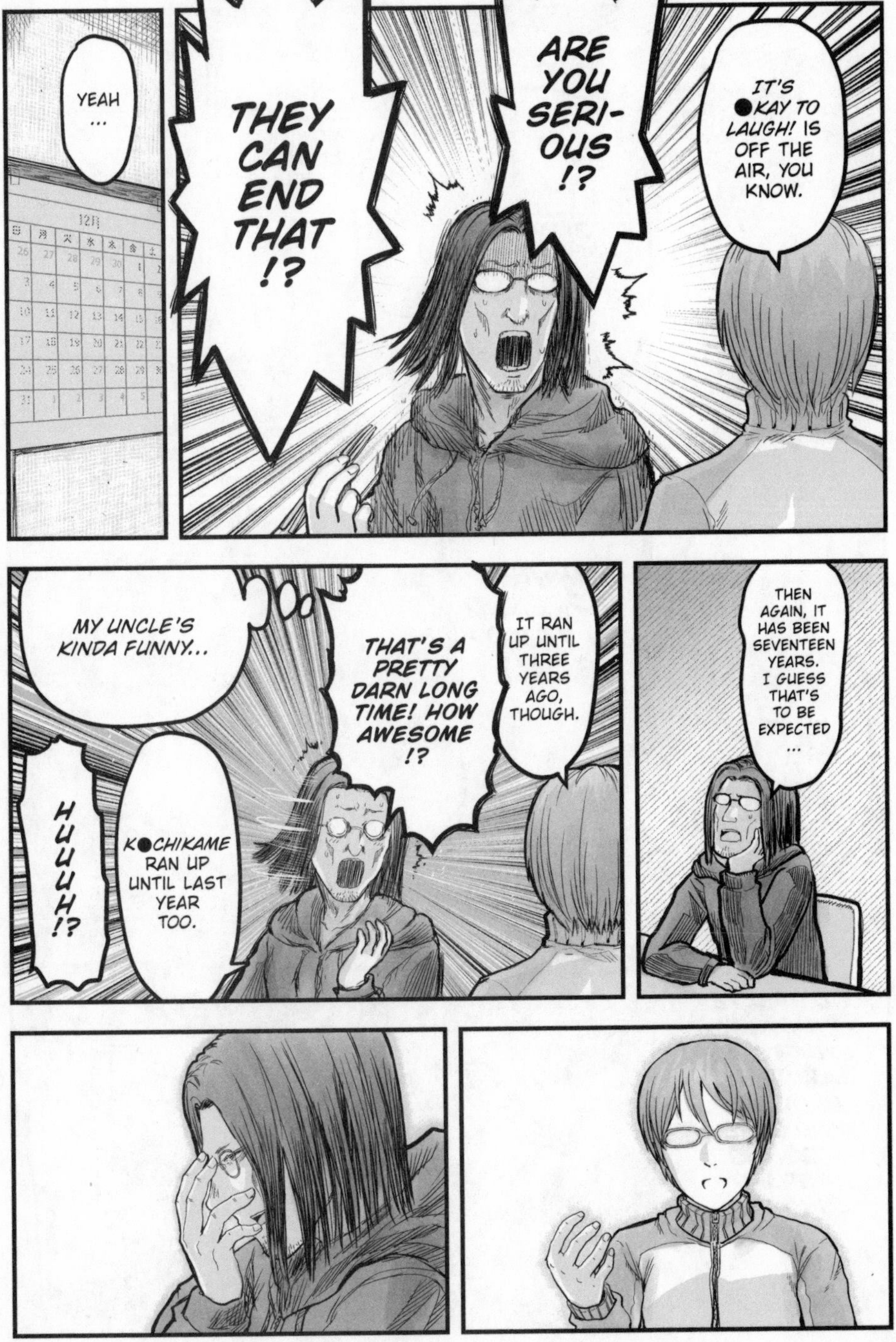
IT'S ●KAY TO LAUGH! IS OFF THE AIR, YOU KNOW.
ARE YOU SERI-OUS!?
THEY CAN END THAT!?
YEAH ...
THEN AGAIN, IT HAS BEEN SEVENTEEN YEARS. I GUESS THAT'S TO BE EXPECTED ...
IT RAN UP UNTIL THREE YEARS AGO, THOUGH.
THAT'S A PRETTY DARN LONG TIME! HOW AWESOME!?
MY UNCLE'S KINDA FUNNY...
K●CHIKAME RAN UP UNTIL LAST YEAR TOO.
HUUUH!?

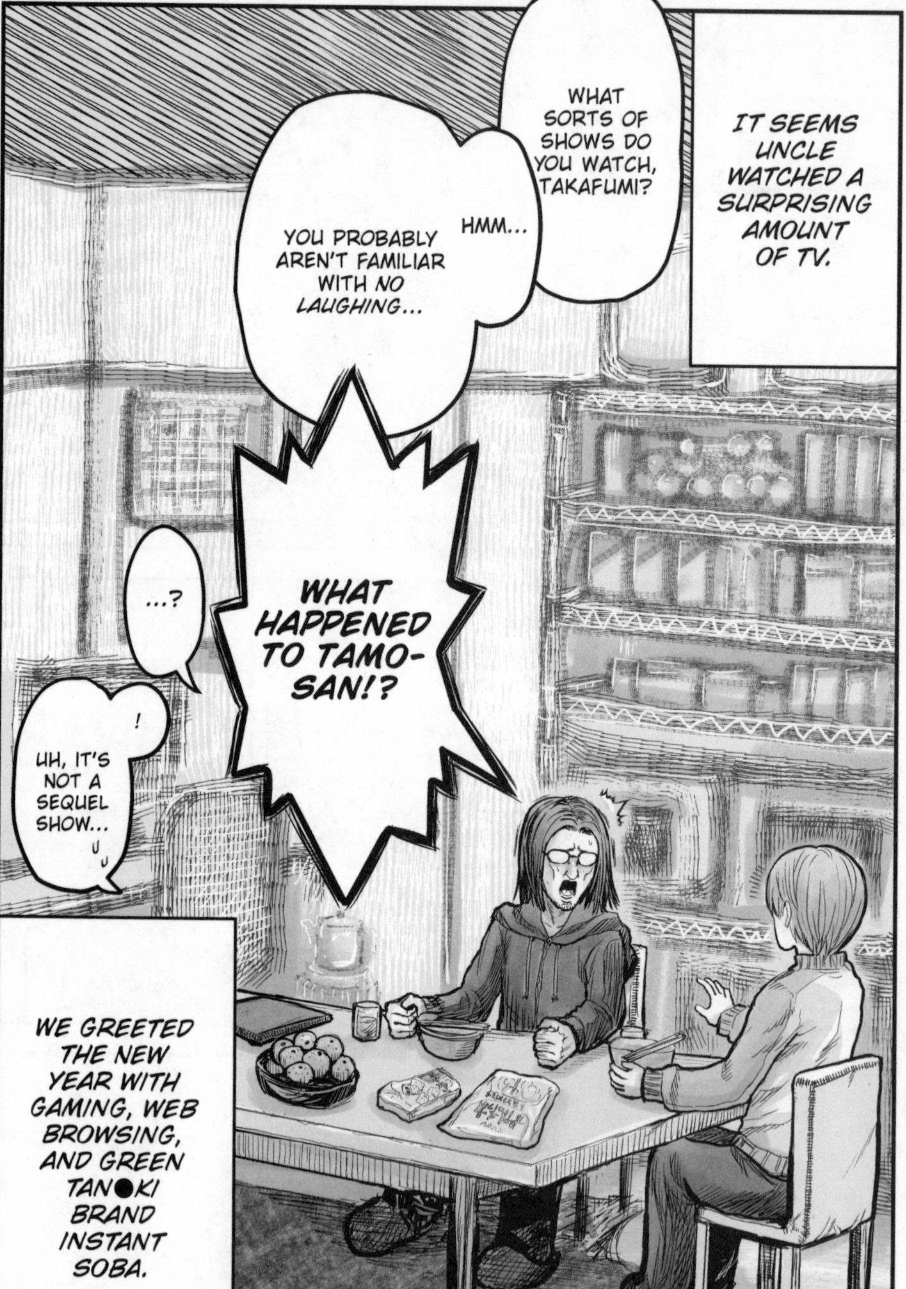
IT SEEMS UNCLE WATCHED A SURPRISING AMOUNT OF TV.
WHAT SORTS OF SHOWS DO YOU WATCH, TAKAFUMI?
HMM...
YOU PROBABLY AREN'T FAMILIAR WITH *NO LAUGHING*...
WHAT HAPPENED TO TAMO-SAN!?
...?
!
UH, IT'S NOT A SEQUEL SHOW...
WE GREETED THE NEW YEAR WITH GAMING, WEB BROWSING, AND GREEN TAN●KI BRAND INSTANT SOBA.

TIPS

Long-Running Serials and Shows

K●chiKame: 1976–2016 (40 years)
Waratte ●itamo! (It's ●kay to Laugh!): 1982–2014 (32 years)

UNCLE from ANOTHER WORLD

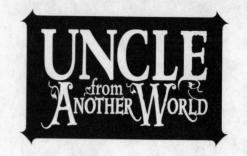

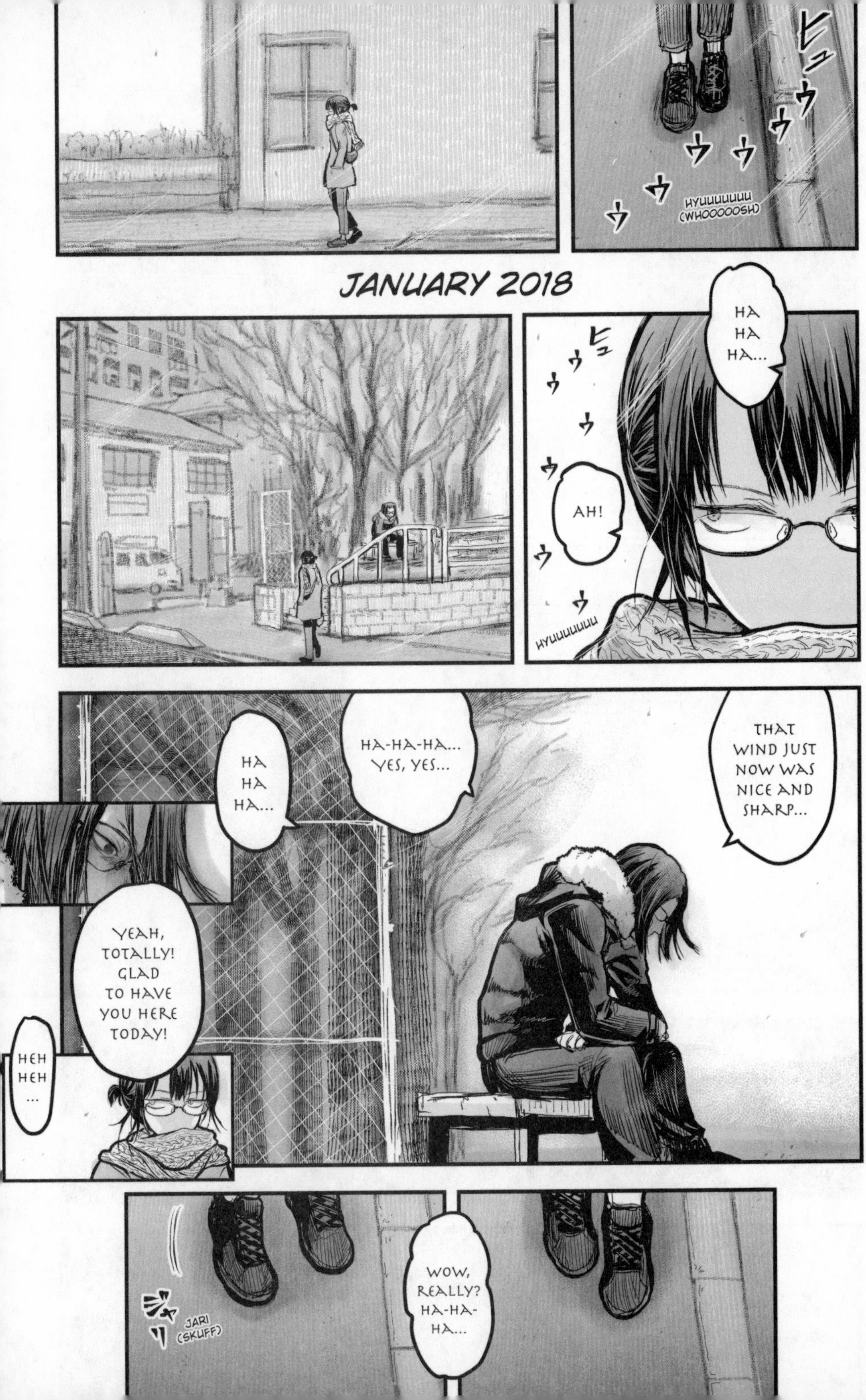
ヒュウウウウウウウ
HYUUUUUUUU (WHOOOOOSH)
JANUARY 2018
HA HA HA...
ヒュウウウウウウ
AH!
HYUUUUUUUU
THAT WIND JUST NOW WAS NICE AND SHARP...
HA-HA-HA... YES, YES...
HA HA HA...
YEAH, TOTALLY! GLAD TO HAVE YOU HERE TODAY!
HEH HEH ...
WOW, REALLY? HA-HA-HA...
ジャリ
JARI (SKUFF)

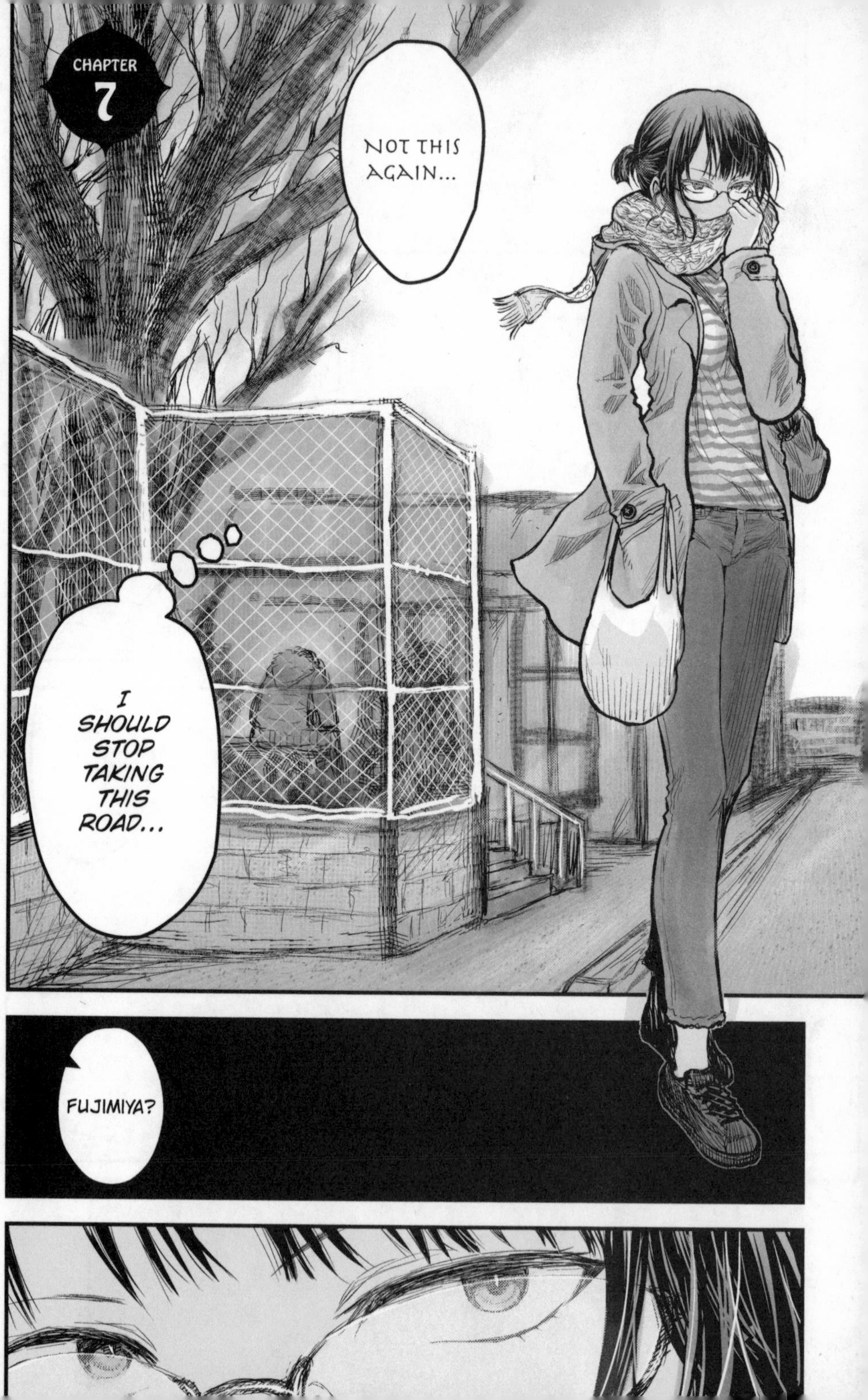
CHAPTER 7
NOT THIS AGAIN...
I SHOULD STOP TAKING THIS ROAD...
FUJIMIYA?

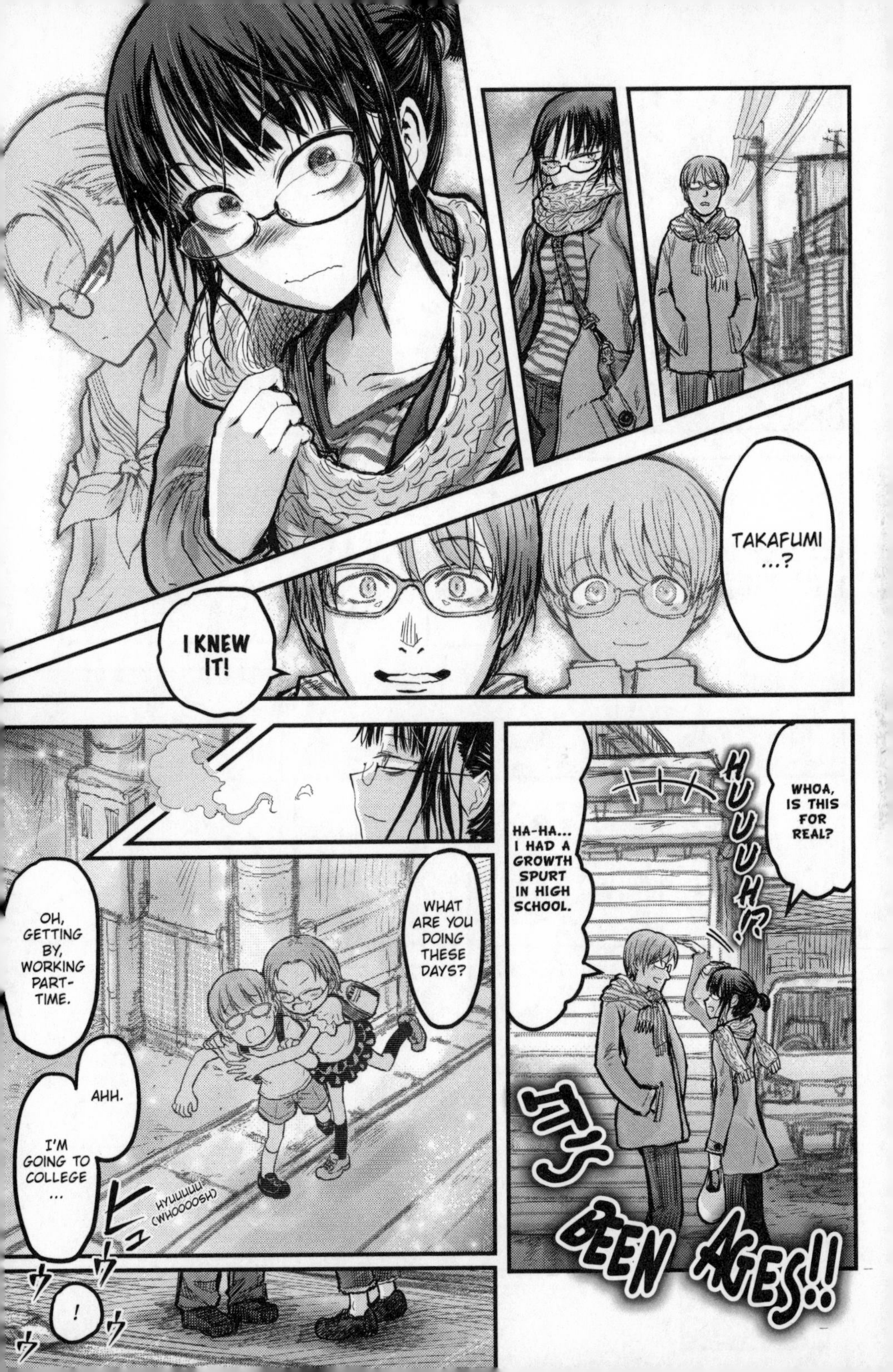
TAKAFUMI ...?
I KNEW IT!
WHOA, IS THIS FOR REAL?
HUUUH!?
HA-HA... I HAD A GROWTH SPURT IN HIGH SCHOOL.
IT'S BEEN AGES!!
WHAT ARE YOU DOING THESE DAYS?
OH, GETTING BY, WORKING PART-TIME.
AHH.
I'M GOING TO COLLEGE ...
HYUUUUU (WHOOOOSH)
!

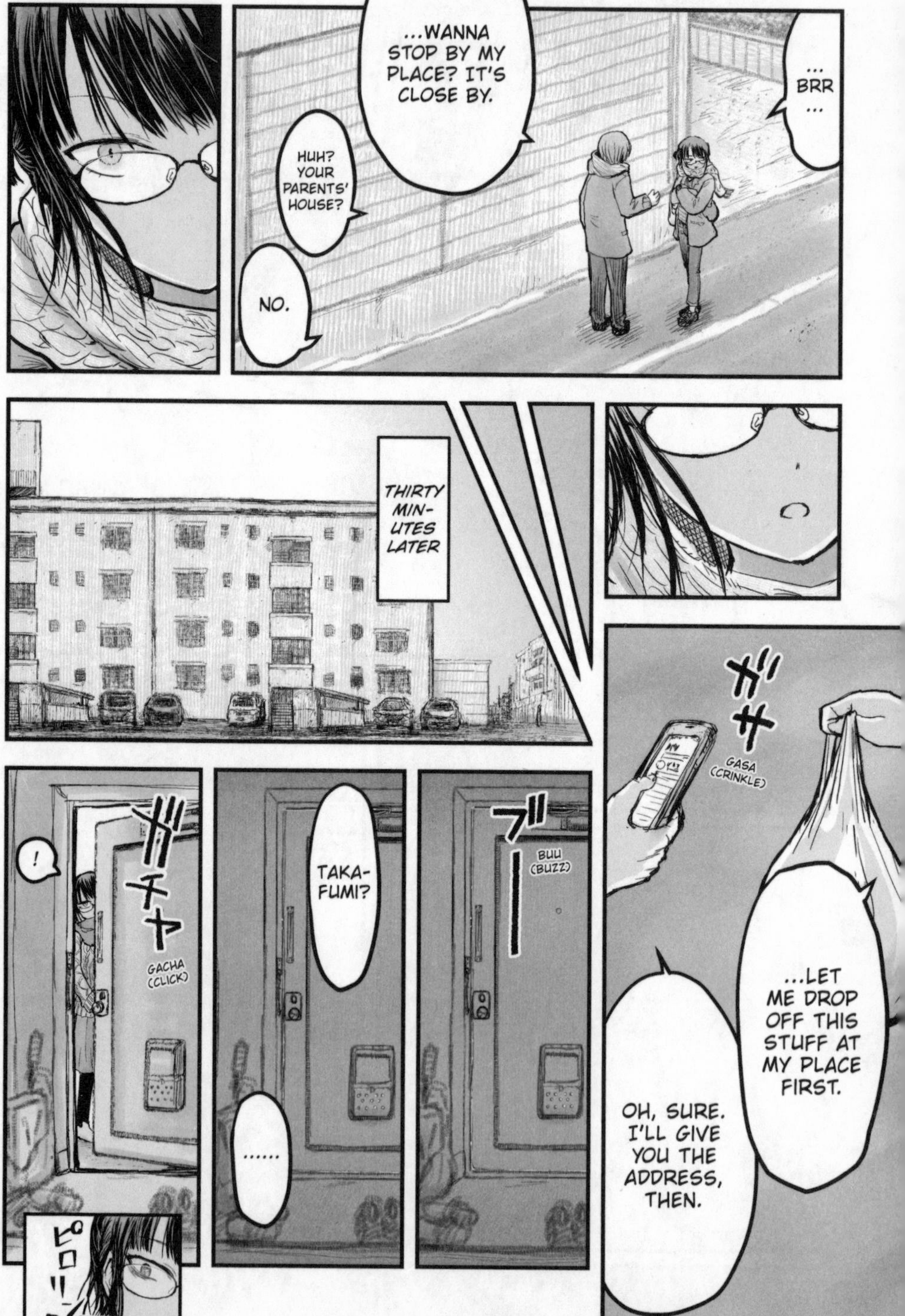
...BRR...
...WANNA STOP BY MY PLACE? IT'S CLOSE BY.
HUH? YOUR PARENTS' HOUSE?
NO.
ガサ
GASA (CRINKLE)
...LET ME DROP OFF THIS STUFF AT MY PLACE FIRST.
OH, SURE. I'LL GIVE YOU THE ADDRESS, THEN.
THIRTY MINUTES LATER
ブー
BUU (BUZZ)
TAKA-FUMI?
......
ガチャ
GACHA (CLICK)
!
ピロリーン♪
PIRORIN (CHIME)

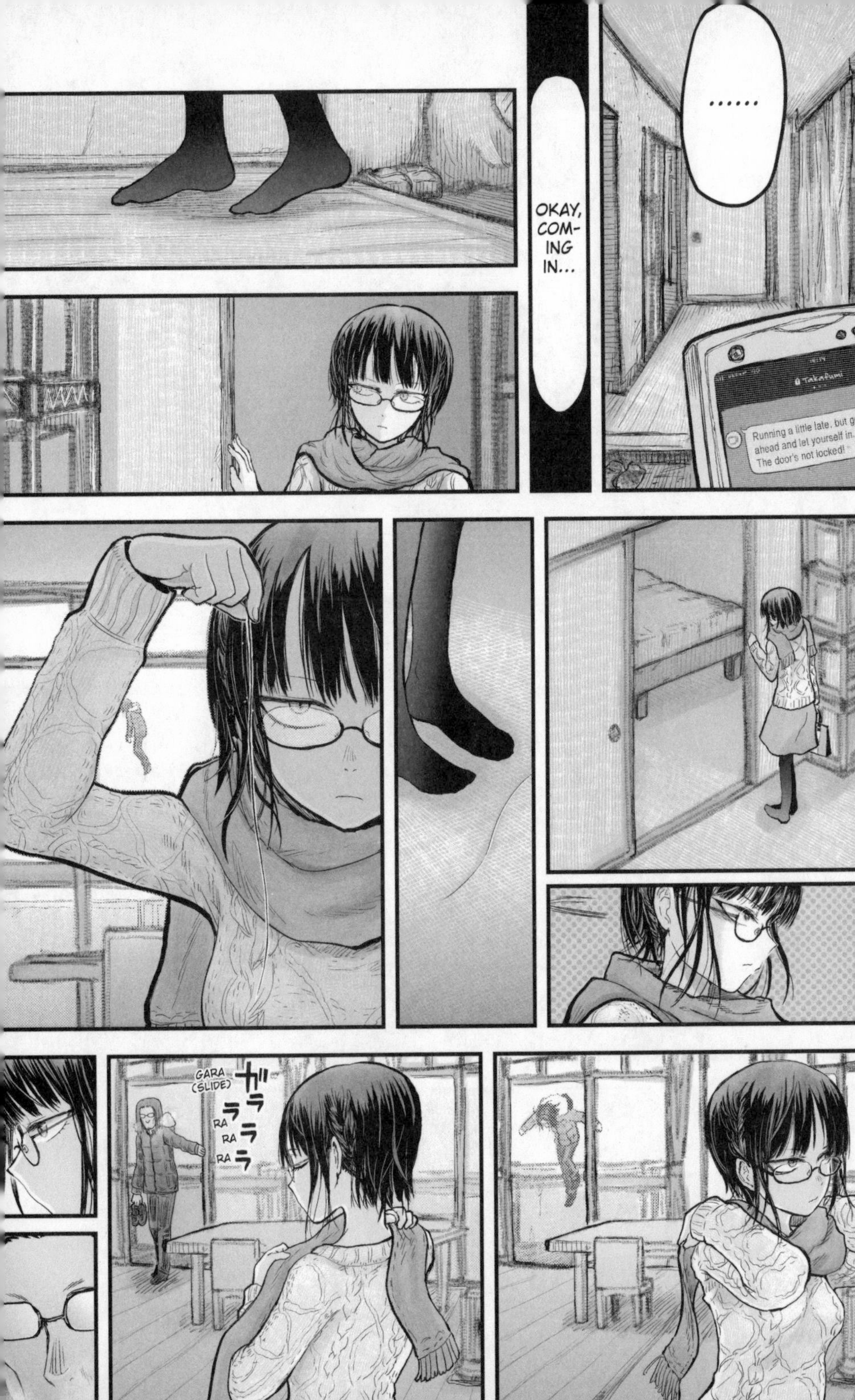
......
Running a little late, but go ahead and let yourself in. The door's not locked!
OKAY, COMING-IN...
ガラララ
GARA (SLIDE) RA RA RA

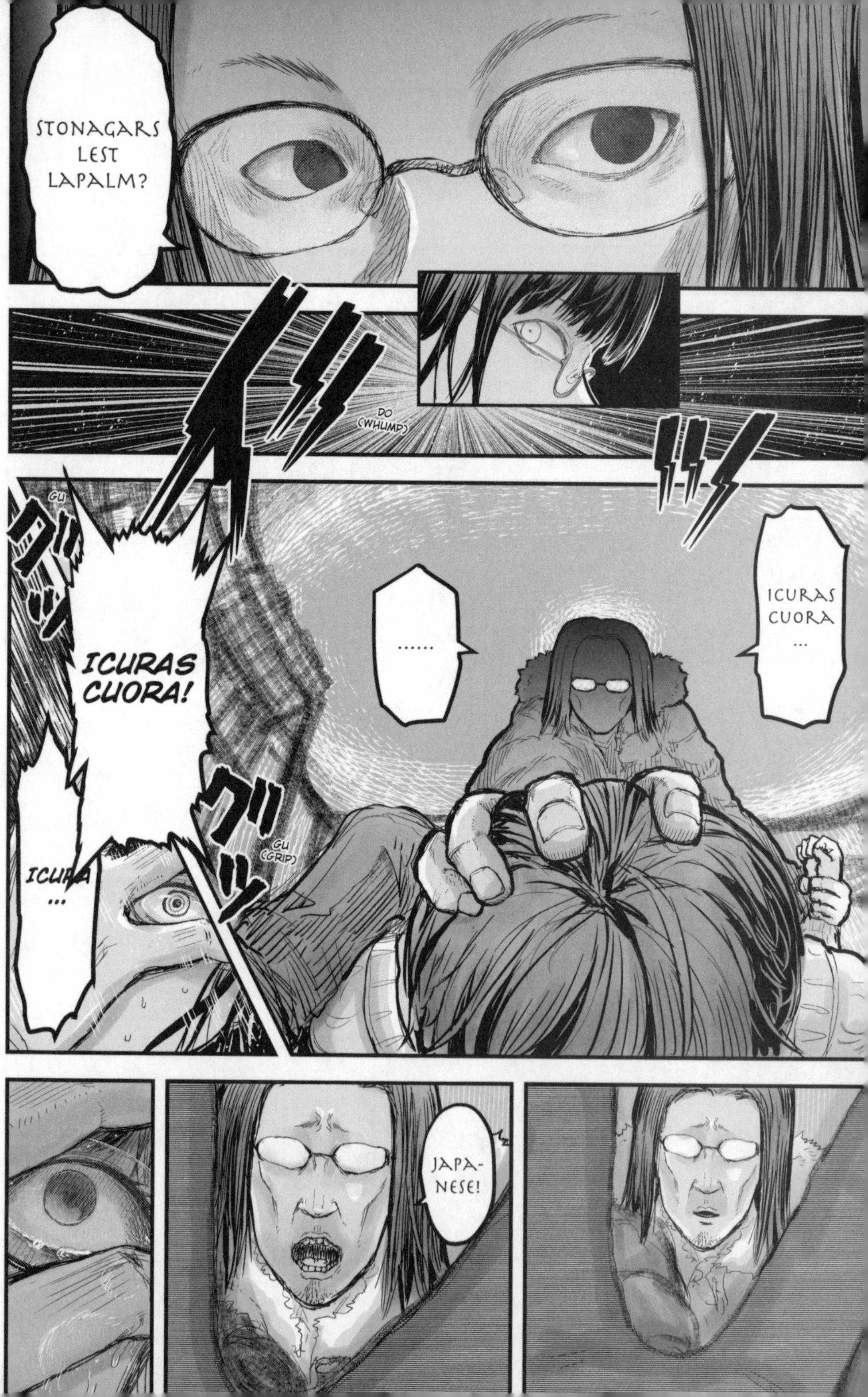
STONAGARS LEST LAPALM?
DO (WHUMP)
ICURAS CUORA ...
......
GU
ICURAS CUORA!
GU (GRIP)
ICURA ...
JAPA-NESE!

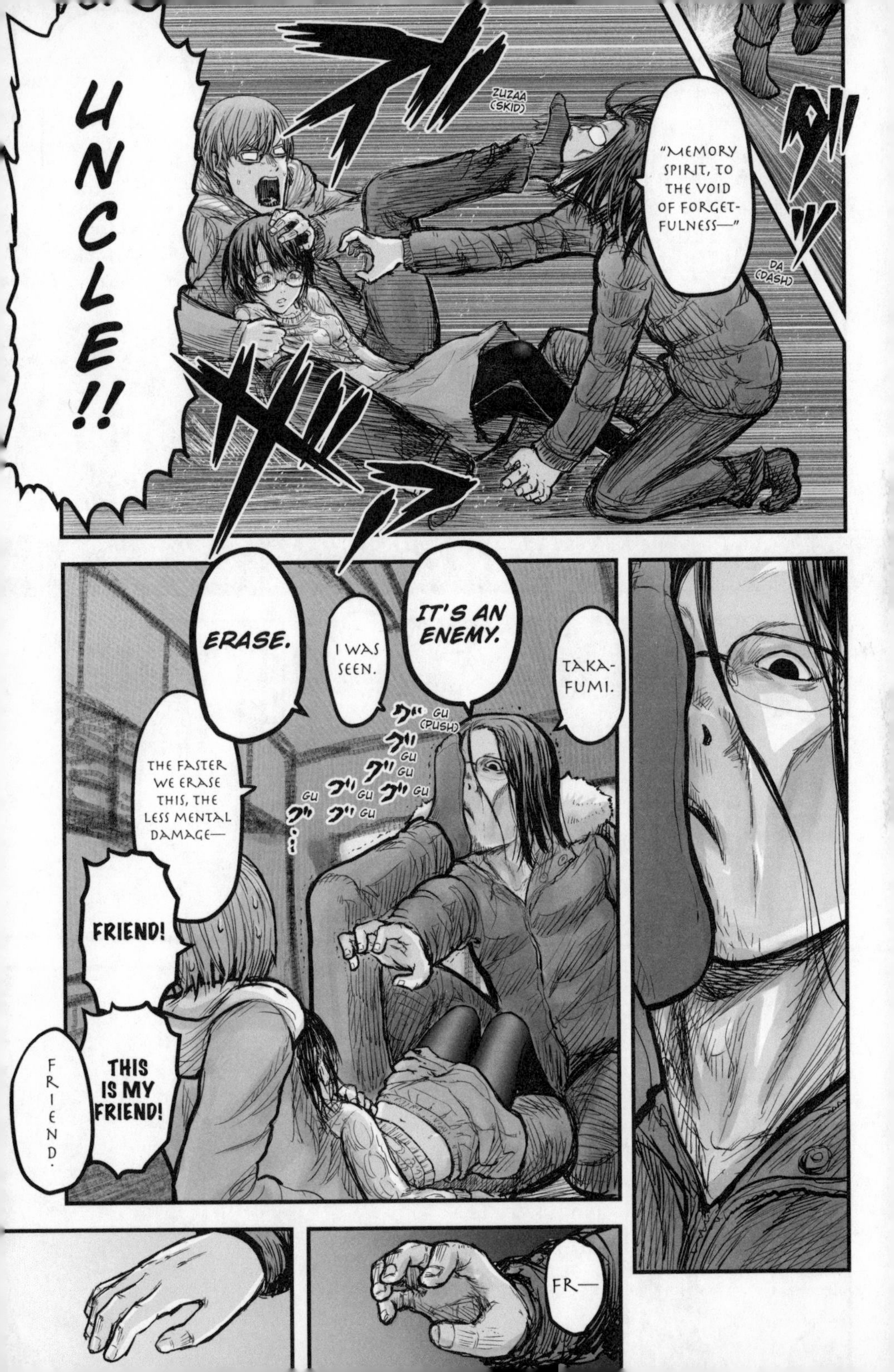
DA (DASH)
"MEMORY SPIRIT, TO THE VOID OF FORGET-FULNESS—"
ZUZAA (SKID)
UNCLE!!
FR—
TAKA-FUMI.
IT'S AN ENEMY.
I WAS SEEN.
ERASE.
GU (PUSH) GU GU GU GU GU GU GU
THE FASTER WE ERASE THIS, THE LESS MENTAL DAMAGE—
FRIEND!
THIS IS MY FRIEND!
FRIEND.

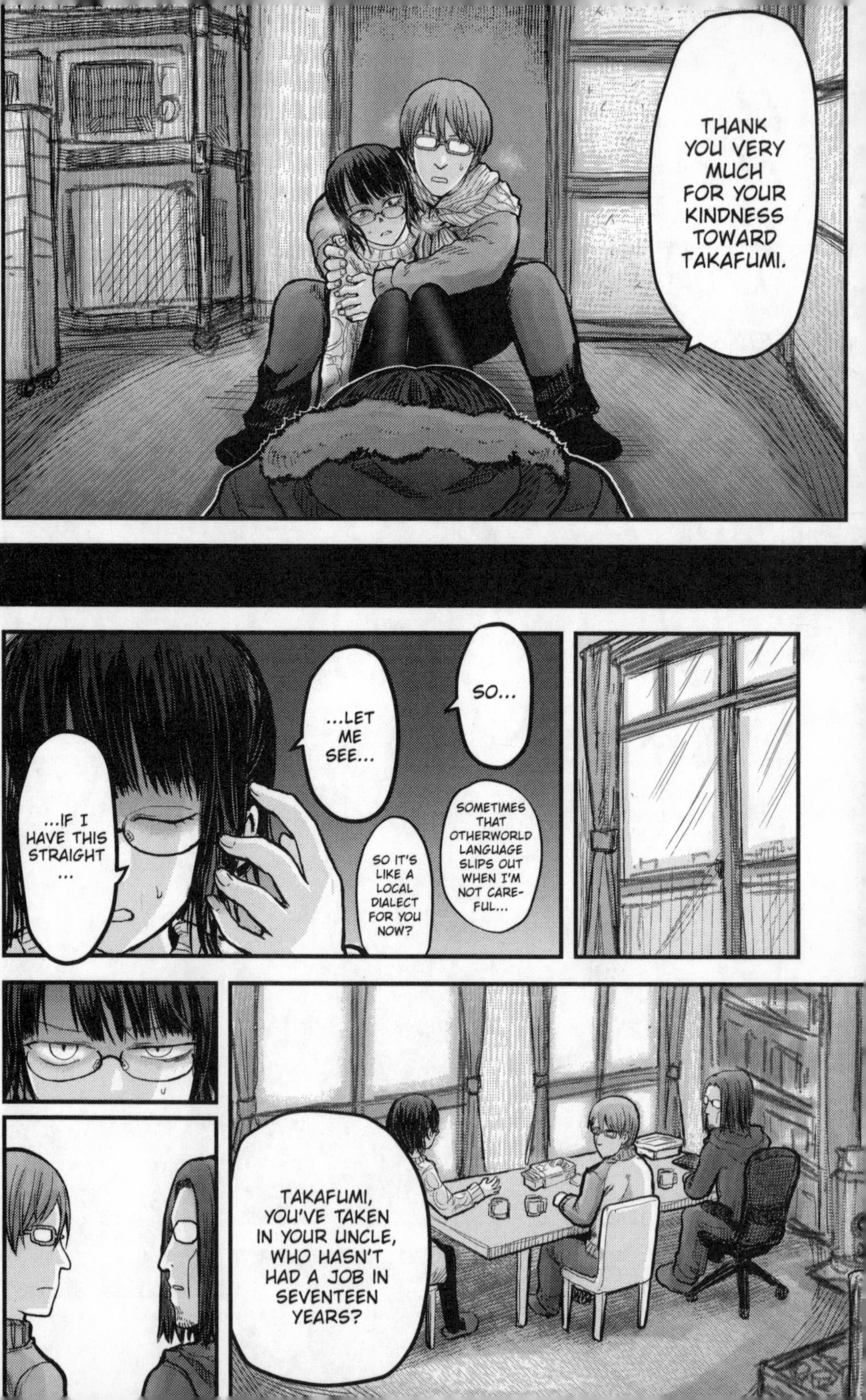
THANK YOU VERY MUCH FOR YOUR KINDNESS TOWARD TAKAFUMI.
SO...
...LET ME SEE...
SOMETIMES THAT OTHERWORLD LANGUAGE SLIPS OUT WHEN I'M NOT CARE-FUL...
SO IT'S LIKE A LOCAL DIALECT FOR YOU NOW?
...IF I HAVE THIS STRAIGHT...
TAKAFUMI, YOU'VE TAKEN IN YOUR UNCLE, WHO HASN'T HAD A JOB IN SEVENTEEN YEARS?

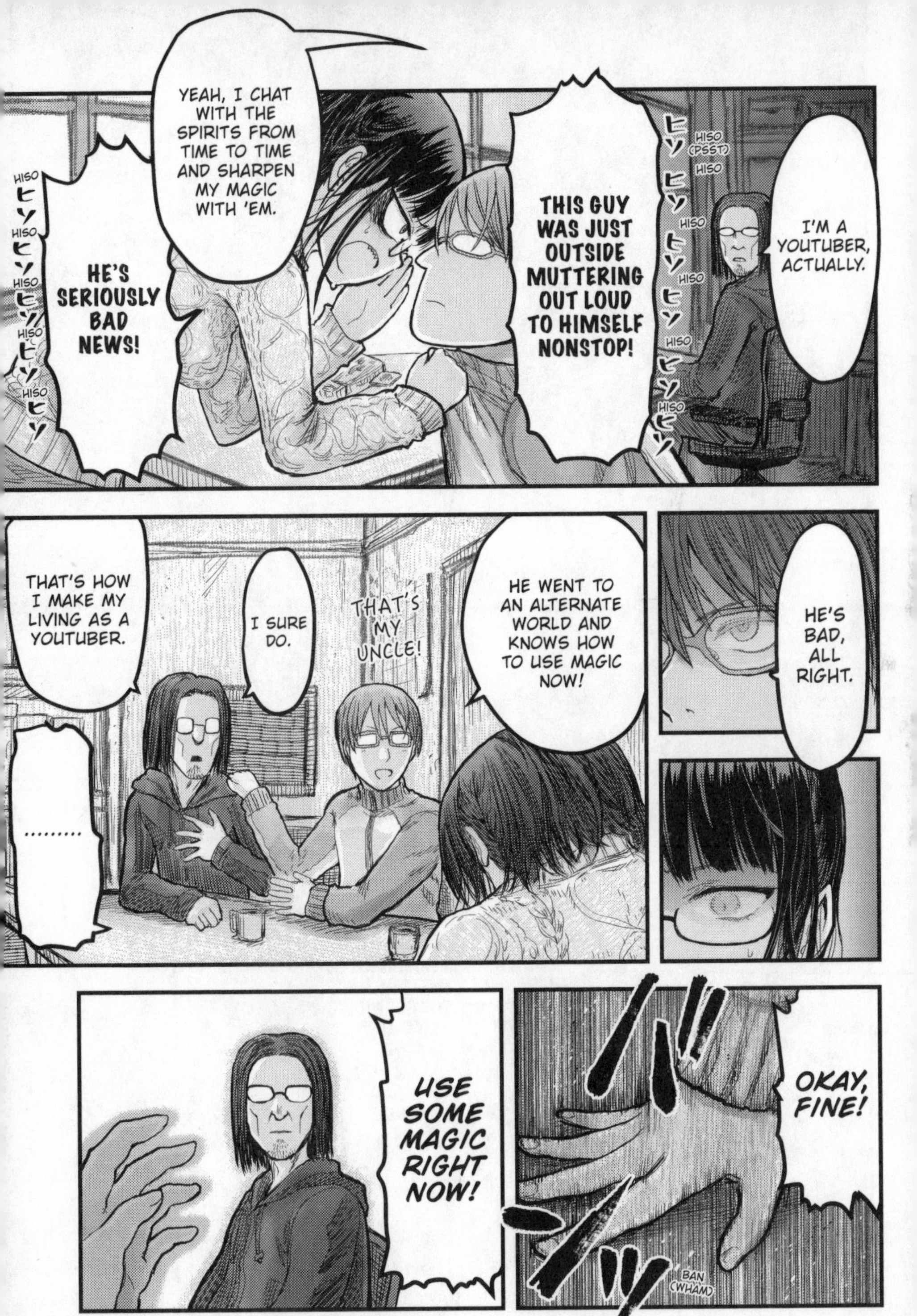
I'M A YOUTUBER, ACTUALLY.
HISO (PSST) HISO HISO HISO HISO HISO
ヒソヒソヒソヒソヒソヒソ
THIS GUY WAS JUST OUTSIDE MUTTERING OUT LOUD TO HIMSELF NONSTOP!
YEAH, I CHAT WITH THE SPIRITS FROM TIME TO TIME AND SHARPEN MY MAGIC WITH 'EM.
HE'S SERIOUSLY BAD NEWS!
HISO HISO HISO HISO HISO
ヒソヒソヒソヒソヒソ
HE'S BAD, ALL RIGHT.
HE WENT TO AN ALTERNATE WORLD AND KNOWS HOW TO USE MAGIC NOW!
THAT'S MY UNCLE!
I SURE DO.
THAT'S HOW I MAKE MY LIVING AS A YOUTUBER.
....
OKAY, FINE!
BAN (WHAM)
USE SOME MAGIC RIGHT NOW!

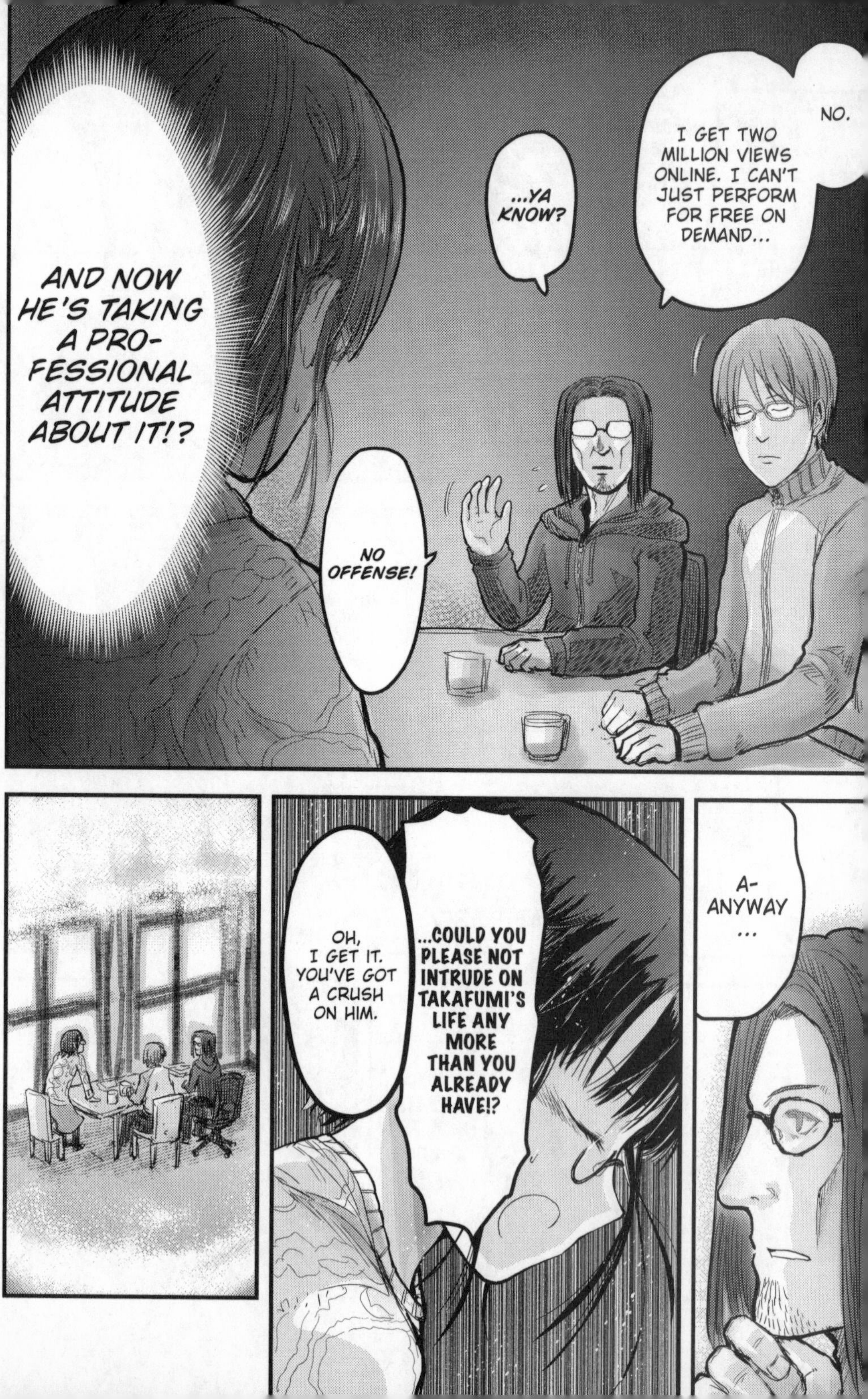
NO.
I GET TWO MILLION VIEWS ONLINE. I CAN'T JUST PERFORM FOR FREE ON DEMAND...
...YA KNOW?
NO OFFENSE!
AND NOW HE'S TAKING A PRO-FESSIONAL ATTITUDE ABOUT IT!?
A-ANYWAY...
...COULD YOU PLEASE NOT INTRUDE ON TAKAFUMI'S LIFE ANY MORE THAN YOU ALREADY HAVE!?
OH, I GET IT. YOU'VE GOT A CRUSH ON HIM.

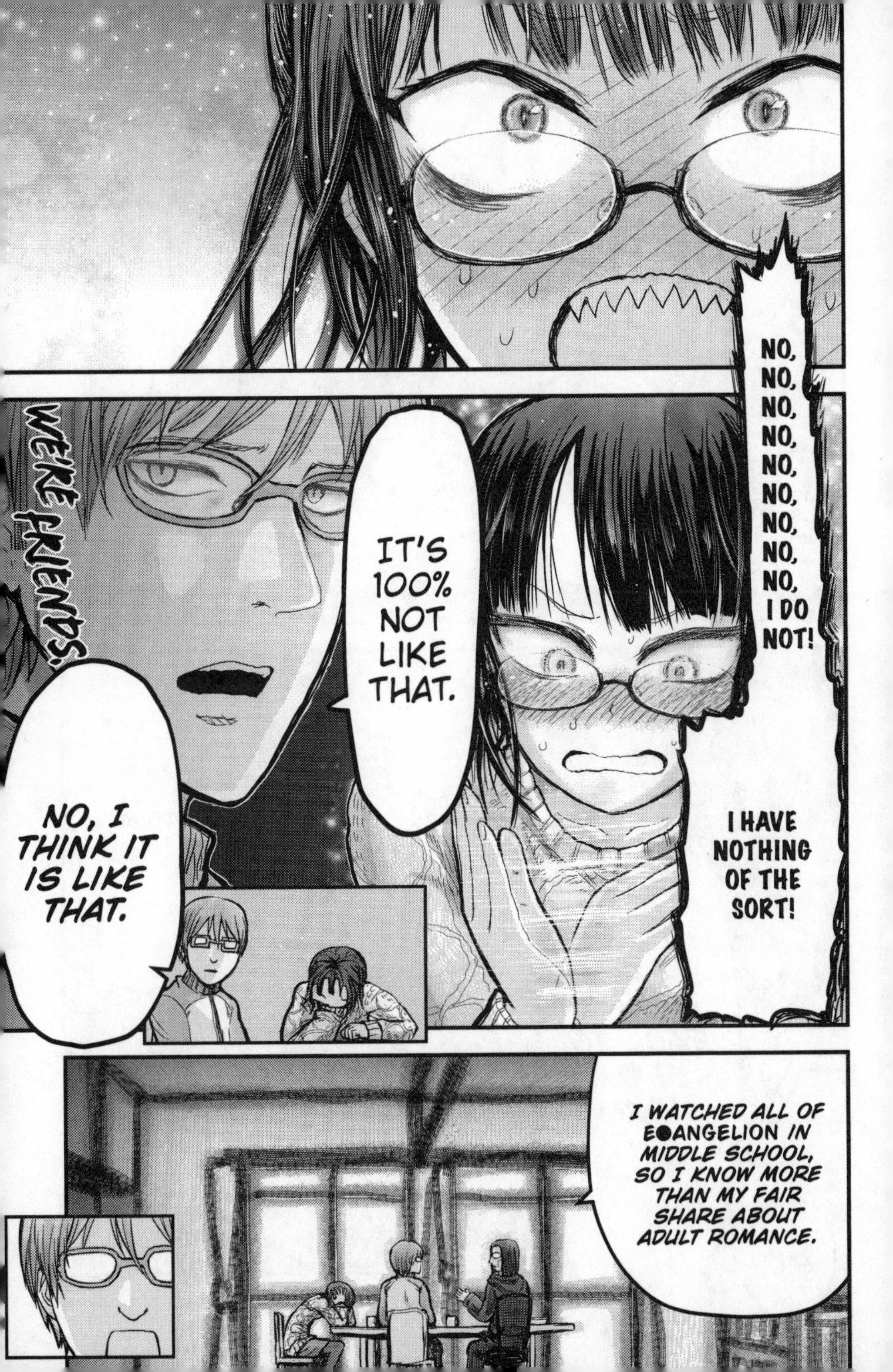
NO, NO, NO, NO, NO, NO, NO, NO, NO, I DO NOT!
I HAVE NOTHING OF THE SORT!
IT'S 100% NOT LIKE THAT.
WE'RE FRIENDS.
NO, I THINK IT IS LIKE THAT.
I WATCHED ALL OF E●ANGELION IN MIDDLE SCHOOL, SO I KNOW MORE THAN MY FAIR SHARE ABOUT ADULT ROMANCE.

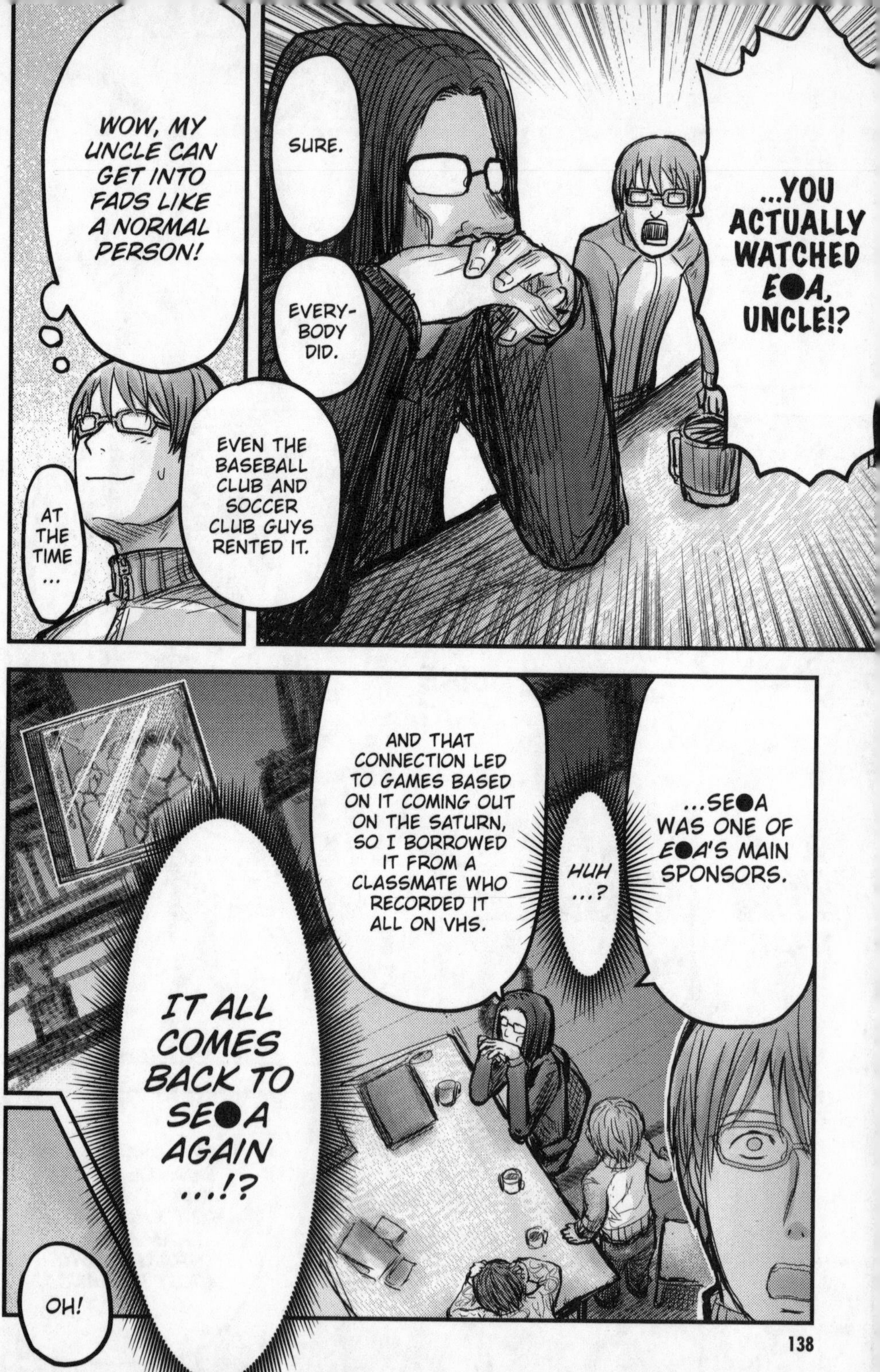
...YOU ACTUALLY WATCHED E●A, UNCLE!?
SURE.
EVERY-BODY DID.
EVEN THE BASEBALL CLUB AND SOCCER CLUB GUYS RENTED IT.
WOW, MY UNCLE CAN GET INTO FADS LIKE A NORMAL PERSON!
AT THE TIME...
...SE●A WAS ONE OF E●A'S MAIN SPONSORS.
HUH...?
AND THAT CONNECTION LED TO GAMES BASED ON IT COMING OUT ON THE SATURN, SO I BORROWED IT FROM A CLASSMATE WHO RECORDED IT ALL ON VHS.
IT ALL COMES BACK TO SE●A AGAIN...!?
OH!

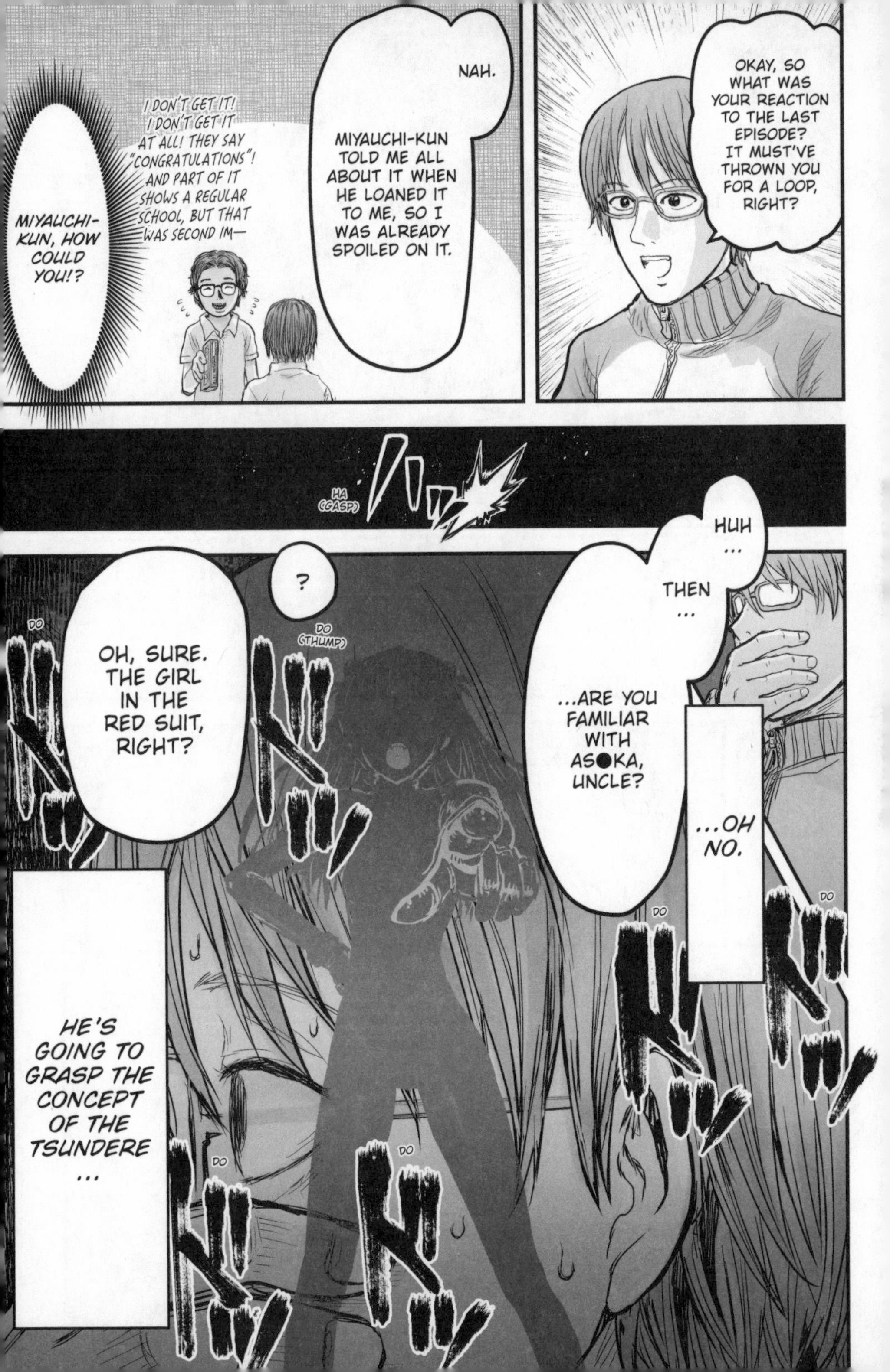
OKAY, SO WHAT WAS YOUR REACTION TO THE LAST EPISODE? IT MUST'VE THROWN YOU FOR A LOOP, RIGHT?
NAH.
MIYAUCHI-KUN TOLD ME ALL ABOUT IT WHEN HE LOANED IT TO ME, SO I WAS ALREADY SPOILED ON IT.
I DON'T GET IT! I DON'T GET IT AT ALL! THEY SAY "CONGRATULATIONS"! AND PART OF IT SHOWS A REGULAR SCHOOL, BUT THAT WAS SECOND IM—
MIYAUCHI-KUN, HOW COULD YOU!?
HA (GASP)
HUH ...
THEN ...
...ARE YOU FAMILIAR WITH AS●KA, UNCLE?
...OH NO.
DO
DO
?
OH, SURE. THE GIRL IN THE RED SUIT, RIGHT?
DO (THUMP)
DO
HE'S GOING TO GRASP THE CONCEPT OF THE TSUNDERE ...
DO
DO

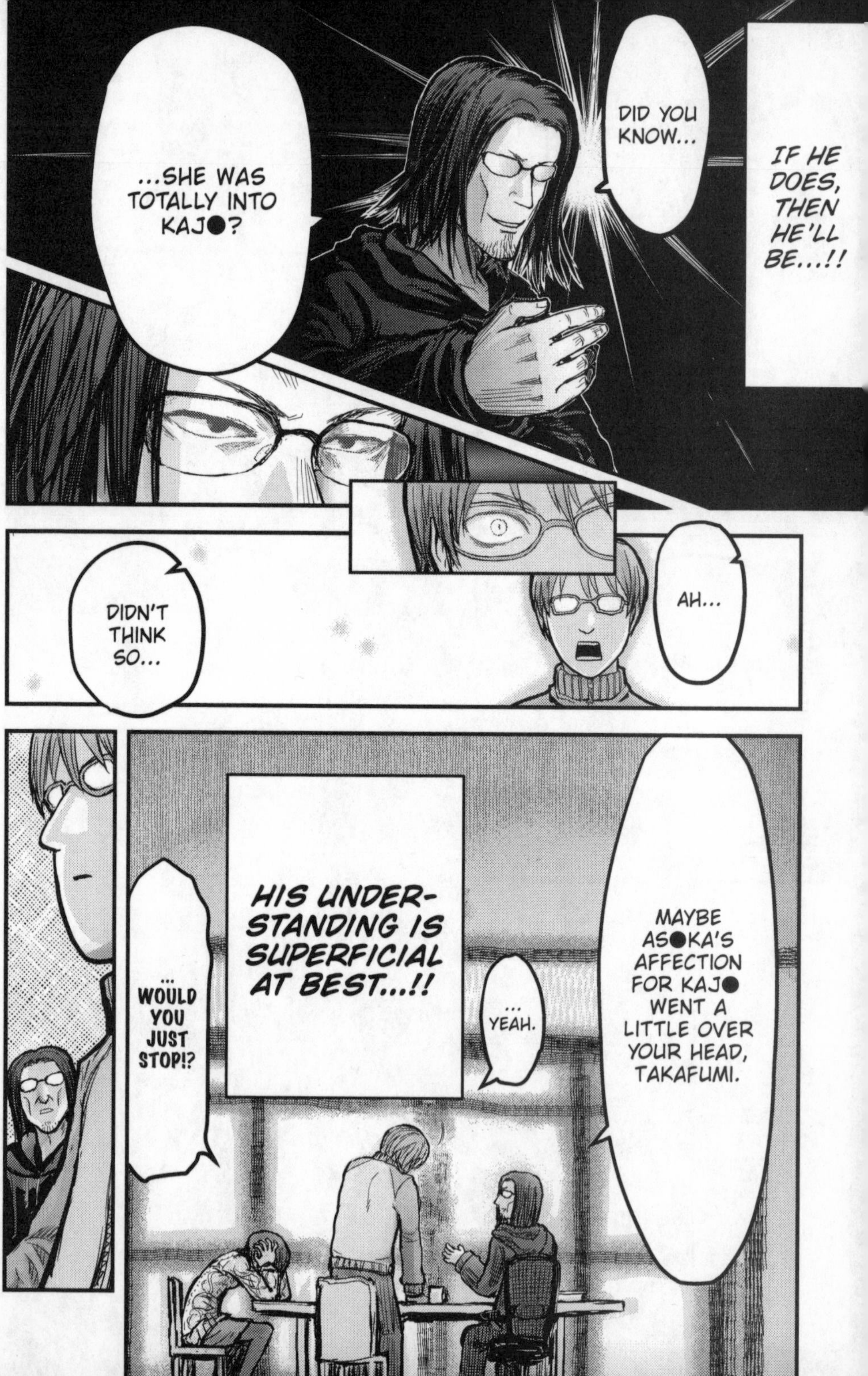
IF HE DOES, THEN HE'LL BE...!!
DID YOU KNOW...
...SHE WAS TOTALLY INTO KAJ●?
AH...
DIDN'T THINK SO...
MAYBE AS●KA'S AFFECTION FOR KAJ● WENT A LITTLE OVER YOUR HEAD, TAKAFUMI.
... YEAH.
HIS UNDER-STANDING IS SUPERFICIAL AT BEST...!!
... WOULD YOU JUST STOP!?

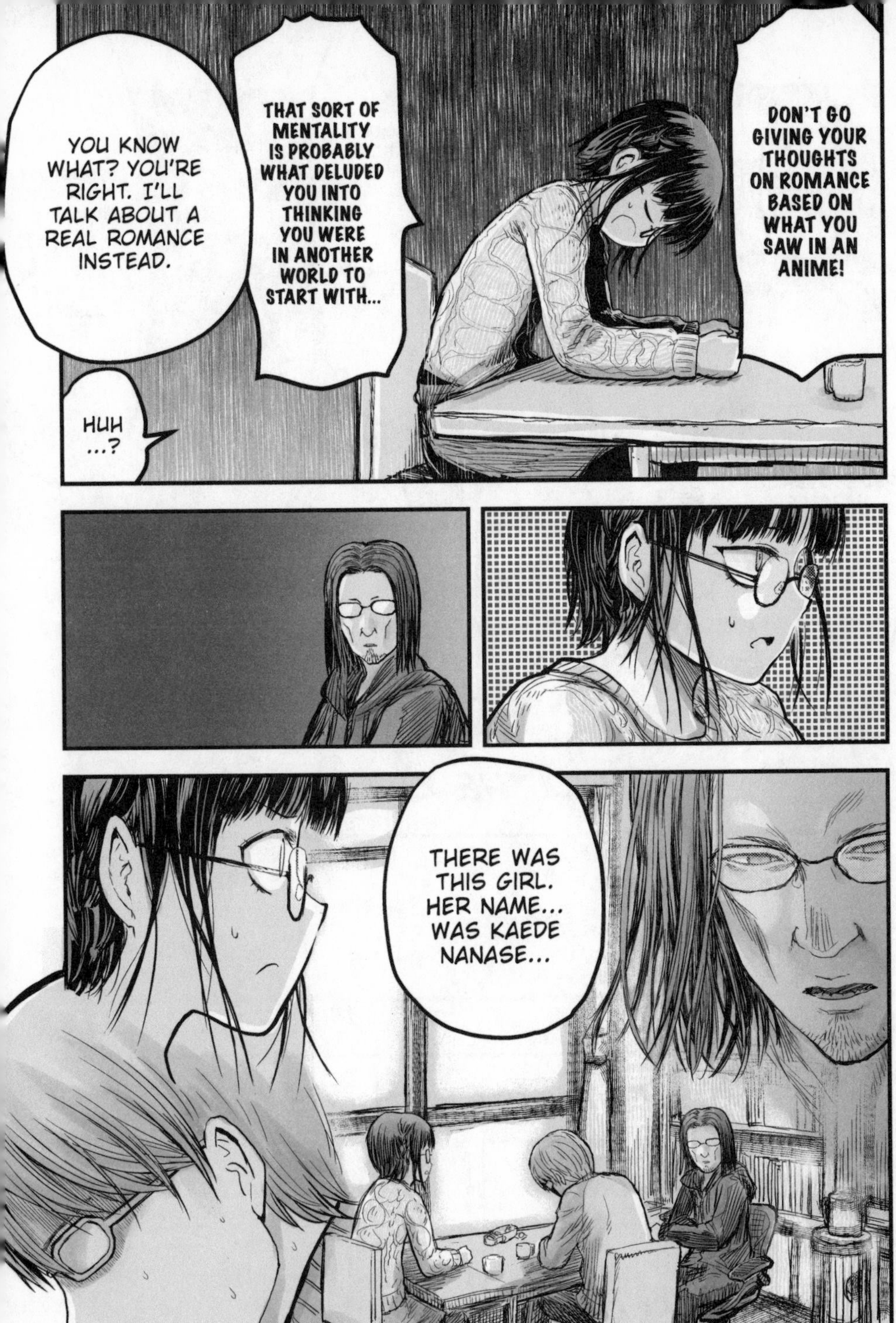
DON'T GO GIVING YOUR THOUGHTS ON ROMANCE BASED ON WHAT YOU SAW IN AN ANIME!
THAT SORT OF MENTALITY IS PROBABLY WHAT DELUDED YOU INTO THINKING YOU WERE IN ANOTHER WORLD TO START WITH...
YOU KNOW WHAT? YOU'RE RIGHT. I'LL TALK ABOUT A REAL ROMANCE INSTEAD.
HUH ...?
THERE WAS THIS GIRL. HER NAME... WAS KAEDE NANASE...

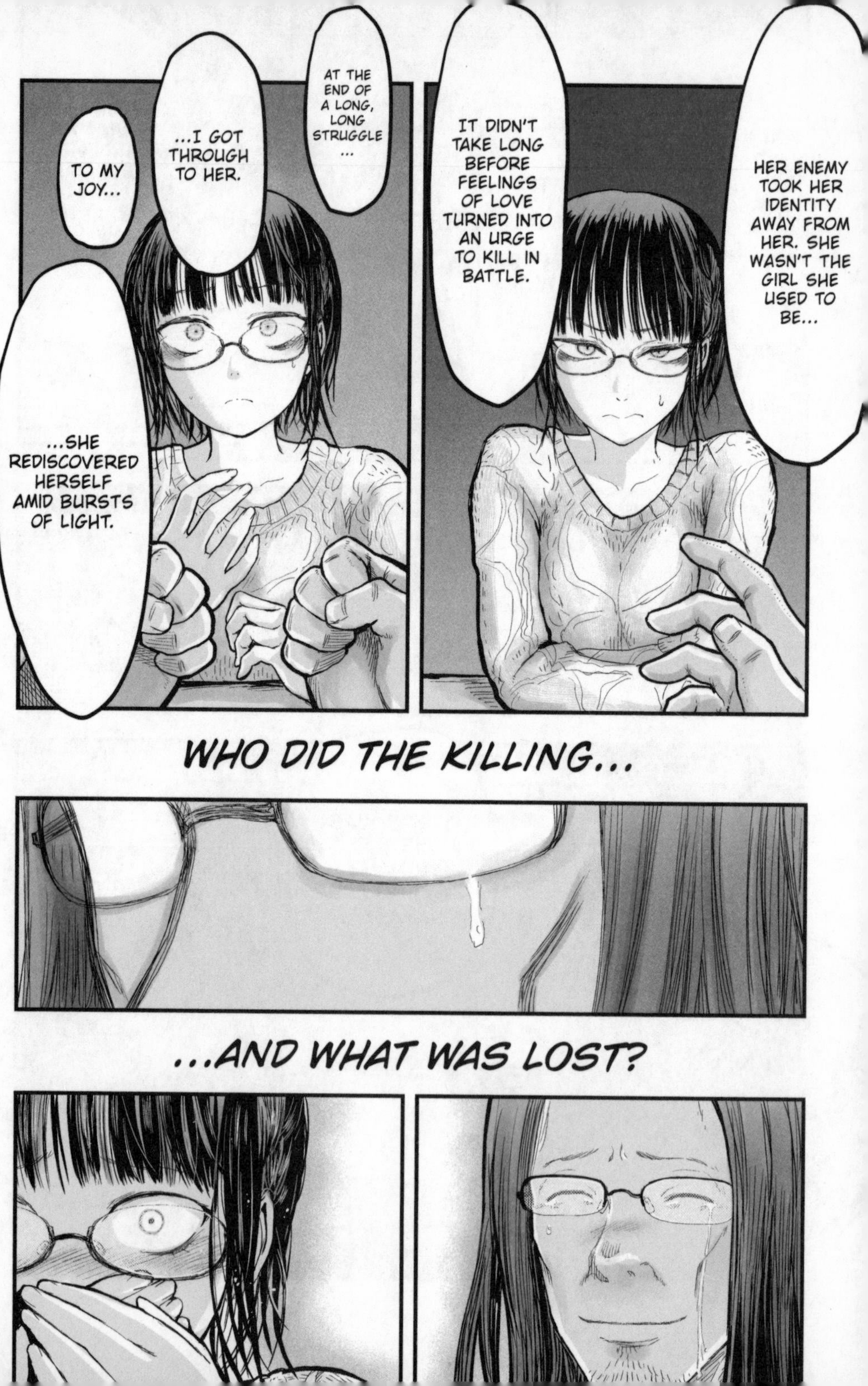
HER ENEMY TOOK HER IDENTITY AWAY FROM HER. SHE WASN'T THE GIRL SHE USED TO BE...
IT DIDN'T TAKE LONG BEFORE FEELINGS OF LOVE TURNED INTO AN URGE TO KILL IN BATTLE.
AT THE END OF A LONG, LONG STRUGGLE...
...I GOT THROUGH TO HER.
TO MY JOY...
...SHE REDISCOVERED HERSELF AMID BURSTS OF LIGHT.
WHO DID THE KILLING...
...AND WHAT WAS LOST?

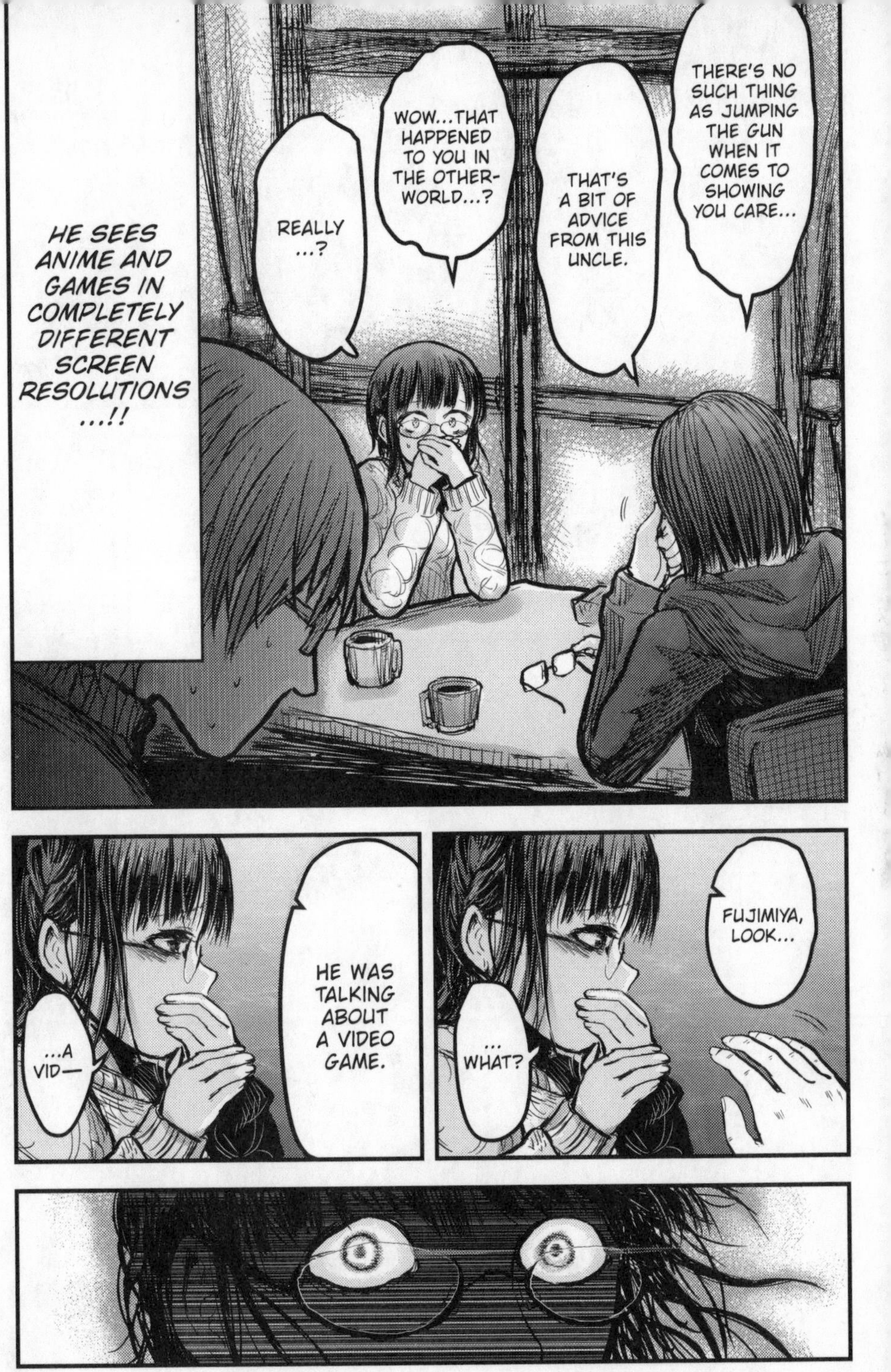
THERE'S NO SUCH THING AS JUMPING THE GUN WHEN IT COMES TO SHOWING YOU CARE...
THAT'S A BIT OF ADVICE FROM THIS UNCLE.
WOW...THAT HAPPENED TO YOU IN THE OTHER-WORLD...?
REALLY ...?
HE SEES ANIME AND GAMES IN COMPLETELY DIFFERENT SCREEN RESOLUTIONS ...!!
FUJIMIYA, LOOK...
... WHAT?
HE WAS TALKING ABOUT A VIDEO GAME.
...A VID—

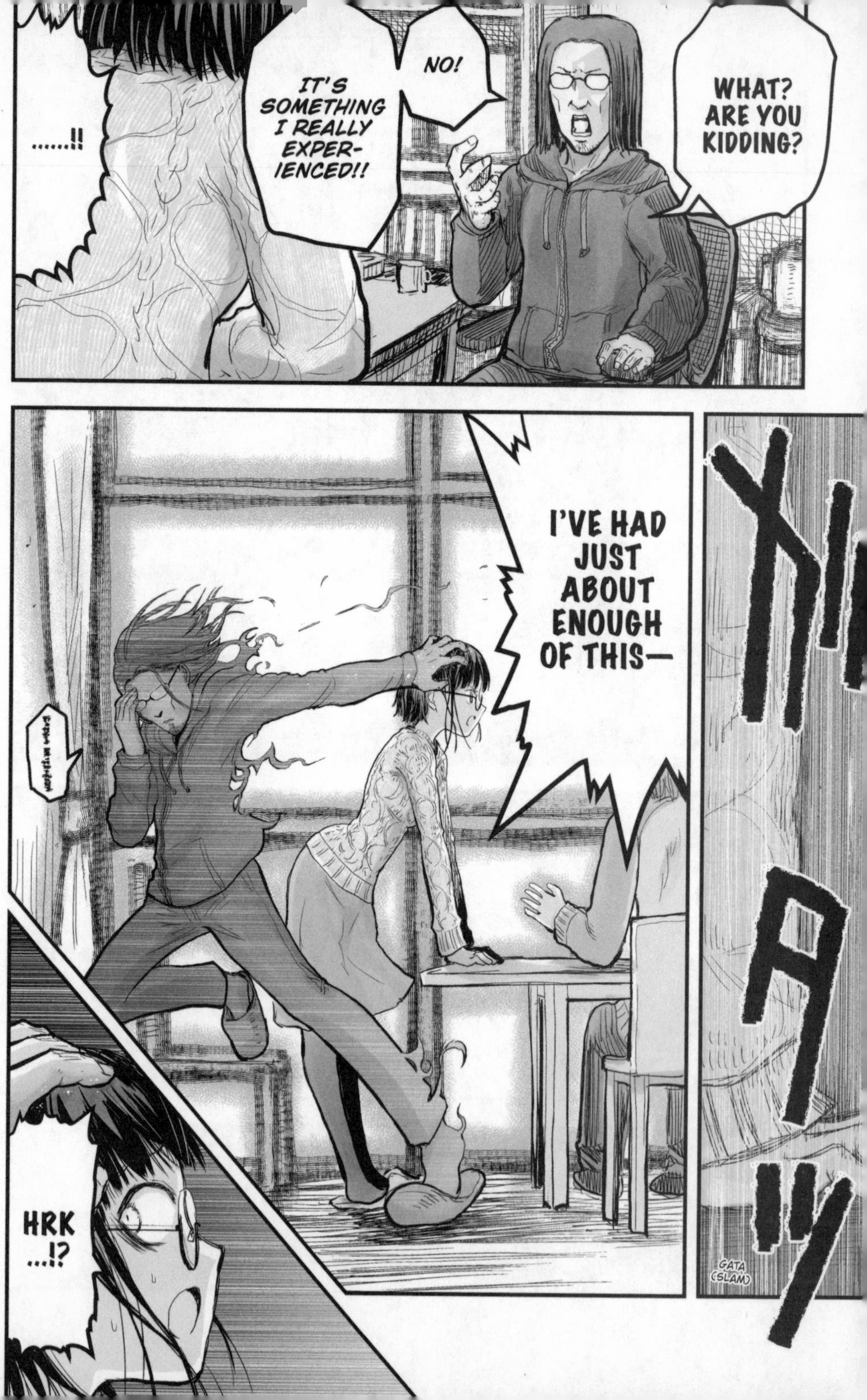
WHAT? ARE YOU KIDDING?
NO!
IT'S SOMETHING I REALLY EXPERIENCED!!
......!!
GATA (SLAM)
I'VE HAD JUST ABOUT ENOUGH OF THIS—
HRK ...!?

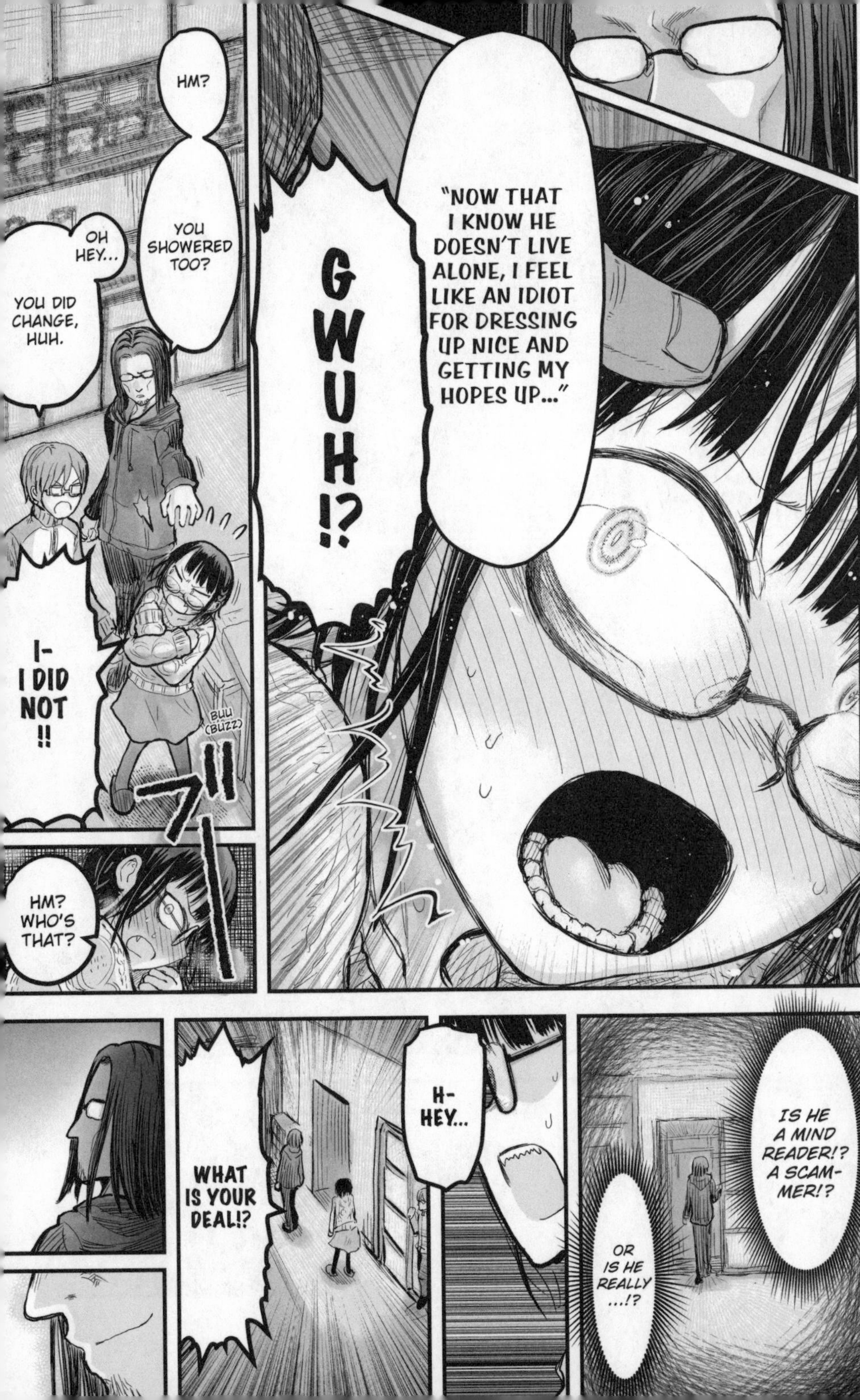
"NOW THAT I KNOW HE DOESN'T LIVE ALONE, I FEEL LIKE AN IDIOT FOR DRESSING UP NICE AND GETTING MY HOPES UP..."
GWUH!?
HM?
YOU SHOWERED TOO?
OH HEY...
YOU DID CHANGE, HUH.
I- I DID NOT!!
BUU (BUZZ)
HM? WHO'S THAT?
IS HE A MIND READER!? A SCAM-MER!?
OR IS HE REALLY ...!?
H- HEY...
WHAT IS YOUR DEAL!?

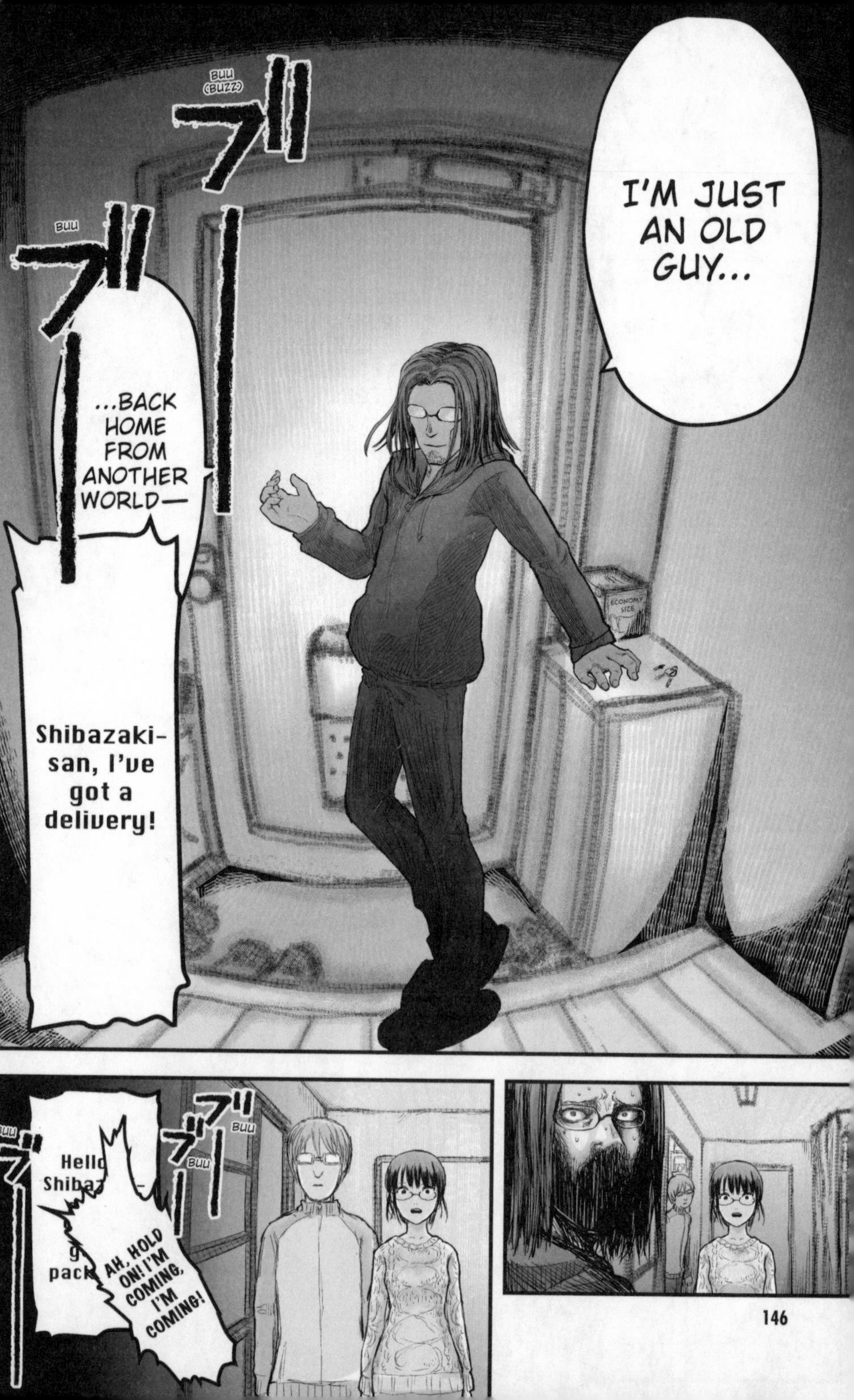
I'M JUST AN OLD GUY...
BUU (BUZZ)
BUU
...BACK HOME FROM ANOTHER WORLD—
Shibazaki-san, I've got a delivery!
BUU
BUU
BUU
Hello
AH, HOLD ON! I'M COMING, I'M COMING!

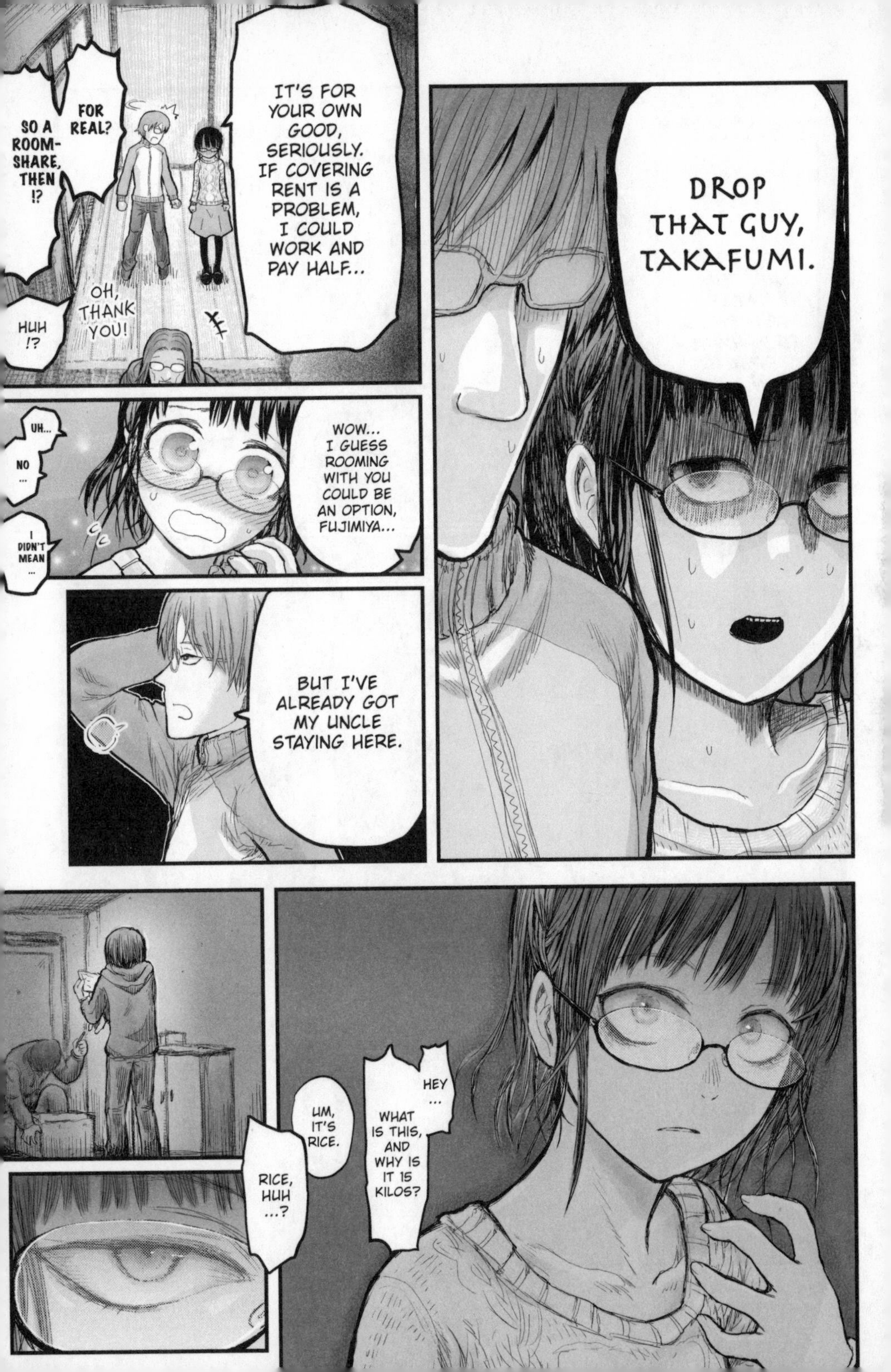
DROP THAT GUY, TAKAFUMI.
IT'S FOR YOUR OWN GOOD, SERIOUSLY. IF COVERING RENT IS A PROBLEM, I COULD WORK AND PAY HALF...
FOR REAL?
SO A ROOM-SHARE, THEN !?
OH, THANK YOU!
HUH !?
WOW... I GUESS ROOMING WITH YOU COULD BE AN OPTION, FUJIMIYA...
UH...
NO ...
I DIDN'T MEAN ...
BUT I'VE ALREADY GOT MY UNCLE STAYING HERE.
HEY ...
WHAT IS THIS, AND WHY IS IT 15 KILOS?
UM, IT'S RICE.
RICE, HUH ...?

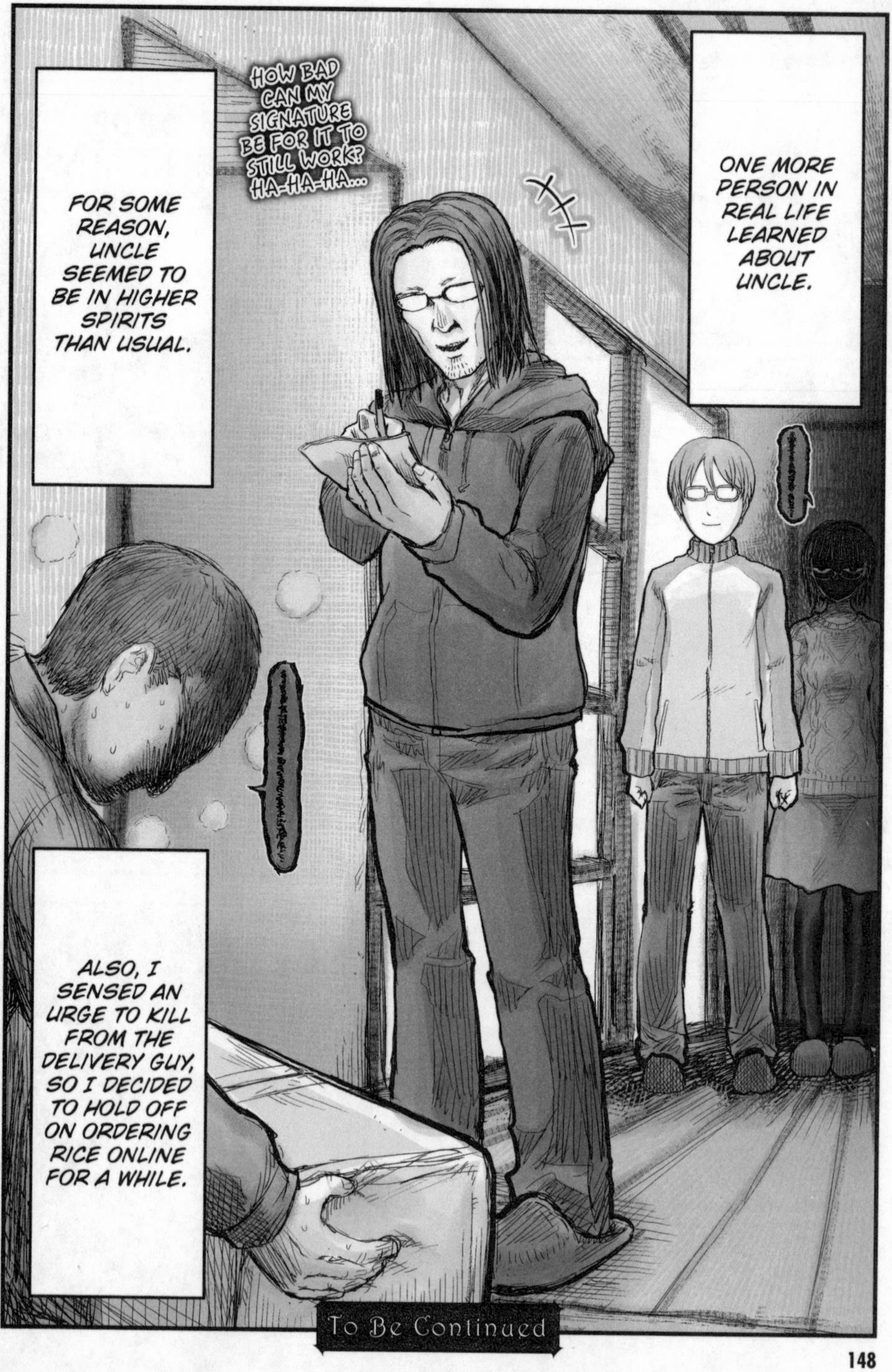
ONE MORE PERSON IN REAL LIFE LEARNED ABOUT UNCLE.
HOW BAD CAN MY SIGNATURE BE FOR IT TO STILL WORK? HA-HA-HA...
FOR SOME REASON, UNCLE SEEMED TO BE IN HIGHER SPIRITS THAN USUAL.
ALSO, I SENSED AN URGE TO KILL FROM THE DELIVERY GUY, SO I DECIDED TO HOLD OFF ON ORDERING RICE ONLINE FOR A WHILE.
To Be Continued

Live-Ins and Roomshares

The main difference between live-in and roomshare arrangements is that only one resident makes a contract in the former, and every resident makes a contract in the latter. In shared living arrangements between members of the opposite sex, whether those arrangements are live-in or roomshare can be a highly subjective question.

TIPS

UNCLE from ANOTHER WORLD

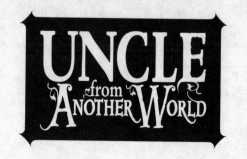

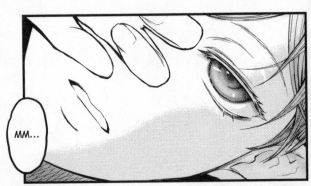

MM...

チュン
チュン
チュン
CHUN
(CHIRP)

NNNGH
...

EXTRA

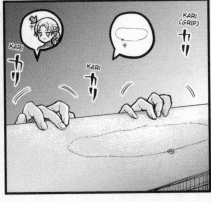

KARI

KARI

KARI
(GRIP)

YO
(HLIP)

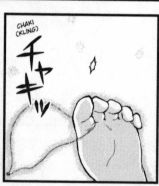

CHAKI
(KLING)

CHARA

CHARA
(JINGLE)

...
GH!

GATA
(CLATTER)

GATA

GATA

WHOA!?

♥

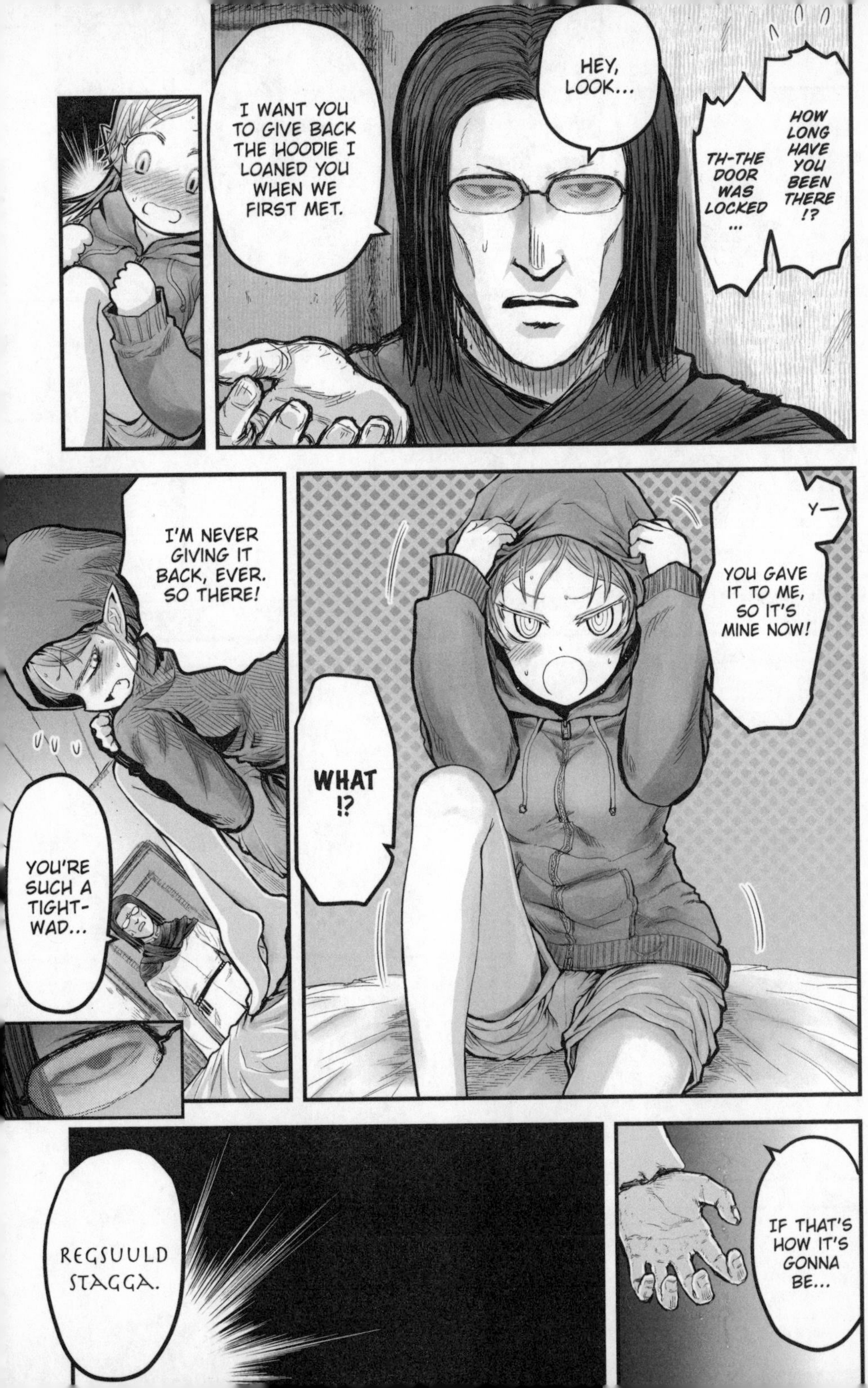
HOW LONG HAVE YOU BEEN THERE!?
TH-THE DOOR WAS LOCKED...
HEY, LOOK...
I WANT YOU TO GIVE BACK THE HOODIE I LOANED YOU WHEN WE FIRST MET.
Y—
YOU GAVE IT TO ME, SO IT'S MINE NOW!
WHAT!?
I'M NEVER GIVING IT BACK, EVER. SO THERE!
YOU'RE SUCH A TIGHT-WAD...
IF THAT'S HOW IT'S GONNA BE...
REGSUULD STAGGA.

NOSHI
(KNEEL)

STAY STILL FOR A SECOND.

WHAT!?

BISHIII
(SNAP)

JI
(ZPP)

JI

JI

JI

JI

JI

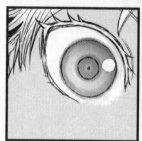

AH!?

! ! ! !

IT'S ALWAYS THE HARD WAY WITH YOU...

JIII
(ZIIIP)

DAMMIT, I CAN'T GET IT OFF WITH THE SPELL IN THE WAY.

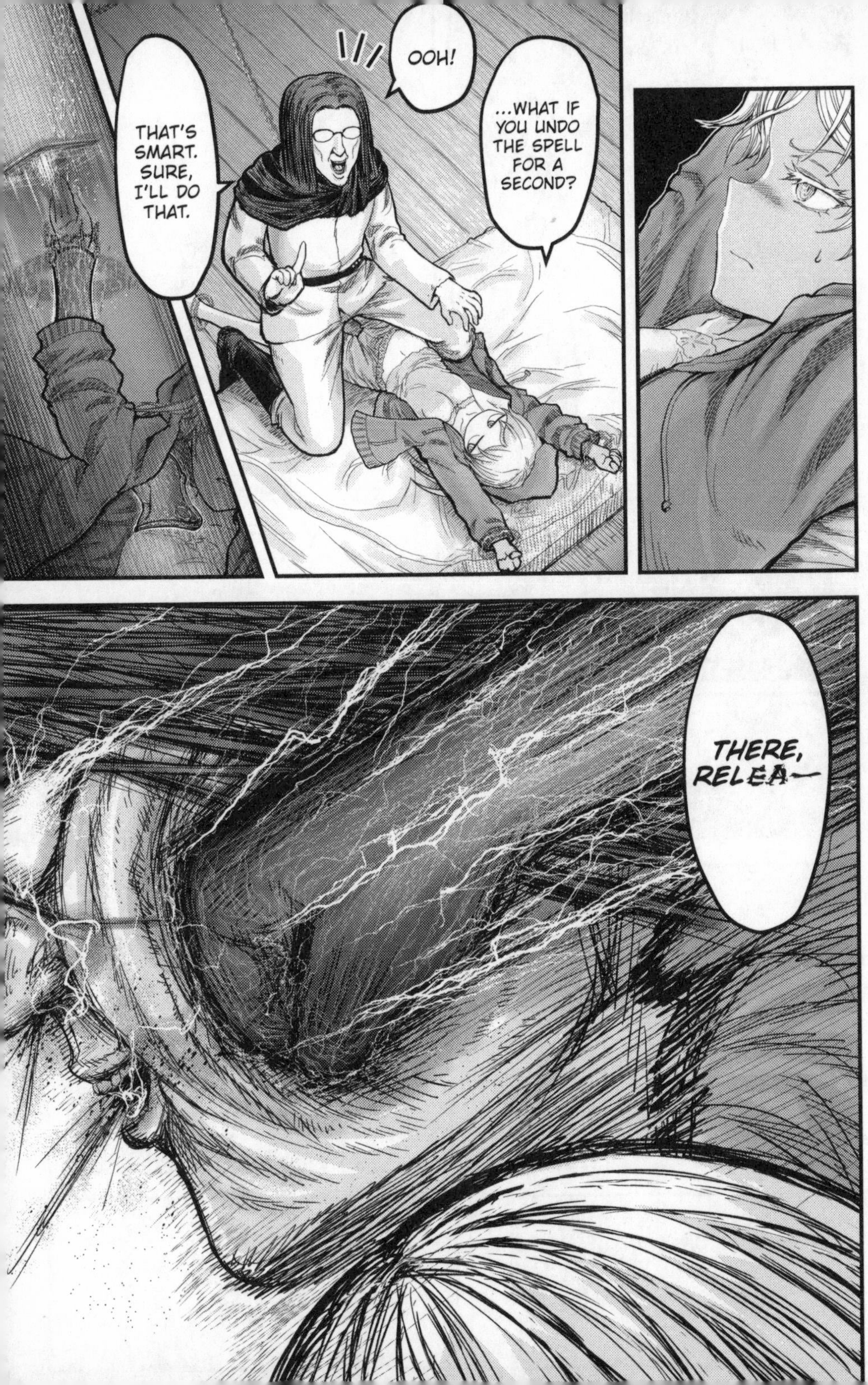
...WHAT IF YOU UNDO THE SPELL FOR A SECOND?
OOH!
THAT'S SMART. SURE, I'LL DO THAT.
THERE, RELEA—

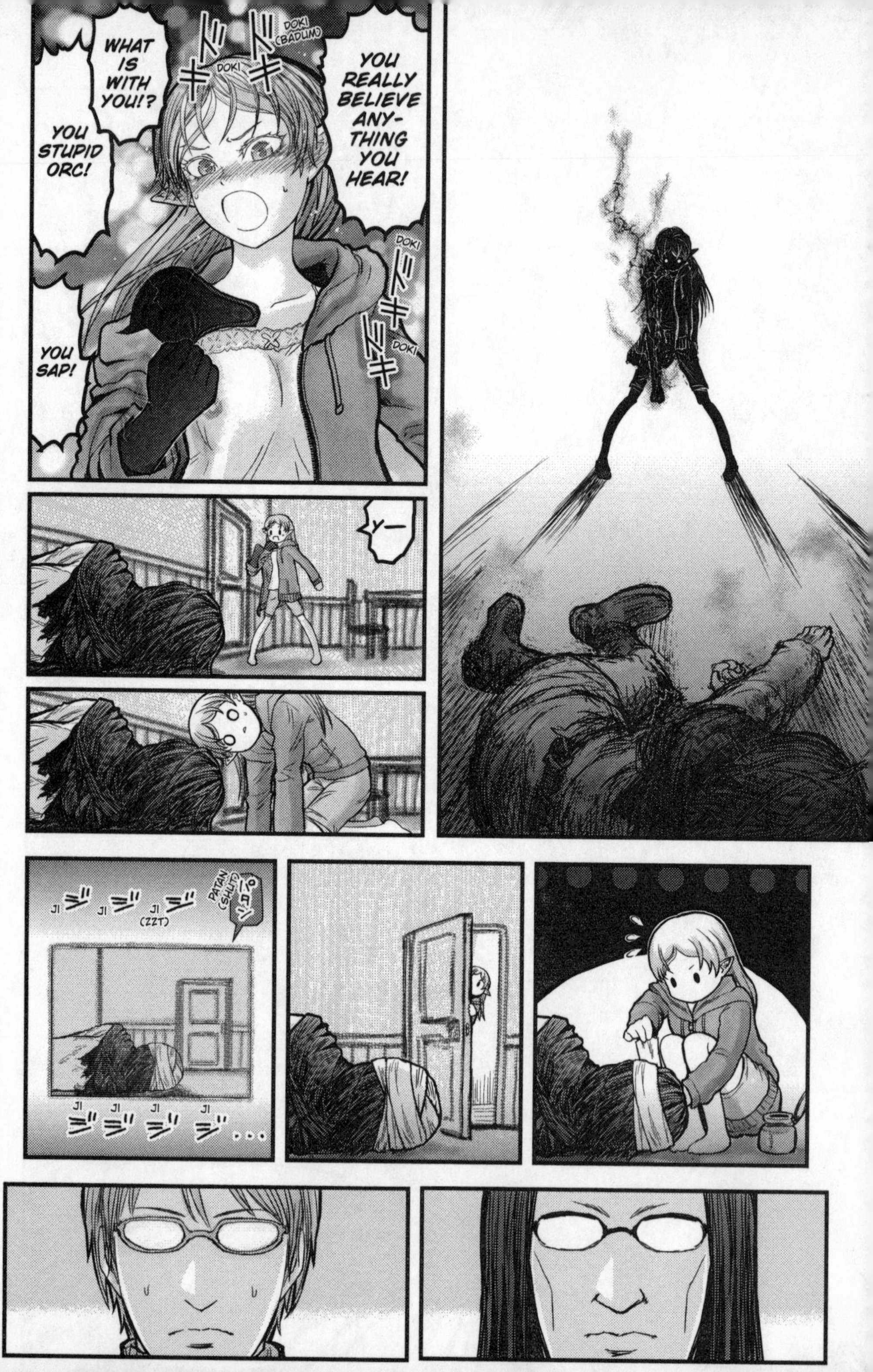
DOKI (BADUM)
DOKI
YOU REALLY BELIEVE ANY-THING YOU HEAR!
WHAT IS WITH YOU!?
YOU STUPID ORC!
DOKI
DOKI
YOU SAP!
Y—
PATAN (SHUT)
JI JI JI (ZZT)
JI JI JI JI . . .

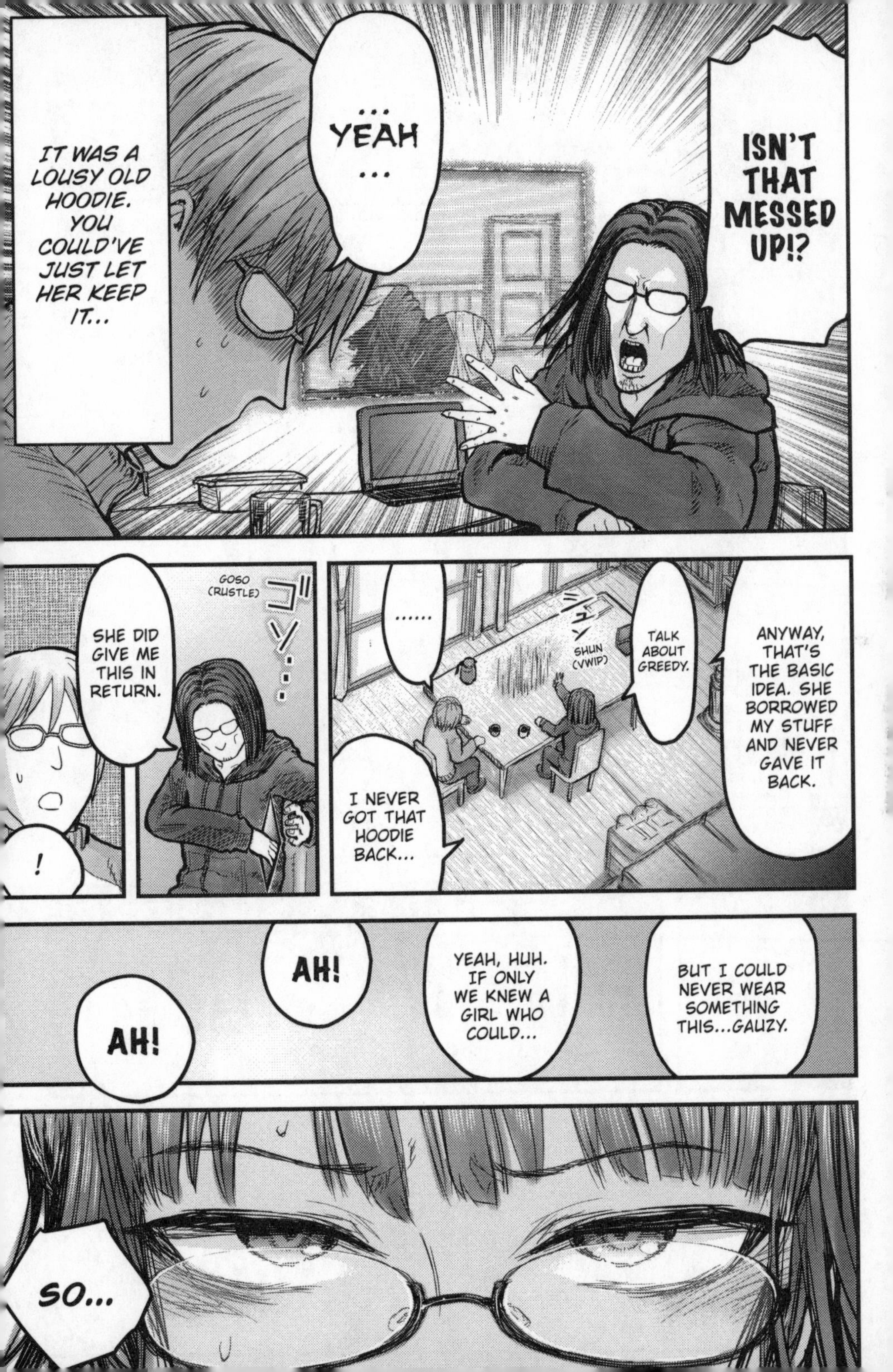
ISN'T THAT MESSED UP!?
... YEAH ...
IT WAS A LOUSY OLD HOODIE. YOU COULD'VE JUST LET HER KEEP IT...
ANYWAY, THAT'S THE BASIC IDEA. SHE BORROWED MY STUFF AND NEVER GAVE IT BACK.
TALK ABOUT GREEDY.
SHUN (VWIP)
......
I NEVER GOT THAT HOODIE BACK...
GOSO (RUSTLE)
SHE DID GIVE ME THIS IN RETURN.
!
BUT I COULD NEVER WEAR SOMETHING THIS...GAUZY.
YEAH, HUH. IF ONLY WE KNEW A GIRL WHO COULD...
AH!
AH!
SO...

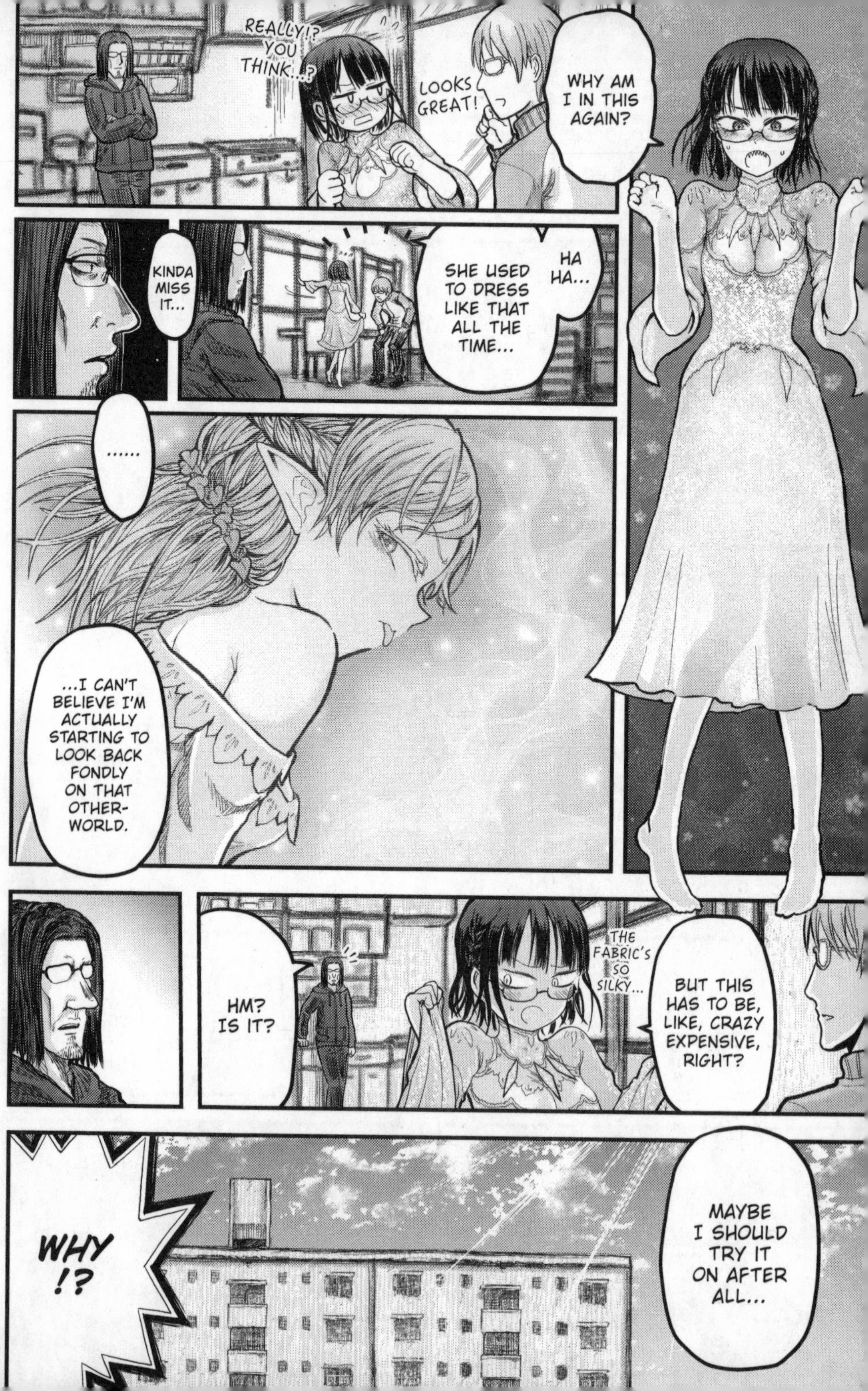
WHY AM I IN THIS AGAIN?
LOOKS GREAT!
REALLY!? YOU THINK...?
HA HA...
SHE USED TO DRESS LIKE THAT ALL THE TIME...
KINDA MISS IT...
......
...I CAN'T BELIEVE I'M ACTUALLY STARTING TO LOOK BACK FONDLY ON THAT OTHER-WORLD.
THE FABRIC'S SO SILKY...
BUT THIS HAS TO BE, LIKE, CRAZY EXPENSIVE, RIGHT?
HM? IS IT?
MAYBE I SHOULD TRY IT ON AFTER ALL...
WHY!?

Translation Notes

COMMON HONORIFICS

no honorific: Indicates familiarity or closeness; if used without permission or reason, addressing someone in this manner would constitute an insult.

-san: The Japanese equivalent of Mr./Mrs./Miss. If a situation calls for politeness, this is the fail-safe honorific.

-sama: Conveys great respect; may also indicate that the social status of the speaker is lower than that of the addressee.

-dono: Roughly equivalent to "master" or "milord."

-kun: Used most often when referring to boys, this indicates affection or familiarity. Occasionally used by older men among their peers, but it may also be used by anyone referring to a person of lower standing.

-chan: An affectionate honorific indicating familiarity, used mostly in reference to girls; also used in reference to cute persons or animals regardless of gender.

-senpai: An honorific for one's senior classmate, colleague, etc., although not as senior or respected as a *sensei* (teacher).

PAGE 13

Se●a is a certain multimedia entertainment company that was one of the two biggest home video game console manufacturers of the early to mid 1990s, alongside **Nint●ndo**. Their last console was released in Japan in 1998 before they retired from that market, supplanted by S●ny.

PAGE 16

The **Xb●x ●ne** is a video game console that was first released in 2013.

PAGE 32

Tsundere is an archetype common to anime and manga where a character either grows from hating someone to loving someone, or acts especially prickly toward a character they have feelings for.

PAGE 36

In Japanese, Uncle asks why there are so many "w"s, a reference to Japanese Internet slang denoting laughter: "wwwww." Similar in usage to "lol," this is translated as **lulz** to reflect Uncle's lack of experience with post-'90s online lingo.

PAGE 62

The Se●a **Saturn** was a 1994 32-bit home video game console. While it was capable of 3D graphics and was home to many innovative games, its original emphasis on superior 2D sprite graphics put it at a disadvantage against its competitors in a time when 3D games were fast becoming the norm.

PAGE 64

Gal games, also known as *bishoujo games* ("beautiful girl games") are a genre where the presence of attractive female characters is one of the primary selling points. This includes, but is not limited to, dating and romance games.

PAGE 68

Guardian H●roes is a 1996 beat-em-up video game with elements of fighting games (special move inputs) and role-playing games (magic and experience levels). It also includes branching story paths leading to multiple different endings.

PAGE 80

EVE Burst Err●r began as a 1995 mystery-themed visual novel game for the PC-98 computer. It is known for its high production values relative to other similar games at the time.

PAGE 87

The **Mega Drive** was a 1988 16-bit home video game console, and was released in North America as the Genesis. It was the system that launched the 1990s console wars, as it was the first true competitor against the near monopoly by Nint●ndo that had existed prior.

PAGE 88

Kaede Nanase comes from a 1995 action-shooter by the same company as *Guardian H●roes*, in which you play as a soldier of alien origins. It's famous for its focus on elaborate boss fights and for being impossibly ambitious in scope.

PAGE 105

Alien St●rm is a 1990 arcade game in the beat-em-up genre in which players have to fend off an alien invasion. It was later ported to both 16-bit and 8-bit consoles.

PAGE 107

K●chiKame is the nickname for an extremely long-running comedy manga about a middle-aged police officer in Tokyo. It ran in the weekly magazine *J●mp*, which has been home to some of the most popular boys manga of all time.

PAGE 121

It is a common Japanese tradition to eat *soba* (buckwheat noodles) on New Year's Eve as a way to symbolize crossing over into the New Year.

PAGE 122

It's ●kay to Laugh! was a long-running Japanese variety show that began in 1982 and lasted nearly thirty-two years.

PAGE 124

No Laughing! is an annual New Year's Eve special T.V. program in Japan in which the hosts, a group of comedians, are put in a variety of odd situations for twenty-four hours, and must not laugh. If they fail, they must participate in humorous penalty games.

Green Tan●ki is a brand of instant *soba* sold in Japan that comes with deep-fried *tempura* batter.

PAGES 137–140

E●angelion is a 1995 anime series about middle schoolers who use giant biomechanical robots to fight invading "Angels," which has had an enduring influence on anime narratives and character tropes. One character, *As●ka*, is regarded as an early version of the *tsundere* character archetype, particularly due to her kind yet spiteful attitude toward the protagonist. When she's first introduced, she displays very outward affection toward the older character Kaj●, making Uncle's "astute" observation painfully obvious to anyone who has watched the anime.

INSIDE COVER (FRONT)

Str●kers 1945 is a 1995 arcade game that was later ported to home consoles. It's a vertically-scrolling shoot-em-up that takes place directly after World War II, when a hidden power unleashes its hyper-advanced weaponry on the world. Whenever a boss fight comes up, a characteristic jingle plays.

INSIDE COVER (BACK)

Genocide Crash is a massive explosion by an undead ally in *Guardian H●roes*. Reverse Thunder Kick is an electrified diving kick used by the playable ninja character.

Hotondoshindeiru

TRANSLATOR: **Christina Rose**
LETERER: **Alexis Eckerman**

ISEKAI OJISAN Vol. 1
©Hotondoshindeiru 2018
©SEGA

First published in Japan in 2018 by KADOKAWA CORPORATION, Tokyo.
English translation rights arranged with KADOKAWA CORPORATION, Tokyo through
TUTTLE-MORI AGENCY, Inc.

Yen Press
150 West 30th Street, 19th Floor
New York, NY 10001

Visit us at yenpress.com ✦ facebook.com/yenpress
twitter.com/yenpress ✦ yenpress.tumblr.com ✦ instagram.com/yenpress

First Yen Press Edition: May 2021

Yen Press is an imprint of Yen Press, LLC.
The Yen Press name and logo are trademarks of Yen Press, LLC.

Library of Congress Control Number: 2021932161

ISBNs: 978-1-9753-2344-8 (paperback)
978-1-9753-2345-5 (ebook)

10 9 8 7 6 5 4 3 2 1

WOR

Printed in the United States of America